高职高专汽车专业系列教材

汽车专业英语
(第 2 版)

何宝文　杨雪松　主　编

张国新　陈海燕　李　源　副主编

清华大学出版社

北 京

内 容 简 介

本书按照高职高专职业技术教育的特点和培养方案，本着"适用、管用、够用"的原则，联系现代汽车技术发展的实际情况，结合知识与实践，精心编写而成。

本书共分为 5 章。第 1 章为汽车发展简史。第 2 章以发动机为主，共分为 10 个单元，包含发动机的工作原理和构成，重点突出电控发动机、电控共轨柴油直喷技术。第 3 章以汽车底盘为主，共分为 10 个单元，除了底盘的基本构造，还包含最新的自动变速器、GPS 定位导航系统、ABS 制动防抱死系统、ESP 电控车身稳定系统等。第 4 章以汽车电器为主，共分为 6 个单元。除了电器基本系统，还包括空调和汽车安全气囊系统。第 5 章为汽车营销英语，包含营销基本原理和销售实务两个单元。

本书体例包括 5 个环节：课文、生词、注释、练习和阅读材料。阅读材料主要涉及汽车维修、故障诊断和设备维护保养。练习环节题型多样，既有对课文的巩固，又有对相关知识的拓展。本书图文并茂，将汽车英语的识读、理解和记忆融会贯通，便于读者学习和掌握。本书可作为高职高专汽车相关专业的教材，也可供汽车从业人员阅读和参考。

图书在版编目(CIP)数据

汽车专业英语/何宝文，杨雪松主编. —2 版. —北京：清华大学出版社，2017（2020.9重印）
(高职高专汽车专业系列教材)
ISBN 978-7-302-45427-4

Ⅰ. ①汽…　Ⅱ. ①何…　②杨…　Ⅲ. ①汽车工程—英语—高等职业教育—教材　Ⅳ. ①U46

中国版本图书馆 CIP 数据核字(2016)第 260863 号

责任编辑：桑任松
封面设计：刘孝琼
责任校对：周剑云
责任印制：丛怀宇

出版发行：清华大学出版社
　　　　网　　　址：http://www.tup.com.cn, http://www.wqbook.com
　　　　地　　　址：北京清华大学学研大厦 A 座　　邮　　编：100084
　　　　社 总 机：010-62770175　　邮　　购：010-62786544
　　　　投稿与读者服务：010-62776969, c-service@tup.tsinghua.edu.cn
　　　　质量反馈：010-62772015, zhiliang@tup.tsinghua.edu.cn
　　　　课件下载：http://www.tup.com.cn, 010-62791865
印 装 者：三河市金元印装有限公司
经　　销：全国新华书店
开　　本：185mm×260mm　　印　张：17　　字　数：415 千字
版　　次：2010 年 3 月第 1 版　2017 年 3 月第 2 版　　印　次：2020 年 9 月第 3 次印刷
定　　价：39.00 元

产品编号：069609-01

第 2 版前言

《汽车专业英语》自 2010 年出版以来受到了读者的广泛好评，也收到了一些中肯的建议，为了适应当今汽车行业的发展需要，为了更好地服务读者，我们对《汽车专业英语》进行了增删与修订，决定出版第 2 版。

据中国汽车工业协会统计，我国 2015 年累计生产汽车 2450.33 万辆，同比增长 3.25%，销售汽车 2459.76 万辆，同比增长 4.68%。其中，乘用车产销 2107.94 万辆和 2114.63 万辆，同比分别增长 5.78% 和 7.30%；商用车产销 342.39 万辆和 345.13 万辆。继续保持世界第一汽车产销大国的位置。在我国成为汽车大国、汽车进入老百姓日常生活的情况下，我国急需汽车理论知识扎实、实践技能熟练的专业人才。而汽车专业英语是汽车服务技术人员尤其是高级技术人才不可或缺的必备知识。在这样的背景下，我们编写了这本《汽车专业英语》。

在编写过程中，我们紧紧联系当前汽车技术发展的实际状况，按照高职高专职业技术教育的特点和培养方案，本着"适用、管用、够用"的原则，将知识与实践紧密结合。

根据第 1 版读者的反馈和实际教学应用中发现的问题，本书内容进行了适当增删与调整。增加了新技术方面的内容，对练习环节进行了更有针对性的修订。本书共分为 5 章，各章包括课文、生词、注释、练习等环节。前 4 章以汽车构造为主线，涵盖发动机、底盘和电气设备等内容，同时侧重于最新汽车技术的内容。所选的阅读材料以汽车维修、故障诊断和维护保养设备的内容为主。第 5 章为汽车营销英语，主题涉及营销基本原理和销售实务。本书所选素材均选自英文原文，练习环节题型多样，既有对课文的巩固，又有相关知识的扩展。本书整体上图文并茂，将汽车英语的识读、理解和记忆融会贯通，便于读者学习和掌握。本书除了可以作为高职高专汽车相关专业的教材之外，也可供汽车从业人员阅读使用。

参加本书编写工作的有：北京城市学院何宝文(编写第 4 章)、云南交通职业技术学院杨雪松(编写第 1 章和第 2 章前 6 个单元)，昆明冶金高等专科学校李源和北京城市学院何宝文(编写第 2 章后 4 个单元)，河南职业技术学院陈海燕(编写第 3 章前 5 个单元)，河北机电职业技术学院张国新(编写第 3 章后 5 个单元)。邢台职业技术学院胡慧敏(编写第 5 章)。本书由何宝文、杨雪松担任主编，张国新、陈海燕和李源担任副主编。

由于编者水平有限，疏漏之处在所难免，恳请读者不吝指正。

编　者

第 1 版前言

中投顾问产业研究中心发布的《2010—2015 年中国汽车行业投资分析及前景预测报告》中指出:"经过近 30 年的努力,特别是过去十多年国家汽车生产和消费政策的调整,我国汽车产业呈现爆发式增长,产销规模在 1998—2008 年的 10 年间保持了 20%以上的年均增幅。目前我国已跃居世界第二大汽车消费国和第三大汽车生产国。2008 年,受国际金融危机的影响,我国汽车产销量分别为 934.5 万辆和 938.1 万辆,增幅低于 2007 年。而自 2009 年以来,汽车市场回暖,从 2009 年 3 月起我国汽车产销已连续 9 个月超过百万辆水平,创历史纪录。2009 年 1—11 月,我国汽车产销分别为 1226.58 万辆和 1223.04 万辆,同比增长 41.59%和 42.39%。中国汽车工业总体发展趋势良好。"

未来的十几年既是我国汽车工业稳健发展的时期,又是汽车市场群雄逐鹿、竞争日益激烈的时期,既有国内大大小小汽车厂家的市场争夺,又有进口车辆的强大威胁。在这种情况下,我国急需汽车理论知识扎实、实践技能熟练的专业人才。而相应的专业英语知识是汽车服务技术人员尤其是高级技术人才不可或缺的技能。在这样的背景下,我们编写了这本《汽车专业英语》。

在编写过程中,我们按照高职高专职业技术教育的特点和培养方案,本着"适用、管用、够用"的原则,紧紧联系当前汽车技术发展的实际状况将知识与实践紧密结合。

本书共 5 章,各章包括课文、生词、注释、练习和阅读材料共 5 个环节。前 4 章以汽车构造为主线,涵盖发动机、底盘和电气设备等内容,同时侧重于最新汽车技术的内容。所选的阅读材料以汽车维修、故障诊断和设备维护保养的内容为主。第 5 章为汽车营销英语,主题涉及营销基本原理和销售实务。本书素材均选自英文原文,练习环节题型多样,既有对课文的巩固,又有对相关知识的扩展。本书图文并茂,将汽车英语的识读、理解和记忆融会贯通,便于读者学习和掌握。本书除了可以作为高职高专汽车相关专业的教材之外,也可供汽车从业人员阅读使用。

参加本书编写工作的有:邢台职业技术学院何宝文(编写第 4 章),李英、陈超、刘学明(整理附录及文图),云南交通职业技术学院杨雪松(编写第 1 章、第 2 章前 6 个单元),昆明冶金高等专科学校李源和邢台职业技术学院何宝文(编写第 2 章后 4 个单元),河南职业技术学院陈海燕(编写第 3 章前 5 个单元),河北机电职业技术学院张国新(编写第 3 章后 5 个单元),邢台职业技术学院胡慧敏(编写第 5 章)。本书由何宝文、杨雪松担任主编,张国新、陈海燕和李源担任副主编。

由于编者水平有限,疏漏之处在所难免,恳请读者不吝指正。

编 者

目 录

Chapter 1   Brief History of Automobile 1

    Words and Expressions 3

    Notes 4

    Exercises 4

    Reading Material............................5

Chapter 2   Engine 9

  Unit 1   Four-stage Engine Operation 9

    Words and Expressions 11

    Notes 11

    Exercises 12

    Reading Material...........................13

  Unit 2   Main Components of Internal
    Combustion Engine..........................17

    Words and Expressions 20

    Notes 21

    Exercises 22

    Reading Material...........................23

  Unit 3   Power Mechanism of the Engine 26

    Words and Expressions 29

    Notes 30

    Exercises 30

    Reading Material............................32

  Unit 4   Valves and Valve Train.....................36

    Words and Expressions 38

    Notes 39

    Exercises 40

    Reading Material...........................41

  Unit 5   Engine Fuel System 44

    Words and Expressions 47

    Notes 48

    Exercises 49

    Reading Material...........................50

  Unit 6   Engine Cooling System...................53

    Words and Expressions 55

    Notes 57

    Exercises 57

    Reading Material.............................59

  Unit 7   Engine Lubrication System 62

    Words and Expressions 64

    Notes 64

    Exercises 65

    Reading Material............................66

  Unit 8   Electronic Fuel Injection System 70

    Words and Expressions 72

    Notes 73

    Exercises 74

    Reading Material............................76

  Unit 9   Emission Control System 78

    Words and Expressions 81

    Notes 82

    Exercises 82

    Reading Material............................84

  Unit 10   Intake and Exhaust Systems...........87

    Words and Expressions 89

    Notes 90

    Exercises 91

    Reading Material............................93

Chapter 3   Chassis.........................97

  Unit 1   Power Train 97

    Words and Expressions 99

    Notes 100

    Exercises 100

    Reading Material............................101

  Unit 2   Clutch 103

    Words and Expressions 105

    Notes 106

    Exercises 106

    Reading Material...........................108

Unit 3　Manual Transmission 110
　　　　Words and Expressions 112
　　　　Notes 112
　　　　Exercises 113
　　　　Reading Material 114
Unit 4　Automatic Transmission 116
　　　　Words and Expressions 119
　　　　Notes 121
　　　　Exercises 121
　　　　Reading Material 123
Unit 5　The Steering System 127
　　　　Words and Expressions 129
　　　　Notes 129
　　　　Exercises 130
　　　　Reading Material 131
Unit 6　Automobile Braking System 133
　　　　Words and Expressions 135
　　　　Notes 136
　　　　Exercises 136
　　　　Reading Material 138
Unit 7　Antilock Brake System 141
　　　　Words and Expressions 143
　　　　Notes 143
　　　　Exercises 143
　　　　Reading Material 145
Unit 8　GPS Navigation System 147
　　　　Words and Expressions 149
　　　　Notes 150
　　　　Exercises 150
　　　　Reading Material 151
Unit 9　Frame and Suspension 154
　　　　Words and Expressions 157
　　　　Notes 157
　　　　Exercises 157
　　　　Reading Material 159
Unit 10　Electronic Stability Program 161
　　　　Words and Expressions 163
　　　　Notes 164

Exercises 164
Reading Material 165

Chapter 4　Electrical Equipment 171
Unit 1　Charging System 171
　　　　Words and Expressions 173
　　　　Notes 173
　　　　Exercises 174
　　　　Reading Material 175
Unit 2　Starting System 178
　　　　Words and Expressions 179
　　　　Notes 180
　　　　Exercises 181
　　　　Reading Material 182
Unit 3　Ignition System Basic 184
　　　　Words and Expressions 186
　　　　Notes 187
　　　　Exercises 188
　　　　Reading Material 189
Unit 4　Electronic Ignition System 191
　　　　Words and Expressions 193
　　　　Notes 194
　　　　Exercises 194
　　　　Reading Material 196
Unit 5　Air Bag System 199
　　　　Words and Expressions 201
　　　　Notes 202
　　　　Exercises 202
　　　　Reading Material 204
Unit 6　Air Conditioning 209
　　　　Words and Expressions 210
　　　　Notes 211
　　　　Exercises 211
　　　　Reading Material 213

Chapter 5　Car Selling 216
Unit 1　Some Basic Marketing Theory 216
　　　　Words and Expressions 218
　　　　Notes 219

Exercises 219

Reading Material.........................221

Unit 2　How to Be a Good Car

Salesman 224

Words and Expressions 225

Notes 226

Exercises 226

Reading Material.........................230

APPENDIX.........................236

Ⅰ　Vocabulary 236

Ⅱ　Abbreviation 256

Ⅲ　Special Words 259

Ⅳ　Example of Engine Specifications........ 261

Ⅴ　2016 Volkswagen Passat　Technical

Data.......................... 262

参考文献 264

Chapter 1　Brief History of Automobile

It has already been over one hundred years since the first automobile was invented in the world. One of the most important landmarks in engine design came from Nicolaus Otto who invented an effective gas motor engine in 1876. Nicolaus Otto built the first practical four-stroke internal combustion engine (ICE) called the "Otto Cycle Engine", and when he completed his engine, he built it into a motorcycle. In spite of the vital role that the gas-driven internal combustion engine played in the evolution of automobile, it had one great drawback — the engine had to be connected to a gas supply for re-fuelling. The solution was an engine that ran on liquid fuels, which were available more easily and readily transportable.

The turning point in the development of automobile was the introduction of the petrol engine in 1885, which started an entirely new era and actually made the automobile a practical and safe proposition. The automobile produced in this period were more like the automobile we can see today and thus began the era of the modern automobile.

In terms of the lives of average people, there is little doubt that the automobile is the most revolutionary invention in the history of transportation since the wheel. In 1886, Karl Benz from Germany designed and built the first machine driven by an internal combustion engine (ICE) at Mannheim. From then on, the transportation on land shifted from the age of coaches to the age of automobiles.

The birth of the automobile as we know it today occurred over a period of years. It was not invented in a single day by a single inventor. The history of the automobile reflects an evolution that took place worldwide. It is estimated that over 100,000 patents created the modern automobile. A typical automobile of today contains more than 15,000 separate, individual parts that must work together. These parts can be grouped into four major categories, i. e. , engine, body, chassis and electrical equipment，as shown in Figure 1-1.

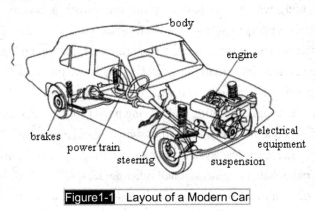

Figure1-1　Layout of a Modern Car

The engine is the source of power that makes the wheels go around and move. It can convert thermal energy into mechanical energy which is used to drive the vehicle, including the fuel, lubricating, cooling, ignition and starting system. Generally, an automobile is operated by internal combustion engine (ICE). The ICE burns fuel within the cylinders and converts the expanding force of the combustion or "explosion" into rotary force used to propel the vehicle.

The chassis which is considered as a support frame for an auto body is used to assemble all auto spare parts on it. In fact, when power from engine continues to be transmitted to chassis, it begins with power train, goes on to steering, wheel suspension, brakes and tires. These individual components interact with each other closely. Therefore, the chassis itself is divided into four systems including transmission system, suspension system, steering system and brake system.

The transmission system applies to the components needed to transfer the drive from the engine to the road wheels. The main components contain a clutch, gear box, propeller shaft, universal joint, final drive and differential, rear axle, etc.

The suspension system is used to absorb the road shocks and reduce the impact and dynamic loads which are transmitted to the sprung weight. The primary purpose of the suspension system is to increase strength and durability of components and to meet customers' requirements for riding comfort and driving safety. In automobile suspension, the major component is spring. The springs used on today's vehicles are designed in a wide variety of types, sizes, rates and capacities.

The function of the steering system is to provide the driver with a means for controlling the direction of the vehicle as it moves. It is composed of steering wheel, steering shaft, worm gear sector, pitman arm, drag link, steering knuckle arm, king pin, steering arms, tie rod and front axle.

The brake system is a balanced set of mechanical and hydraulic devices used to retard the motion of the vehicle by means of friction. It is used to convert the power of momentum of the moving vehicle (kinetic energy) into heat by means of friction, in other words, brake caliper (shoe) is forced against machined surfaces of rotating disc or drum at each wheel to slow and stop the vehicle. Structurally, the brake system consists of the drum or disc brake assembly, brake lever assembly, etc. Functionally, the brake system can be divided into wheel brake mechanism and parking brake mechanism.

The automobile body which is regarded as the framework is seated on the chassis. The function is obvious for occupants to provide comfort, protection and shelter. The automobile body is generally divided into four sections, i. e. , the front, the rear, the top and the underbody. These sections can further be divided into small units, such as the hood, the fenders, the roof panels, the door, the instrument panel, the bumpers and the luggage compartment.

The electrical system supplies lighting and driving power for the vehicle. It cranks the engine for starting and offers high-voltage surges that ignite the compressed air fuel mixture in combustion chambers. The electrical system includes starting system, ignition system, lighting system, horn system, radio, battery, generator and other devices.

With the rapid development of automobile industry, the new models of automobiles are becoming better and better in design and performance. Nowadays automobiles are very popular with people, meanwhile many negative problems corresponding to the facts have to be considered by scientists, such as energy crisis, air pollution and traffic jam. In order to mitigate the negative effects of automobiles, scientists and auto manufactures are doing their best to improve fuel economy, control exhaust emissions, and the governments are taking active measures to resolve traffic problem at the same time.

Words and Expressions

1. landmark　['lændmɑːk]　*n.* 重大事件；里程碑；地界标

2. combustion　[kəm'bʌstʃən]　*n.* 燃烧，燃尽；发火；爆震燃烧

3. evolution　[ˌiːvə'luːʃən]　*n.* 进化；进展

4. transportation　[ˌtrænspɔː'teiʃən]　*n.* 运输；交通业；输送

5. chassis　['ʃæsi]　*n.* 底盘

6. suspension　[səs'penʃən]　*n.* 悬挂，悬吊；悬置

7. component　[kəm'pəunənt]　*n.* 元件，组件　*adj.* 组成的，构成的

8. clutch　[klʌtʃ]　*n.* 离合器；控制　*v.* 抓住；攫取

9. hood　[hud]　*n.* 车篷，遮罩　*vt.* 覆盖

10. fender　['fendə]　*n.* 挡泥板

11. bumper　['bʌmpə]　*n.* 汽车保险杠；防撞器；缓冲器

12. surge　[səːdʒ]　*n.* 电涌；冲击波；浪涌　*v.* 汹涌；澎湃

13. differential　[ˌdifə'renʃəl]　*n.* 差动器；差别；微分　*adj.* 差别的，微分的

14. dynamic　[dai'næmik]　*adj.* 动态的，有活力的　*n.* 动力力学

15. retard　[ri'tɑːd]　*n.* 减速，延迟；阻滞　*v.* 延迟，阻止，使减速；减慢

16. hydraulic　[hai'drɔːlik]　*adj.* 水力的，水压的

17. gearbox　['giəbɔks]　*n.* 齿轮箱，变速箱

18. propeller shaft　传动轴

19. universal joint　万向节

20. final drive　主减速器

21. worm gear sector　扇形蜗轮

22. pitman arm　转向摇臂

23. drag link　直拉杆

24. steering knuckle arm　转向节臂

25. king pin　主销

26. kinetic energy　动能

27. combustion chamber　燃烧室

28. brake caliper　制动钳

29. power train　动力传动系

Notes

1. The solution was an engine that ran on liquid fuels, which were available more easily and readily transportable.

解决方案是采用更方便和易于运输的液体燃料来驱动发动机。

2. In terms of the lives of average people, there is little doubt that the automobile is the most revolutionary invention in the history of transportation since the wheel.

对一般人来说，汽车无疑是交通运输史上自车轮以来最具革命性的发明。

3. From then on, the transportation on land shifted from the age of coaches to the age of automobiles.

从那时起，陆路交通运输就从马车时代过渡到汽车时代。

4. The suspension system is used to absorb the road shocks and reduce the impact and dynamic loads which are transmitted to the sprung weight.

悬挂系统用来吸收路面震动，减少冲击和传到簧上的动态载荷。

5. The brake system is a balanced set of mechanical and hydraulic devices used to retard the motion of the vehicle by means of friction.

制动系统是一套通过摩擦力作用阻碍车辆运动的平衡的机械和液压装置。

Exercises

A. Vocabulary

I. Translate the following expressions into Chinese.

1. internal combustion engine

2. power train

3. parking brake mechanism

4. thermal energy

5. instrument panel

6. luggage compartment

7. traffic jam

8. fuel economy

9. exhaust emission

10. combustion chamber

II. Identify the English names of the automobile according to the picture.

1. _____   2. _____

3. _____   4. _____

5. _____   6. _____

7. _____   8. _____

9. _____   10. _____

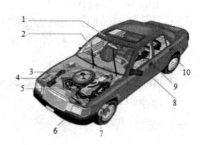

B. Comprehension

I. Discuss the following questions in groups and write down your answers.

1. What are the main parts of an automobile?

_____

2. Which systems does a chassis include and what are the main functions of the chassis?

_____

3. Why is suspension system used on vehicles?

_____

4. Is the brake system used to slow and stop the motion of the vehicle by means of friction?

_____

II. Read the following passage carefully and fill in the blanks with the proper forms of the given words.

consider	*train*	*frame*	*component*	*transmit*
steering	*spare*	*divide*	*suspension*	*assemble*

The chassis which is _____ as a support _____ for an auto body is used to _____ all auto _____ parts on it. In fact, when power from engine continues to be _____ to chassis, it begins with power _____, goes on to steering, wheel suspension, bakes and tires. These individual _____ interact with each other closely. Therefore, the chassis itself is _____ into four systems like transmission system, _____ system, _____ system and brake system.

C. Translation

I. Translate the following sentences into Chinese.

1. The engine is the source of power that makes the wheels go around and move.

2. The function of the steering system is to provide the driver with a means for controlling the direction of the vehicle as it moves.

3. It cranks the engine for starting and offers high-voltage surges that ignite the compressed air fuel mixture in combustion chambers.

II. Translate the following sentences into English.

1. 解决方案是采用更为方便和易于运输的液体燃料来驱动发动机。
2. 悬挂系统用来吸收来自路面的震动、减少冲击和降低传到簧上重量动态载荷的影响。
3. 从功能说，制动系统可分为行车制动系统和驻车制动系统。

Reading Material

Read the following passages and answer the questions according to the information given in the passages.

Passage One　Electric Vehicle

An electric vehicle, or EV, is a vehicle driven by an electric motor instead of by an internal combustion engine (ICE), and fueled by electricity from a battery instead of by a tank of gasoline.

As such, there are only three major components, i. e. , the motor, the battery, and a controller of energy between the two. These three major components, in their simplest form, have been around for decades in machinery that is used for months on end without rest.

EVs are presently used where their advantages outweigh their shortcomings, such as passenger transport in airport terminals and parks, industrial lift trucks in factories, or golf carts.

An EV for road use, as either an automobile or as a delivery van, is most suitable for urban areas or the payloads are light. With further research, people constantly are improving the performance of the batteries used for EVs, to reduce their cost and weight and to increase the range of vehicles.

To overcome the limitations of batteries, we use hybrid EVs, and use a combination of a battery and an ICE. In such a vehicle the battery supplies high energy for acceleration while a small ICE runs efficiently at a constant speed while moving the vehicle on highway. Extended range, high performance, reduced pollution and increased efficiency are the results.

Most present-day EVs don't look much different from ICE vehicles; they are conversions of existing ICE vehicles. The advantages of using an existing vehicle is that it eliminates the problem of designing from scratch, but it sacrifices performance and efficiency due to the heavy weight and poor aerodynamics. However, some electric cars have an unusual appearance for a number of reasons. They may be more aerodynamic to reduce the energy consumption. Some use a large number so that the car body can last longer because electric drive trains tend to have very long life spans. Some have unusual shapes to accommodate a large battery pack low in the vehicle to lower the center of gravity, allowing for better handling; whereas some EV makers just want to be sure that you know that this vehicle is something special and worth a second look.

We must use energy wisely, more efficiently, and an EV uses less than half the energy of an ICE. In cities, where 80%-90% of driving occurs, the gasoline engine gets its worst mileage whereas the EV gets its best. The electric motor in an EV is not running when stopped in traffic and therefore uses no energy. Also, EVs can be equipped with regenerative braking which puts energy back into the batteries while slowing to a stop. Because of the increased efficiency of EVs and the fact that recharging would take place mostly at night, millions of electric vehicles could be put into use in North America with no increase in electrical generating capacity being required. In the most extreme case, an all-electric car in North America would only increase electric power plant demand by about 20%.

The ICE automobile is responsible for almost 80% of the air pollution in our cities. Air quality is thus the driving force for finding a replacement for the ICE auto. An EV produces no emissions by itself and is responsible for only a small portion of power plant wastes. In Canada, 60% of the electricity is generated by hydro, which causes no air pollution. Furthermore, EVs reduce more air pollution. They reduce water pollution by virtue of reducing the amount of petroleum products being produced, transported, stored, used and disposed of. Each of these activities contributes to pollution, refinery waste products and emissions, spills from tanker ships and tanker trucks, leaks from storage tanks and vehicle crankcases, and disposal by burning or being dumped into waterways and sewage systems. EVs are quieter than Otto and Diesel cycle engine so they reduce the level of noise pollution. EVs produce far less waste heat than combustion engines (also known as heat engines), so they reduce the amount of heat pollution being produced.

One of the best Characteristics of EVs is how little they cost to operate. EVs' fuel cost is much less than gasoline vehicles. Battery replacement costs over the life of the car are less than the costs of ICE tune-ups. The purchase price of an EV is presently higher than a comparable car, but total lifetime costs are about equal. Continuing research and mass production will lower both electric vehicle and battery costs in the future.

Questions

1. What are the three sections of an electric vehicle?

2. Please describe the operational principle of an electric vehicle.

3. Please describe the advantage and disadvantage of an electric vehicle.

Passage Two   Gasoline Octane

It is the least amount that's necessary to prevent detonation (spark knock). On most vehicles, that's 87 octane regular grade, unleaded gasoline. But on higher compression engines, or turbocharged or supercharged engines, the engine may require premium grade 91 to 93 octane fuel.

Detonation, which can be very damaging to your engine, occurs when the octane rating of the fuel isn't high enough to handle the heat and pressure. Instead of a single flame front forming when the fuel is ignited, multiple flame fronts form spontaneously throughout the combustion chamber. When these collide, the shock waves make a pinging noise, and the piston receives a hammer-like blow.

One way to prevent detonation is to use a higher octane fuel. The octane rating of a motor fuel is a measure of its detonation resistance. The octane that's posted on the filling station pump is "pump octane," which is an average of something called "research" and "motor" octane ratings(which are two different laboratory methods of measuring octane). The higher the pump octane number, the better able the fuel is to resist detonation.

A gasoline's octane rating depends on the blend of hydrocarbons in the fuel and other ingredients that are added to it. Tetraethyl lead was long used as an anti-knock additive to improve gasoline octane. In fact, it was the most effective and least expensive octane-boosting additive that could be used for this purpose. But leaded fuel cannot be used in a vehicle with a catalytic converter because the lead fouls the catalyst. So unleaded fuel must contain other octane-boosting additives such as MTBE(methyl tert-butyl ether) or alcohol.

Most unleaded gasoline today is rated at 87 octane, which is sufficient for engines with compression ratios of up to about 9 to 1. Higher compression engines, engines with turbochargers or superchargers, or those used frequently for towing should use a higher grade or premium gasoline.

CAUTION: Follow the fuel recommendations in your vehicle owner's manual. If your

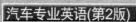 
vehicle requires premium 91 or higher octane fuel, then you must use premium.

If you can't find pump gas with a high enough octane to prevent detonation, you can always add an aftermarket octane boosting fuel additive to your fuel tank. Such products can boost the octane rating of ordinary pump gas several points depending on the concentration used (always follow directions). But even this might not be enough to eliminate a persistent spark knock if your engine has an underlying problem.

Questions

1. What is a spark knock?

2. How much octane does our engine really need?

3. What should we pay more attention to ?

Chapter 2　Engine

Unit 1　Four-stage Engine Operation

There are various types of engines such as electric motors, stream engines and internal combustion engines. However, the internal combustion engine seems to be the most commonly used in the automotive field. According to the fuel energy used, internal combustion engines are further divided into gasoline engines and diesel engines.

The internal combustion engine, as its name indicates, burns fuel within the cylinders and converts the expanding force of the combustion into rotary force used to propel the vehicle. The actions taking place in the engine cylinder can be classified into four stages, or stroke. The "stroke" refers to piston movement — a stroke occurs when the piston moves from one limiting position to the other. The upper limit of piston movement is called TDC (top dead center). The lower limit of the piston movement is called BDC (bottom dead center). A stroke is the movement from TDC to BDC or from BDC to TDC. In other words, the piston completes a stroke, each time it changes its direction of motion, as shown in Figure 2-1.

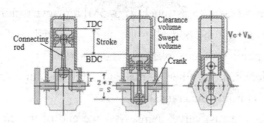

Figure 2-1　Four-stroke Engine

Almost all cars currently use the so-called four-stroke cycle engine to convert gasoline into motion. The four-stroke approach is also known as the Otto cycle, in honor of Nicolaus Otto, who invented it in 1867. The four strokes are intake stroke, compression stroke, power stroke and exhaust stroke, as shown in Figure 2-2.

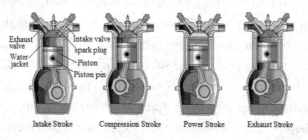

Figure 2-2　The Operation of a Four-stroke Cycle Engine

Intake stroke. The piston is connected to the crankshaft by a connecting rod. On the intake stroke, the piston moves down from the TDC to the BDC as the crankshaft revolves. This downward movement of the piston creates a vacuum, a difference in pressure in the space above the piston. The intake valve opens automatically as or slightly before the piston starts down, therefore, the air fuel mixture pushed by the atmospheric pressure outside the engine, rushes through the intake manifold and into the engine cylinder. At the same time, the exhaust valve remains closed and prevents the entering air fuel charge from escaping through the exhaust port. The mixture of air and vaporized gasoline is delivered to the cylinder by the fuel system and carburetor.

Compression stroke. After the piston reaches the BDC, the piston moves back up to compress this combustible mixture within the combustion chamber and the intake valve and the exhaust valve are all closed. Since both valves are closed, the piston compresses the air fuel mixture in the small space between the top of the piston and the cylinder head. When the mixture is compressed, not only does the pressure in the cylinder go up, but also the temperature increases. As the piston reaches the TDC again during its upward travel, the compression stroke of the piston is over. The air fuel charge is now under compression so that it will produce a great deal of power when the spark plug ignites it.

Power stroke. Just as or slightly before the piston reaches the TDC on the compression stroke with the air fuel mixture fully compressed, a timed electrical spark appears at the spark plug. This spark ignites the compressed air fuel mixture. The burning mixture begins to expand, and the cylinder pressure increase to as much as 3-5MPa or even more. This tremendous force pushed the piston downward on the power stroke, and a power impulse transmitted through the connecting rod to the crankpin on the crankshaft. The crankshaft is rotated as the piston is pushed down by the pressure above it. In other words, the force resulting from the expansion of the burning air fuel mixture is turning the crankshaft.

Exhaust stroke. The exhaust valve opens, near the end of the downward movement of the piston on the power stroke, although much of the gas pressure has expended itself driving the piston downward, some pressure still remains when the exhaust valve opens. This remaining pressurized gas flows comparatively freely from the cylinder through the passage port opened by the exhaust valve. Then, as the piston again moves up in the cylinder, it drives any remaining gases out of the cylinder past the open exhaust valve. In other words, while the exhaust valve is open, the upward movement of the piston provides an effective method for discharging all waste gases from the engine cylinder and combustion chamber. As the crankshaft nears the end of its second complete revolution, the piston again approaches the TDC position. At this point the exhaust valve is closing and the intake valve starts to open. Both valves are open together for a short period of time in order to accelerate the fresh charge to flow into the cylinder.

As the piston travels through the TDC position and starts downward again in the cylinder, a new operating cycle begins. This four-stroke cycle of piston within the cylinder is repeated time and again to put the vehicle forward.

Words and Expressions

1. various ['vɛəriəs] *adj.* 各种各样的

2. diesel ['di:zəl] *n.* 柴油机；内燃机

3. propel [prə'pel] *v.* 推进；驱使

4. stage [steidʒ] *n.* 阶段；舞台；驿站 *vt.* 上演；实行，进行

5. approach [ə'prəutʃ] *n.* 接近；途径；方法 *v.* 靠近，接近

6. crankshaft ['kræŋkʃɑ:ft] *n.* 曲轴

7. vacuum ['vækjuəm] *n.* 真空；空间；真空吸尘器 *adj.* 真空的

8. atmospheric [ˌætməs'ferik] *adj.* 大气的，大气层的

9. manifold ['mænifəuld] *n.* 多种；歧管 *adj.* 多种的，多方面的 *v.* 繁殖，增多

10. vaporize ['veipəraiz] *v.* (使)蒸发

11. combustible [kəm'bʌstəbl] *adj.* 易燃的，燃烧性的 *n.* 燃质物，可燃物

12. ignite [ig'nait] *vi.* 着火，发光 *vt.* 点燃，(使)燃烧，引发

13. slightly ['slait·ly] *adv.* 轻微地；微小地；稍微地；纤细地

14. transmit [trænz'mit] *vt.* 传输，传送；代代相传；传达

15. tremendous [tri'mendəs] *adj.* 巨大的；可怕的；非常的

16. comparatively [kəm'pærətivli] *adv.* 比较地；相对地

17. gasoline engine 汽油机

18. diesel engine 柴油机

19. top dead center (TDC) 上止点；上死点

20. bottom dead center (BDC) 下止点；下死点

21. connecting rod 连杆

22. spark plug 火花塞

23. inlet (intake) valve 进气阀

24. exhaust valve 排气阀

25. swept volume 有效容积

Notes

1. The internal combustion engine, as its name indicates, burns fuel within the cylinders and converts the expanding force of the combustion into rotary force used to propel the vehicle.

内燃发动机，正如其名字所示，在汽缸内燃烧燃料并转换燃烧的膨胀力为回转力来推动车辆运动。

2. The intake valve opens automatically at or slightly before the piston starts down, therefore, the air fuel mixture pushed by the atmospheric pressure outside the engine, rushes through the intake manifold and into the engine cylinder.

进气门自动打开或者稍微提前于活塞开始向下运动时打开，因此，空燃混合气在发动机外部大气压力的推动下，急速通过进气歧管并进入发动机汽缸。

3. When the mixture is compressed, not only does the pressure in the cylinder go up, but also the temperature increases.

当混合物被压缩时，不仅汽缸里的压力会上升，而且温度也会上升。

4. This tremendous force pushed the piston downward on the power stroke, and a power impulse transmitted through the connecting rod to the crankpin on the crankshaft.

在做功行程中，这样巨大推力作用于活塞使它向下运动，并且脉冲推力通过连杆传到曲轴轴颈上。

5. This remaining pressurized gas flows comparatively freely from the cylinder through the passage port opened by the exhaust valve.

气体的余压使废气能相对自由地从汽缸通过排气门的排气口。

Exercises

A. Vocabulary

I. Translate the following expressions into Chinese.

1. power stoke

2. clearance volume

3. compression ratio

4. revolution

5. intake stroke

6. compression stroke

7. exhaust stroke

8. engine block

9. bore

10. engine capacity

II. Identify the English names of the four-stroke engine according to the picture.

1. _____ 2. _____

3. _____ 4. _____

5. _____ 6. _____

7. _____ 8. _____

9. _____ 10. _____

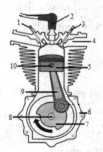

B. Comprehension

I. Discuss the following questions in groups and write down your answers.

1. Would you please tell different types of engines?

_____

2. What does internal combustion engine mean?

_____

3. How does the engine produce power for the automobile?

_____

4. What is the function of each stroke?

_____

II. Read the following passage carefully and fill in the blanks with the proper forms of the given words.

expand　appear　rotate　reach　transmit

compress　tremendous　crankshaft　push　increase

Just as or slightly before the piston ____ TDC on the compression stroke with the air fuel mixture fully ____, a timed electrical spark ____ at the spark plug. This spark ignites the compressed air fuel mixture. The burning mixture begins to ____, and the cylinder pressure ____ to as much as 3–5MPa or even more. This ____ force pushed the piston downward on the power stroke, and a power impulse ____ through the connecting rod to the crankpin on the ____. The crankshaft is ____ as the piston is ____ down by the pressure above it.

C. Translation

I. Translate the following sentences into Chinese.

1. The mixture of air and vaporized gasoline is delivered to the cylinder by the fuel system and carburetor.

2. The air fuel charge is now under compression so that it will produce a great deal of power when the spark plug ignites it.

3. Both valves are open together for a short period of time in order to accelerate the fresh charge to flow into the cylinder.

II. Translate the following sentences into English.

1. "冲程"，是指活塞运动，一个冲程发生时，活塞从一个极限位置运动到另外一个极限位置。

2. 活塞每完成一个冲程，活塞将改变其运动方向一次。

3. 与此同时，排气门仍然关闭，阻止进入的可燃混合气通过排气口逸出。

Reading Material

Read the following passages and answer the questions according to the information given in the passages.

Passage One　Two-stroke Engine

We are familiar with two types of engines found in nearly every car and truck on the road today. They are gasoline and diesel engines. Both are classified as four-stroke reciprocating internal combustion engines and two-stroke engines. The two-stroke engines are commonly found in lower power applications such as jet skis. The two-stroke engines have three important advantages over four-stroke engines as follows:

- Two-stroke engines do not have valve, which simplifies their construction and lowers their weight.
- Two-stroke engines fire once every revolution, while four-stroke engines fire once every other revolution. This gives two-stroke engines a signification power boost.

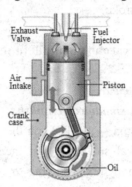

- Two-stroke engines can work in any orientation. A standard four-stroke engine may have problem with oil flow unless it is upright, and solving this problem can add complexity to the engine.

These advantages make two-stroke engines lighter, simpler and less expensive to manufacture. Two-stroke engines also have the potential to pack about twice the power into the same space because there are twice as many power strokes per revolution. The combustion of light weight and twice the power gives two-stroke engines a great power-to-weight ratio compared to many four-stroke engine designs.

Start with the point where the spark plugs fire. Fuel and air in the cylinder have been compressed when the spark plugs fire the mixture. The resulting explosion drives the piston downward. Note that as the piston moves downward, it is compressing the air fuel mixture in the crankcase. As the piston approaches the bottom of its stroke, the exhaust port is uncovered. The pressure in the cylinder drives most of the exhaust gases out of cylinder. As the piston finally bottoms out, the intake port is uncovered. The piston's movement has pressurized the mixture in the crankcase, so it rushes into the cylinder, displacing the remaining exhaust gases and filling the cylinder with a fresh charge of fuel. Note that in many two-stroke engines which use a cross-flow design, the piston is shaped so that the incoming fuel mixture doesn't simply flow right over the top of the piston and out the exhaust port. Now the momentum in the crankshaft starts driving the piston back toward the spark plug for the compression stroke. As the air fuel mixture in the piston is compressed, a vacuum is created in the crankcase. This vacuum opens the reed valve and sucks air-fuel mixture from the carburetor.

Once the piston moves up to the end of the compression stroke, the spark plug fires again to repeat the cycle. It's called a two-stroke engine because there is a compression stroke and then a combustion stroke. In a four-stroke engine, there are separate intake, compression, combustion and exhaust strokes. You can see that the piston is really doing the following different things in a two-stroke engine:

1. On one side of the piston is the combustion chamber, where the piston is compressing the

air fuel mixture and capturing the energy released by the ignition of the fuel.

2. On the other side of the piston is the crankcase, where the piston is creating a vacuum to suck in air fuel from the carburetor through the reed valve and then pressurize the crankcase so that air fuel is forced into the combustion chamber.

3. Meanwhile, the sides of the piston are acting like valves, covering and uncovering the intake and exhaust ports drilled into the sides of the cylinder wall.

You can now see that two-stroke engines have two important advantages over four-stroke engines: they are simpler and lighter, and they produce about twice as much power as four-stroke engines. But why do cars and trucks use four-stroke engines? There are four main reasons as follows:

1. Two-stroke engines don't last nearly so long as four-stroke engines. The lack of a dedicated lubrication system means that the parts of a two-stroke engine wear a lot faster.

2. Two-stroke oil is expensive, and you need about 4 ounces of it per gallon of gas. You would burn about a gallon of oil every 1,000 miles if you use a two-stroke engine in a car.

3. Two-stroke engines do not use fuel efficiently, so you would get fewer miles per gallon.

4. Two-stroke engines produce a lot of pollution. The pollution comes from two sources. The first is the combustion of the oil. The oil makes all two-stroke engines smoky to some extent, and a badly worn two-stroke engine can emit huge clouds of oily smoke. The second is that each time a new charge of air fuel is loaded into the combustion chamber, part of it leaks out through the exhaust port. That's why you see a sheet of oil around any two-stroke boat motor. The combustion of the leaking hydrocarbons from the fresh fuel and the leaking oil is real mess for the environment.

These disadvantages mean that two-stroke engines are used only in applications where the motor is not used very often and a fantastic power-to-weight ratio is important.

Questions

1. What are the shortcomings of two-stroke engines?

2. Please describe different things that a piston can do in a two-stroke engine.

3. Why do cars and trucks use four-stroke engines?

Passage Two　From Carburetors to Fuel Injection

Why did the car makers change from carburetors to fuel injection? The standard reply to this question is that fuel injection provides a better way to meet government fuel economy and emission standards, which is true. But equally important is the fact that fuel injection is an all-round better fuel delivery system.

Fuel injection has no choke, but sprays atomized fuel directly into the engine. This eliminates most of the cold start problems associated with carburetors. Electronic fuel injection also integrates more easily with computerized engine control systems because the injectors are more easily controlled than a mechanical carburetor with electronic add-ons. Multiport fuel injection (where each cylinder has its own injector) delivers a more evenly distributed mixture of air and fuel to each of the engine's cylinders, which improves power and performance. Sequential fuel injection (where the firing of each individual injector is controlled separately by the computer and timed to the engine's firing sequence) improves power and reduces emissions. So there are

some valid engineering reasons as well for using fuel injection.

Types of Fuel Injection

The earliest fuel injection systems were mechanical and were more complex than carburetors. Consequently, they were expensive and their use was limited. Chevrolet introduced a Rochester mechanical fuel injection system back in 1957, and it became the "hot" setup on Corvettes up through 1967.

The Europeans, however, were the real leaders in fuel injection technology. Bosch offered an early electronic system on Volkswagen Squarebacks in the late 1960s and early 1970s. By the early 1980s, almost all of the European auto makers were using some type of Bosch multiport fuel injection system.

In the mid-1980s, the domestic auto makers first turned to "throttle body" injection as a stop-gap system as they made the transition from electromechanical carburetors to fuel injection.

Throttle Body Injection (TBI)

Throttle body injection is much like a carburetor except that there's no fuel bowl, float, needle valve, venturi, fuel jets, accelerator pump or choke. That's because throttle body injection does not depend on engine vacuum or venturi vacuum for fuel metering. Fuel is sprayed directly into the intake manifold instead of being siphoned in by intake vacuum.

A TBI fuel delivery system consists of a throttle body with one or two injectors and a pressure regulator. Fuel pressure is provided by an electric pump. It's a relatively simple setup and causes few problems — but doesn't provide all of the advantages of a multiport or sequential fuel injection system.

Multiport Injection

The next step up from TBI was multiport injection. Engines with multiport injection have a separate fuel injector for each cylinder, mounted in the intake manifold or head just above the intake port. Thus, a four cylinder engine would have four injectors, a V6 would have six injectors and a V8 would have eight injectors.

Multiport injection systems are more expensive because of the added number of injectors. But having a separate injector for each cylinder makes a big difference in performance. The same engine with multiport injection will typically produce 10–40 more horsepower than one with TBI because of better cylinder-to-cylinder fuel distribution. Injecting fuel directly into the intake ports also eliminates the need to preheat the intake manifold since only air flows through the manifold. This, in turn, provides more freedom for tuning the intake plumbing to produce maximum torque. It also eliminates the need to preheat the incoming air by forcing it to pass through a stove around the exhaust manifold.

There are other differences between multiport injection systems. One is the way in which the injectors are pulsed. On some systems, all the injectors are wired together and pulse simultaneously (once every revolution of the crankshaft). On the others, the injectors are wired separately and are pulsed sequentially (one after the other in their respective firing order). The latter approach is more complicated and requires more expensive electronic controls, but provides better performance and throttle response by allowing more rapid changes in the fuel mixture.

Questions

1. Why did the car makers change from carburetors to fuel injection?

2. What fuel injection engine types are there in the world now ?

3. What are the differences between two-stroke engines and four-stroke engines?

Unit 2   Main Components of Internal Combustion Engine

Of all automobile components, an automobile engine is the most complicated assembly with dominant effects on the function of an automobile, so the engine is generally called the "heart" of an automobile.

The internal combustion engine, as its name indicates, burns fuel within the cylinders and converts the expanding force of the combustion into rotary force used to propel the vehicle. Heat energy released in the combustion chamber raises the temperature of the combustion gases with the chamber. The increase in gas temperature causes the pressure of the gases to increase. The pressure developed within the combustion chamber is applied to the head of a piston to produce a usable mechanical force, which is then converted into useful mechanical power.

Each of the engines has a few main working parts. The auxiliary parts are necessary to hold the working parts together or to assist the main working parts in their performance. All of the major units such as the engine crankcase and cylinder block, the piston and connecting rod, and the crankshaft and flywheel work in close cooperation to convert thermal energy into mechanical energy which is used to drive the vehicle, as shown in Figure 2-3.

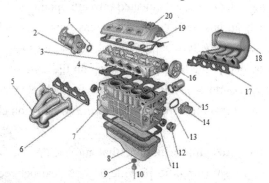

Figure 2-3   Main Components of Internal Combustion Engine

1—distributor washer   2—distributor   3—cylinder head   4—head gasket
5—exhaust manifold   6—exhaust manifold gasket   7—engine block   8—oil pan
9—drain bolt crush washer   10—oil pan drain bolt   11—oil pan gasket   12—timing belt drive pulley
13—water pump gasket   14—water pump   15—oil filter   16—camshaft grommets
17—intake manifold gasket   18—intake manifold   19—cylinder head cover gasket   20—cylinder head cover

Engine Crankcase and Cylinder Block

The engine crankcase and cylinder block are usually cast in one piece and therefore can be seen as the largest and most intricate piece of metal in automobile. Figure 2-3 shows the engine crankcase and cylinder block. It has two main sections: the crankcase section and the cylinder section. The crankcase section is used to house the crankshaft and oil pan. Cooling passageways are built within the block. These passageways, also known as water sockets, surround the cylinders. They allow coolant to circulate throughout the cylinder area to keep engine cool. There is also a drilled passageway within some blocks for camshaft. Many oil holes are drilled internally so that engine parts can be adequately lubricated.

The cylinders are cast into the block. They are usually made of high-grade cast alloy iron to improve wear characteristics of the cylinders. This major unit must be strong and rigid enough to withstand any bending or distortion. The cylinders are circular, tube like openings in the block, which act as guides for the pistons as they move up and down. Some blocks are cast from aluminum. The block contains not only the cylinders but also the water jackets that surround them. In aluminum blocks, cast iron or steel cylinder sleeves (also called bore liners) are used. These metals have better wearing qualities than aluminum and can better withstand the wearing effect of the pistons and rings moving up and down in the cylinders. Finally, the block has cast in bores for the camshaft and crankshaft.

Many parts are also attached by fastening devices to the engine block. These items include the water pump, oil pan, the flywheel or clutch housing, the ignition distributor, oil and fuel pump and the cylinder head.

Cylinder Head

The cylinder head is used to hold the valves, and it has ports to allow air, fuel and exhaust to move through the engine. In addition, cylinder head contains water jackets for cooling in the assembled engine; these water jackets are connected through openings to the cylinder-block water jackets. After the cylinder head has been cast, some areas must be machined so that intake and exhaust manifolds can be attached; valves can be seated; spark plugs and injectors can be installed and a good seal can be provided to the block. Depending on the style of engine, the cylinder head serves many functions. For example, in all engine type the head forms an upper cover for the cylinders; therefore, the head forms the upper portion of the combustion chamber.

Piston

The piston is essentially a cylindrical plug that moves up and down inside the engine cylinder. It is equipped with piston rings to provide a good seal between the cylinder wall and piston. The piston converts the potential energy of the fuel into the kinetic energy that turns the crankshaft. The piston absorbs heat from the gas, and this heat must be carried away and the metal temperature is to be held within safe limits.

The piston is composed of piston head, piston rings, piston lands, piston skirt and piston pin hole. The piston head or "crown" is the top surface against which the explosive force is exerted. It may be flat, concave and convex or any one of a great variety of shapes to promote turbulence or

help control combustion. The piston lands are parts of piston between the ring grooves. The lands provide a seating surface for the sides of the piston rings.

The rings are installed in grooves in the piston. Actually, there are two types of rings, compression rings and oil-control rings. The compression rings seal in the air fuel mixture as it is compressed and also the combustion pressures as the mixture burns. The oil-control rings control the amount of oil being deposited on the cylinder wall. The lower grooves often have holes or slots in the bottom of the grooves to permit oil drainage from behind the ring, and then the oil-control rings scrape off excessive oil from the cylinder wall and return it to the oil pan.

The main section of a piston is known as the skirts. It forms a bearing area in contact with the cylinder wall. The piston pin hole in the piston also serves as a bearing for the piston pin, which is used to connecting rod. In addition, because pistons operate under exceedingly difficult mechanical and thermal conditions, piston must be strong enough to stand the force of the expansion. The piston must be able to withstand the heat from the burning air-fuel mixture, plus the heat generated by friction.

Connecting Rod

The connecting rod is attached at one end to a crankpin on the crankshaft and at the other end to a piston, through a piston pin or wrist pin. In operation, the connecting rod is subjected to both gas pressure and inertia loads, therefore, it must be adequately strong and rigid and also as light as possible. So they are generally fabricated from high quality steel. The connecting rod is in form of a bar with ring shaped heads at its end. They are composed of connecting rod small, connecting rod shank, connecting rod big end, connecting rod cap, and connecting rod bearing half shells. To avoid misplacing the rod caps during assembly, the connecting rods and their mating caps are marked on one side with serial numbers, starting with the first rod from the radiator, to identify their location in the engine, as shown in Figure 2-4.

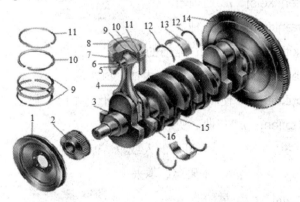

Figure 2-4 The Connecting Rod and Crankshaft

1—V-belt pulley 2—timing gear 3—crankshaft 4—connecting rod
5—latch hook 6—piston pin 7—piston ring groove 8—piston
9—oil rings 10—the second compression ring 11—the first compression ring 12—crankshaft thrust
13—central main bearing half shell 14—flywheel 15—connecting rod bolt 16—connecting rod cap

Crankshaft

The crankshaft can change the reciprocating motion of the piston into rotary motion and handles the entire power output.

The periodic gas and inertia forces taken by the crankshaft may cause it to suffer wear and bending and tensional strain. The crankshaft therefore must be adequately strong and wear-resistant. So the crankshaft is either forged from high quality steel or cast in a high-strong iron. The crankshaft is actually made up of various parts such as main bearing journals, rod journal, crank arm bearing, counter-balanced weight and flywheel end.

The front end of the crankshaft carries three devices: the gear or sprocket that drives the camshaft, the vibration damper, and the fan belt pulley. The pulley drives the engine fan, water pump, and generator with a V-belt.

Flywheel

The flywheel is a comparatively heavy wheel bolted to the rear end of the crankshaft. The inertia of the flywheel tends to keep it turning at constant speed. Thus, the flywheel absorbs energy as the crankshaft tries to speed up and gives back energy as the crankshaft tries to slow down. In effect, the flywheel function is to run smoothly by absorbing some of the energy during the power stroke and then releasing it during the other strokes of the cycle.

In conclusion, the main components of engine are composed of various units, and each of these units has its own function in producing power for vehicle.

Words and Expressions

1. dominant ['dɔminənt] *adj.* 占优势的；主导的；显性的 *n.* 主宰者

2. auxiliary [ɔ:g'ziljəri] *n.* 帮助者；辅助物；助动词 *adj.* 附加的，辅助的

3. crankcase ['kræŋkkeis] *n.* 曲轴箱

4. crankshaft ['kræŋkʃɑ:ft] *n.* 曲轴

5. intricate ['intrikit] *adj.* 复杂的；难懂的

6. internally [in'tənəli] *adv.* 内部地，国内地，内在地

7. lubricate ['lu:brikeit] *v.* 使润滑，涂油，起润滑剂作用

8. distortion [dis'tɔ:ʃən] *n.* 扭曲，变形；曲解

9. bore [bɔ:] *n.* 孔，口径；令人讨厌的人或事 *v.* 钻孔，凿孔

10. essentially [i'senʃəli] *adv.* 本质上；本来

11. kinetic [kai'netik] *adj.* 运动的

12. groove [gru:v] *n.* 槽，凹槽；切口 *v.* 开槽

13. deposit [di'pɔzit] *v.* 存放，堆积；使沉淀 *n.* 押金；存款；定金；堆积物

14. drainage ['dreinidʒ] *v.* 排水 *n.* 排水系统；污水

15. fabricate ['fæbrikeit] *v.* 制造，组装；伪造，杜撰；装配

16. reciprocating [ri'siprəkeitiŋ] *n.* 往复(摆动, 往复式发动机) *adj.* 摆动的

17. sprocket ['sprɔkit] *n.* 链齿；带齿盘；星轮

18. connecting rod 连杆；结合杆；活塞杆

19. ignition distributor 点火分电器

20. water jacket 水冷套，水套

21. clutch housing 离合器壳

22. cylinder head 汽缸盖

23. counter-balanced weight 配重，平衡重

24. cylinder block 汽缸体

25. vibration damper 振动阻尼器，减振器

26. belt pulley 皮带轮，带式运输机滚筒

27. combustion chamber 燃烧室

28. power stroke 做功行程

29. bearing journal 支承轴颈

Notes

1. The increase in gas temperature causes the pressure of the gases to increase. The pressure developed within the combustion chamber is applied to the head of a piston to produce a usable mechanical force, which is then converted into useful mechanical power.

气体温度的增加会导致气体压力的增加。在燃烧室内逐渐形成的压力作用于活塞的头部，产生一个可用的机械力，继而转换成有用的机械功。

2. Each of the engines has a few main working parts; the auxiliary parts are necessary to hold the working parts together or to assist the main working parts in their performance.

每台发动机都有一些主要的工作部件，而辅助部件在使工作部件协调统一工作或辅助主要工作部件运行时也是非常必需的。

3. After the cylinder head has been cast, some areas must be machined so that intake and exhaust manifolds can be attached; valves can be seated; spark plugs and injectors can be installed and a good seal can be provided to the block.

汽缸盖被铸好后，有些地方必须进行机加工，以使进气和排气管可以被安装好，气门、火花塞和喷油器可以被装入并且与缸体间有良好的密封性。

4. The lower grooves often have holes or slots in the bottom of the grooves to permits oil drainage from behind the ring, and then the oil-control rings scrape off excessive oil from the cylinder wall and return it to the oil pan.

较低的环槽底部经常会有孔或槽，它允许润滑油从环后面排出，并且油环从缸壁上刮下过多的润滑油能回到油底壳中。

5. The crankshaft can change the reciprocating motion of the piston into rotary motion and handles the entire power output.

曲轴能将活塞的上下往复运动变为回转运动，并实现整个动力的输出。

6. The flywheel absorbs energy as the crankshaft tries to speed up and gives back energy as the crankshaft tries to slow down.

当曲轴加快运动时，飞轮能够吸收能量；当曲轴运动减慢时，飞轮能够释放能量。

Exercises

A. Vocabulary

I. Translate the following expressions into Chinese.

1. cylinder block

2. oil pan

3. connecting rod

4. water socket

5. piston head

6. piston pin hole

7. connecting rod cap

8. connecting rod bearing half shells

9. main bearing journals

10. counter-balanced weight

II. Identify the English names of the main components of internal combustion engine according to the picture.

1 _____ 2 _____

3 _____ 4 _____

5 _____ 6 _____

7 _____ 8 _____

9 _____ 10 _____

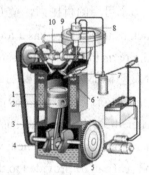

B. Comprehension

I. Discuss the following questions in groups and write down your answers.

1. What does the main components of engine consist of?

_____

2. Which component is the piston attached to?

_____

3. What is the function of the crankshaft?

_____

4. What is the function of the flywheel?

_____

II. Read the following passage carefully and fill in the blanks with the proper forms of the given words.

smoothly	speed up	release	bolted	tend
constant	absorb	rear	slow down	comparatively

The flywheel is a ____ heavy wheel ____ to the ____ end of the crankshaft. The inertia of the flywheel ____ to keep it turning at ____ speed. Thus, the flywheel ____ energy as the crankshaft tries to ____ and gives back energy as the crankshaft tries to ____. In effect, the flywheel function is to run ____ by absorbing some of the energy during the power stroke and then ____ it during the other strokes of the cycle.

C. Translation

I. Translate the following sentences into Chinese.

1. The internal combustion engine, as its name indicates, burns fuel within the cylinders and converts the expanding force of the combustion into rotary force used to propel the vehicle.

2. To avoid misplacing the rod caps during assembly, the connecting rods and their mating caps are marked on one side serial numbers, starting with the first rod from the radiator, to identify their location in the engine.

3. The crankshaft can change the reciprocating motion of the piston into rotary motion and handles the entire power output.

II. Translate the following sentences into English.

1. 汽车发动机是汽车上最复杂的总成，它对于汽车性能有着决定性影响。

2. 由于活塞在极度恶劣的机械和热环境下工作，因此它必须有足够的强度来承受燃气爆炸力。

3. 实际上，飞轮的主要作用是通过吸收发动机在做功冲程中的能量并在其他循环冲程中释放出来，使发动机运转更平稳。

Reading Material

Read the following passages and answer the questions according to the information given in the passages.

Passage One　The Modern Engine

Internal combustion gasoline engines run on a mixture of gasoline and air. The ideal mixture is 14.7 parts of air to one part of gasoline (by weight). Since gas weighs much more than air, we are talking about a whole lot of air and a tiny bit of gas. One part of gas that is completely vaporized into 14.7 parts of air can produce tremendous power when ignited inside an engine.

Let's see how the modern engine uses that energy to make the wheels turn.

Air enters the engine through the air cleaner and proceeds to the

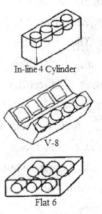

In-line 4 Cylinder

V-8

Flat 6

throttle plate. You control the amount of air that passes through the throttle plate and into the engine with the gas pedal. It is then distributed through a series of passages called the intake manifold to each cylinder. At some point after the air cleaner, depending on the engine, fuel is added to the air-stream by either a fuel injection system or, in older vehicles, by the carburetor.

The majority of engines in motor vehicles today are four-stroke, spark-ignition internal combustion engines. The exceptions like the diesel and rotary engines will not be covered in this article.

Engine Types

There are several engine types which are identified by the number of cylinders and the way the cylinders are laid out. Motor vehicles will have from 3 to 12 cylinders which are arranged in the engine block in several configurations. The most popular of them are shown in the upper figure. In-line engines have their cylinders arranged in a row. 3, 4, 5 and 6 cylinder engines commonly use this arrangement. The "V" arrangement uses two banks of cylinders side-by-side and is commonly used in V-6, V-8, V-10 and V-12 configurations. Flat engines use two opposing banks of cylinders and are less common than the other two designs. They are used in Subaru's and Porsche's in 4 and 6 cylinder arrangements as well as in the old V W beetles with 4 cylinders. Flat engines are also used in some Ferrari's with 12 cylinders.

Each cylinder contains a piston that travels up and down inside the cylinder bore. All the pistons in the engine are connected through individual connecting rods to a common crankshaft.

The crankcase is located below the cylinders on an in-line engine, at the base of the V-type engine and between the cylinder banks on a flat engine. As the pistons move up and down, they turn the crankshaft just like your legs pump up and down to turn the crank that is connected to the pedals of a bicycle.

A cylinder head is bolted to the top of each bank of cylinders to seal the individual cylinders and contains the combustion process that takes place inside the cylinder. The cylinder head contains at least one intake valve and one exhaust valve for each cylinder. This allows the air fuel mixture to enter the cylinder and the burned exhaust gas to exit the cylinder. Most engines have two valves per cylinder, one intake valve and one exhaust valve. Some newer engines sing multiple intakes and exhaust valves per cylinder for increased engine power and efficiency. These engines are sometimes named for the number of valves that they have such as "24 Valve V-6" (which indicates a V-6 engine with four valves per cylinder). Modern engine designs can use anywhere from 2 to 5 valves per cylinder.

The valves are opened and closed by means of a camshaft. A camshaft is a rotating shaft that has individual lobes for each valve. The lobe is a "bump" on one side of the shaft that pushes against a valve lifter moving it up and down. When the lobe pushes against the lifter, the lifter in turn pushes the valve open. When the lobe rotates away from the lifter, the valve is closed by a spring that is attached to the valve. A very common configuration is to have one camshaft located in the engine block with the lifters connecting to the valves through a series of linkages. The camshaft must be synchronized with the crankshaft so that it makes one revolution for every two revolutions of the crankshaft. In most engines, this is done by a "Timing Chain" that connects the camshaft with the crankshaft. Newer engines have the camshaft located in the cylinder head directly over the valves. This design is more efficient but it is more costly to manufacture and requires multiple camshafts on Flat and V-type engines. It also requires much longer timing chains or timing belts which are prone to wear. Some engines have two camshafts on each head, one for the intake valves and one for the exhaust valves. These engines are called Double Overhead Camshaft (D.O.H.C) Engines while the other type is called Single Overhead Camshaft (S.O.H.C) Engines. Engines with the camshaft in the block are called Overhead Valve (O.H.V) Engines.

Questions

1. What does the Double Overhead Camshaft (D.O.H.C) Engines mean?

2. Please describe tell different types of engines.

3. Which component is the "Timing Chain" attached to?

Passage Two   Air Filter Service

How often should I replace my air filter? It's hard to give a specific time or mileage figure because the life of the filter depends on how much crud it ingests. A filter that lasts 20,000 or even 30,000 miles on a vehicle that's driven mostly on expressways may last only a month or two in a rural setting where the vehicle is driven frequently on gravel roads. Changing it annually or every 15,000 miles for preventative maintenance may be a good recommendation for the city driver, but not its country cousin.

Regardless of the mileage or time, a filter should be replaced before it reaches the point where it creates a significant restriction to airflow. But when exactly that point is reached is subject to opinion.

A slightly dirty filter actually cleans more efficiently than a brand new filter. That's because the debris trapped by the filter element helps screen out smaller particles that try to get through. But eventually every filter reaches the point where it causes enough of a pressure drop to restrict airflow. Fuel economy, performance and emissions begin to deteriorate and get progressively worse until the dirty filter is replaced.

Many heavy-duty trucks have a "restriction" meter on the air filter housing that signals when the filter is dirty enough to need replacing. But lacking such a device, the best you can do is guess.

Removing the filter and holding it up to a light will show you how dirty it is. If it's really caked with dirt, it obviously needs to be replaced. Trying to shake or blow the dirt out is a waste of time because too much of it will be embedded in the filter fibers.

NOTE: Many filters that appear to be dirty are in fact still good and do not really need to be replaced. So whether you replace a filter or not is up to you. If you think it's dirty, replace it. If you don't think it's dirty enough to need replacing, then don't.

Questions

1. What does the sentence "a slightly dirty filter actually cleans more efficiently than a brand new filter" mean?

2. How often should you replace your air filter?

3. Why do we say it's hard to give a specific time or mileage figure to change an air fillter?

Unit 3 Power Mechanism of the Engine

In a reciprocating engine, the power mechanism is called the crankshaft and connecting rod assembly. In this assembly, all of the major units such as the engine crankcase and cylinder block, the piston and connecting rod, and the crankshaft and flywheel work in close cooperation to convert thermal energy into mechanical energy used to drive the vehicle.

The engine crankcase and block are usually cast into one piece and therefore can be seem as the largest and most intricate piece of metal in automobile. They are usually made of high-grade cast alloy iron to improve wear characteristics of the cylinder. This major unit must be strong and rigid enough to withstand any bending or distortion.

The piston converts the potential engines of the fuel into the kinetic energy that turns the crankshaft, as shown in Figure 2-5, the piston is a cylindrical shaped hollow part that moves up and down inside the engines cylinder. The piston is composed of piston head, piston rings, piston lands, piston skirt and piston pin hole. The piston head or "crown" is the top surface against which the explosive force is exerted. It may be flat, concave, and convex or any one of a great variety of shapes to promote turbulence or help control combustion. In some application, a narrow groove is cut into the piston above the top ring to serve as a "heat dam" to reduce the amount of heat reaching the top ring. The piston rings carried in the ring groove are of two basic types: compression rings and oil-control ring. Both types are made in a wide variety of designs. The upper ring or rings are to prevent compression leakage; the lower ring or rings control the amount of oil being deposited on the cylinder wall. The lower groove or grooves often have holes or slots in the bottom of the grooves to permit oil drainage from behind the rings. The piston lands are parts of the piston between the ring grooves. The lands provide a seating surface for the sides of piston rings.

The main section of a piston is known as the skirts. It forms a bearing area in contact with the cylinder wall. The piston pinhole in the piston also serves as a bearing for the piston pin, which is used to connect the connecting rod. In addition, because pistons operate under exceedingly difficult mechanical and thermal conditions, piston must be strong enough to stand the force of the expansion, yet light enough to avoid excessive inertia forces when their direction of travel is reversed twice each revolution. Piston must be able to withstand the heat from the burning air-fuel mixture, plus the heat generated by friction.

The connecting rod is attached to the crankshaft at one end and to the piston at the other end. In operation, the connecting rod is subjected to both gas pressure and inertia loads, and therefore, it must be adequately strong and rigid and light in weight as well. So they are generally fabricated from high quality steel composed of connecting rod small end, connecting rod shank, connecting rod big end, connecting rod cap, and connecting rod bearing half shells. Shank of the connecting rod is provided with an I-cross section to give the rod maximum rigidity with the minimum of weight. The big end of the rod is split so that it can be connected to the crankshaft. To avoid misplacing the rod caps during assembly, the connecting rods and their mating caps are marked on one side with serial numbers, starting with the first rod from the radiator, to identify their location in the engine.

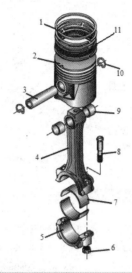

Figure 2-5   A Piston and a Connecting Rod

1—compression rings   2—piston   3—piston pin   4—connecting rod shank   5—connecting rod cap
6—connecting rod nut   7—crank bearing half shells   8—connecting rod bolt   9—connecting rod bushing
10—piston-pin ring   11—oil rings

Some connecting rods have an oil spurt hole in the yoke or at the cap-mating surface to provide cylinder wall lubrication. The small end of the connecting rod is attached to the piston by a piston pin. In some cases the small end of the rod is clamped to the pin or has a bushing in it to allow the pin and rod oscillation. In other designs the pin is bolted to the rod. Connecting rods are usually drilled to provide lubrication to the piston pin and also to spray oil into the bottom of the piston for piston cooling on some designs.

The crankshaft, regarded as the "backbone" of the engine, as shown in Figure 2-6, serves to change the reciprocating motion of the piston into rotary motion and handles the entire power output. The periodic gas and inertia forces taken by the crankshaft may cause it to suffer wear and bending and tensional strains. The crankshaft therefore must be adequately strong and wear-resistant. So the crankshaft is either forged from high quality steel or cast in a high-strong iron. As shown in Figure 2-6, the crankshaft is actually made up of various parts such as main bearing journals, rod journal, crank arm, bearing, counter balanced weight and flywheel end. The crankshaft revolves in bearings located in the engine crankcase, but the number of bearings used

usually depends on the number of cylinders in the engine and the design of the engine. Mechanically, a crankshaft without special balanced weight would have severe vibration when revolving. In order to reduce or eliminate such vibration, it must be provided with counter balanced weights that extend radically from the crankshaft centerline in the opposite direction of the crank arms. In that way, the forces acting on the crankshaft are balanced and vibration is reduced. The rod journals are bored hollow in order to reduce the crankshaft inertia. Drilled diagonally through the crank arms are oil holes to supply oil to the rod journals.

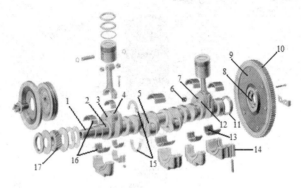

Figure 2-6　The Crankshaft

1—crankshaft front end　2—front main journal　3—oil passage hole　4—crank pin

5—crank web　6—oil passage plug　7—oil passage　8—clutch shaft bearing　9—flywheel

10—flywheel gear ring　11—crankshaft collar　12—counter-balanced weight　13—oil groove

14—connecting rod cap　15—crankshaft thrust　16—front main bearing half shell　17—timing gear

The flywheel is a relatively heavy metal wheel, which is firmly attached to the crankshaft. Its function is to help the engine to run smoothly by absorbing some of the energy during the power stroke and releasing it during the other strokes.

The flywheel acquires kinetic energy because of its rotation; when the flywheel speeds up, it stores additional kinetic energy; and when the flywheel slows down, it gives back that energy. The amount of energy that a flywheel will store for a given change in speed depends on its inertia, which, in turn, depends on its mass and its effective diameter. The heavier the flywheel or the larger its diameter the smaller will be the speed changes. For an engine of a given horsepower, single cylinder engines require large flywheels to keep the momentary speed variations; while multi-cylinder require fewer flywheels which can do it. In practice, the automobile engine is usually multi-cylinder engine. Flywheels, however, because of its inertia, an excessively heavy flywheel will cause the engine to accelerate and decelerate slowly. For this reason, heavy-duty or truck engines have large and heavy flywheels, while racing engines or high performance engines have light flywheels.

In the front face of the flywheel, there is a shallow indentation used to determine the position of the piston in the first cylinder. When this indentation is aligned with a special hole provided in the bell housing, the piston is at Top Dead Center (TDC) or indicates the start of fuel injection into the first cylinder. The flywheels of some engines also carry marks indicating the serial numbers of the cylinders where the compression occurs. The flywheel marks and indentation are used for setting the valve and ignition systems relative to prescribed positions of the crankshaft.

In conclusion, the connecting rod and crankshaft mechanism of the engine is composed of various units, and each of these units has its own functions in producing power for vehicles.

Words and Expressions

1. reciprocating　[ri'siprəkeitiŋ]　*n.* 往复，往复摆动，往复式发动机　*adj.* 摆动的

2. mechanism　['mekənizəm]　*n.* 机械机构

3. crankcase　['kræŋkkeis]　*n.* 曲柄箱，曲轴箱

4. intricate　['intrikit]　*adj.* 复杂的；难懂的

5. rigid　['ridʒid]　*adj.* 刚性的；刚硬的，坚硬的；不易变形的

6. distortion　[dis'tɔ:ʃən]　*n.* 变形，扭曲；扭转

7. flat　[flæt]　*adj.* 平坦的；单调的；扁平的　*adv.* 平直地；干脆地　*n.* 公寓

8. concave　['kɔn'keiv]　*adj.* 凹的，凹面的

9. convex　['kɔn'veks]　*n.* 凸状；凸透镜　*adj.* 凸面的

10. inertia　[i'nə:ʃə]　*n.* 惯性，惯量

11. drainage　['dreinidʒ]　*v.* 排水　*n.* 排水系统；污水

12. serial　['siəriəl]　*adj.* 连续的；一系列的

13. clamp　[klæmp]　*n.* 夹子　*v.* 夹紧

14. backbone　['bækbəun]　*n.* 脊骨，支柱；骨干

15. vibration　[vai'breiʃən]　*n.* 振动；颤动

16. radially　['reidiəli]　*adv.* 径向地；放射状地

17. spray　[sprei]　*v.* 喷雾；扫射；喷射

18. oscillation　[ˌɔsi'leiʃən]　*n.* 振动；动摇

19. fabricate　['fæbrikeit]　*v.* 制造，建造；装配

20. cylindrical　[si'lindrik(ə)l]　*adj.* 圆柱的

21. distortion　[dis'tɔ:ʃən]　*n.* 扭曲，变形；曲解

22. turbulence　['tə:rbjuləns]　*n.* 紊流，涡流；喧嚣，骚乱，狂暴

23. leakage　['li:kidʒ]　*n.* 泄漏

24. thermal energy　热能

25. kinetic energy　动能

26. piston head　活塞顶部

27. piston land　活塞环槽岸

28. piston pin hole　活塞销孔

29. compression ring 压缩环，气环

30. bearing journal 支承轴颈

31. oil-control ring 控油环，油环

32. counter-balanced weight 平衡重量，平衡块

33. crank arm 曲柄臂

Notes

1. This major unit must be strong and rigid enough to withstand any bending or distortion.
这一部件必须非常坚固刚硬，才足以抗得住任何的弯曲或扭曲。

2. The piston head or "crown" is the top surface against which the explosive force is exerted.
活塞头部或"冠部"是整个活塞的最上端，承受爆炸燃烧所产生的力。

3. In order to reduce or eliminate such vibration, it must be provided with counter balanced weights that extend radically from the crankshaft centerline in the opposite direction of the crank arms.
为了减少或消除振动，它必须装有从曲轴中心线向与曲柄相对的方向延伸的平衡块。

4. The heavier the flywheel or the larger its diameter, the smaller will be the speed changes.
飞轮越重或飞轮直径越大，速度变化就越小。

5. Because of its rotation the flywheel acquires kinetic energy; when the flywheel speeds up, it stores additional kinetic energy; and when the flywheel slows down it gives back that energy.
由于旋转的飞轮需要动能，当飞轮的运动加速时，它存储额外的动能；当飞轮减速时，它释放能量。

6. The flywheel marks and indentation are used for setting the valve and ignition systems relative to prescribed positions of the crankshaft.
飞轮标记和凹口被用来确定阀门和点火装置系统的位置，这要根据曲轴的规定位置来确定。

Exercises

A. Vocabulary

I. Translate the following expressions into Chinese.

1. thermal energy

2. connecting rod cap

3. piston head

4. piston land

5. counter-balanced weight

6. connecting rod bearing half shells

7. bearing journal

8. rod journal

9. oil-control ring

10. crank arm

II. Identify the English names of the automobile according to the picture.

1. _____   2. _____

3. _____   4. _____

5. _____   6. _____

7. _____   8. _____

9. _____   10. _____

B. Comprehension

I. Discuss the following questions in groups and write down your answers.

1. What dose the power mechanism of an engine consist of?

_____

2. What are the functions of the power mechanism of the engine?

_____

3. What components are attached to the piston?

_____

4. What is the function of the flywheel?

_____

II. Read the following passage carefully and fill in the blanks with the proper forms of the given words.

> *shape   concave   convert   combustion   promote*
> *kinetic   compose   groove   reach   serve*

The piston _____ the potential engines of the fuel into the _____ energy that turns the crankshaft. The piston is a cylindrical _____ hollow part that moves up and down inside the engines cylinder. The piston is _____ of piston head, piston rings, piston lands, piston skirt and piston pin hole. The piston head or "crown" is the top surface against which the explosive force is exerted. It may be flat, _____, and convex or any one of a great variety of shapes to _____ turbulence or help control _____. In some application, a narrow groove is cut into the piston above the top ring to _____ as a "heat dam" to reduce the amount of heat _____ the top ring. The piston rings carried in the ring _____ are of two basic types: compression rings and oil-control ring. Both types are made in a wide variety of designs.

C. Translation

I. Translate the following sentences into Chinese.

1. The engine crankcase and block are usually cast into one piece and therefore can be seen as the largest and most intricate piece of metal in automobile.

2. The connecting rod is attached to the crankshaft at one end and to the piston at the other end.

3. The periodic gas and inertia forces taken by the crankshaft may cause it to suffer wear and bending and tensional strains. The crankshaft therefore must be adequately strong and wear-resistant.

II. Translate the following sentences into English.

1. 在这些总成中，所有的组成部件如发动机曲轴箱和缸体、活塞和连杆、曲轴和飞轮密切联系，把热能转换成机械能，用来驱动车辆行驶。

2. 由于活塞在极度恶劣的机械和热性能条件下工作，因此活塞必须有足够的强度来承受膨胀力，同时必须足够轻，以避免两次相反的转动过程产生过度的惯性力。

3. 为避免错误地装配连杆盖，连杆和与它相配合的连杆盖(从散热器旁的第一根连杆开始)一侧用序号进行标注，以识别它们在发动机上的安装位置。

Reading Material

Read the following passages and answer the questions according to the information given in the passages.

Passage One   Benefits of HEV

Hybrid Electric Vehicles (HEVs) are offered by numerous auto manufacturers and are becoming increasingly more available. Today, most people have heard of HEVs and many people have a basic understanding of how they work. Hybrid Electric Vehicles (HEVs) combine the internal combustion engine of a conventional vehicle with the battery and electric motor of an electric vehicle. The combination offers low emissions with the power, range, and convenient fueling of conventional (gasoline and diesel) vehicles, and they never need to be plugged in. The inherent flexibility of HEVs makes them well suited for fleet and personal transportation.

A Hybrid Electric Vehicle (HEV) is an optimized mix of various components. It mainly contains the following parts: electric motor, battery, engine, fuel tank, etc.

A Hybrid Electric Vehicle (HEV) has two or more sources of onboard power. The integration of these power-producing components with the electrical energy storage components allows for many different types of HEV designs. A power control strategy is needed to control the flow of power and to maintain adequate reserves of energy in the storage devices. Although this is an added complexity not found in conventional vehicles it allows the components to work together in an optimal manner to achieve multiple design objectives, such as high fuel economy and low emissions.

Hybrid Electric Vehicles (HEVs) are powered by two energy sources — an energy conversion unit(such as a combustion engine or fuel cell) and an energy storage device (such as batteries or ultra capacitors). The energy conversion unit may be powered by gasoline, methanol, compressed natural gas, hydrogen and other alternative fuels. Hybrid electric vehicles have the potential to be two to three times more fuel-efficient than conventional vehicles.

Low Emissions and High Efficiency

Hybrid Electric Vehicle (HEV) emissions vary depending on the vehicle and its configuration. But in general, HEVs have lower emissions than conventional vehicle because an electric motor is used with an internal combustion engine, reduces fuel use and emissions. In addition, HEVs have the potential to operate in "electric only" mode. In this mode, the vehicle can operate with no emissions, which is optimal in congested areas and in areas where emissions are not tolerated.

An HEV can easily control the engine's operating point, which enables the vehicle to be more efficient and pollute less. The engine can also be downsized because the motor/battery can help power the vehicle and the engine can be turned off during non-use times, such as at stops or coasting. In addition, the engine can have a smoother operation, which decreases power spikes that can cause the engine to use more fuel and produce more pollution. And finally, an HEV engine can power electric compacts, which is more efficient than the mechanical counterparts normally used. An example of this would be using the electric motor instead of hydraulic power for steering.

High Fuel Economy and Low Costs

HEVs can go 40−70 miles per gallon of gasoline. It allows drivers to fuel less often and drives more miles on a tank of fuel than a conventional vehicle.

In addition to the cost savings associated with vehicle operation, the cost of HEVs are very competitive with similar conventional vehicles. Any premium cost that may be associated with HEVs of the future can be offset by overall fuel savings and tax incentives.

Today there are several tax incentives that make purchasing an HEV cost effective. There are federal and state incentives available.

Outstanding Performance

Auto manufactures are making HEVs with performance, safety and cost comparable to a conventional vehicle because they know that these elements are most important to consumers. And by combining gasoline with electric power, Hybrid will have the same or greater range than traditional combustion engines. The HEV is able to operate approximately two times more efficiently than conventional vehicles.

Energy Security

Because HEVs are so efficient and have high fuel economy, less fuel is used than conventional vehicle. In additional, HEVs have the potential of running on alternative fuels, which can be renewable and produced in the United States. Therefore, HEVs can reduce America's dependence on fossil fuels and help decrease foreign oil imports, thereby increasing energy security.

Questions

1. Why do HEVs have lower emissions than conventional vehicles?

2. Which is more efficient between HEVs and conventional vehicles? Why?

3. Please describe the outstanding performance of HEVs.

Passage Two   Fuel Filter Replacement

How can I tell if my fuel filter needs to be replaced? The only way to tell for sure is to remove the filter and blow through it. If there's little resistance, the filter is still okay and does not need to be replaced. But if there's more than minimal resistance, the filter is dirty and should be replaced.

CAUTION: Gasoline is poisonous; does not taste very good and may burn sensitive lips. So don't hold the filter to your mouth to blow through it. Instead, attach a short piece of clean rubber hose to the filter and then blow through the hose to test the filter.

Filter Problems

A completely plugged fuel filter will make your engine cold by choking off the flow of fuel to the carburetor or injectors. The engine may not start, or it may start, then stall and die.

Some filters have a spring-loaded bypass, however, this allows fuel to bypass the filter element if it becomes clogged. Fuel continues to flow, but it may carry dirt to the carburetor or injectors, which can create additional problems.

A partially restricted filter will usually pass enough fuel to keep the engine running at idle or low speed, but may starve the engine for fuel at higher speeds or loads. So your engine may run fine putting around town, but sputter and lack power when you try to drive at highway speeds or pass someone.

Tank Filter

Located inside the fuel tank is a screen or mesh sock that acts like a prefilter to keep big pieces of dirt and rust from being drawn into the fuel pickup tube or tank-mounted electric fuel pump. If the screen becomes clogged with debris, it can have the same effect as a plugged or dirty fuel filter. Therefore, if you've been experiencing a fuel starvation problem and have replaced the fuel filter — and it didn't help — the screen in the tank is probably the culprit. To clean or replace it, the fuel tank usually has to be removed.

WARNING: The fuel tank must be drained prior to removal. The fuel must be stored in a sealed "approved" container. The battery should also be disconnected to prevent any accidental sparks from an in-tank electric fuel pump connection from igniting the vapors. Do not smoke when working on the fuel tank, filter or fuel lines, and keep all other sources of ignition away (electric heaters, pilot lights, etc.) from the work area.

Filter Replacement

Replacing the fuel filter periodically (every year or so) for preventative maintenance can reduce the risk of filter-related driveability problems. Most vehicle manufacturers, however, no longer specify a replacement interval for the fuel filter. Or, if they do, it's some incredibly long interval like once every five years or 50,000 miles. Many mechanics feel this is unrealistic.

Waiting that long to change the filter is asking for trouble, especially if you drive on gravel or dirt roads, buy the cheapest gas you can find from "cut-rate" stations, use gas with alcohol in it, or your vehicle is more than six or seven years old and may have rust in the tank.

The fuel filter on carbureted engines is usually located at the inlet fitting of the carburetor, or an "in-line" filter is used between the fuel pump and carburetor.

When replacing a filter that screws into the inlet fitting on the carburetor, be careful not to overtighten the filter. The threads in the carburetor are relatively soft and can be easily stripped. But also make sure the filter is snug so that it doesn't leak. It's okay to apply some gasket sealer to the filter threads to assure a leak-free connection. But do not use Room Temperatwe Valcanization(RTV) silicone sealer (which gasoline dissolves) or teflon tape (pieces of which can flake loose and end up in the carburetor).

When replacing an in-line filter, most filters come with two new rubber hoses that go on either side of the filter. Use them. Don't reuse the old hoses because rubber hoses deteriorate over time and can leak or shed small flakes or rubber that can end up in the filter or carburetor. Also, make sure the hose clamps are properly positioned and tight.

NOTE: Most in-line filters have an arrow showing the direction fuel should flow through the filter. Install the filter so the arrow points toward the carburetor.

Fuel Injection Filters

Fuel filters on fuel injected engines are usually larger and have a finer filter element than those on carbureted engines. Consequently, they are usually more expensive.

The filter may be located anywhere between the fuel tank and injector fuel supply rail or throttle body. On many cars, light trucks and minivans, the filter is located underneath the vehicle along a frame rail. On some, the filter is part of the electric fuel pump assembly inside the fuel tank! Refer to a shop manual for your fuel filter's location.

CAUTION: Fuel injected engines usually have a lot of residual pressure in the fuel line, even when a vehicle has sat overnight. So either follow the manufacturer's recommended procedure for relieving pressure in the line prior to removing the filter (applying vacuum to the fuel pressure regulator manifold fitting, or cranking the engine with the ignition disabled), or wrap a rag around the hose connections and slowly loosen them.

If the filter has an arrow indicating the direction of flow, it should be installed with the arrow pointing toward the engine and away from the fuel tank.

If the filter is located inside the tank, the tank will probably have to be removed. Follow the same precautions as previously described for replacing a plugged pickup screen.

Questions

1. How can I tell if my fuel filter needs to be replaced?
2. What are the common problems of a filter?
3. Please describe the procedure of changing fuel fillter.

Unit 4　Valves and Valve Train

The valve gear of an internal combustion engine provides timely admission of the fresh charge into the cylinders and exhaust of spent gases from them. For this purpose, the valves at definite moments open and close the intake and exhaust ports in the cylinder head, through which the cylinders communicate with the intake and exhaust manifold.

There are two openings, or ports, in the enclosed end of the cylinder. One of them permits the mixture of air and gasoline vapor to enter the cylinder. The other port permits the burned gases, after combustion, to exhaust, or escape, from the cylinder. The cam lobes on the camshaft are so related to the crankshaft crankpins through the gears or sprockets and chain as to cause the valves to open and close with the correct relationship to the piston strokes.

A valve-opening mechanism opens the valve or lifts it off its seat at certain times. For most engines, this mechanism is called the valve train. It is composed of timing gears, a camshaft, tappets, push rods, rocker arm with fasteners, valves, springs with fasteners and valve guides, as shown in Figure 2-7.

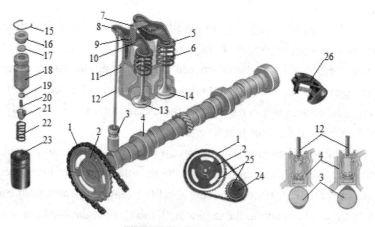

Figure 2-7　Valve Gear

1—timing chain　2—sprocket camshaft　3—hydraulic tappet　4—camshaft　5—retainer　6—valve spring
7—bridge　8—rocker arm　9—cap screws　10—pivot assembly　11—cylinder head　12—push rod
13—exhaust valve　14—intake valve　15—snap ring　16—plunger cap　17—metering valve　18—plunger
19—check valve　20—check valve spring　21—check valve retainer　22—plunger return spring
23—tappet body　24—crankshaft sprocket　25—timing marks　26—tensioner

As the camshaft turns, the cam lobe comes around under the valve lifter. This raises the lifter, which in turn pushes upward on the push rod. The push rod, as it is lifted, causes the end of the rocker arm to move up. The rocker arm pivots around its supporting shaft so that the valve end of the rocker arm is forced downward. This downward movement forces the valve to move downward off its seat so that it opens. After the cam lobe moves out from under the valve lifter, the valve spring forces the valve up onto its seat again.

A spring on the valve stem tends to hold the valve on its seat (closed). The lower end of the spring rests against the cylinder head. The upper end rests against a flat washer, or spring retainer, which is attached to the valve stem by a retainer lock (also called a keeper). The spring is under compression, which means that it tries to expand and therefore spring-loads the valve in the closed position.

The timing gears in most engines are housed in a special case fitted at the front end of the engine. These are necessary to transmit rotation from the crankshaft to the camshaft, fuel injection pump shaft, oil pump and other mechanisms. The gears are made of steel and use helical teeth to reduce noise.

Camshaft's function is to open the engine valves positively and timely, in a definite sequence, and to control their closing against the return action of the valve springs. The shaft is made integral with its cams and bearing journals. Each cam controls a single valve, either intake or exhaust. In some automobile engines, the camshaft is made integral with fuel pump eccentric wheel and oil pump drive gear. The camshaft bearings are lubricated with oil supplied under pressure from the main gallery in the cylinder block.

The tappets serve to transmit the force from the camshaft to the push rods. The tappets are small cylindrical bores receive the push rods. They are made of cast iron or steel and located in the guides, which may be made integral with the cylinder block or removable as in the engine. When the engines operate, the tappets continuously rotate about their axes for uniform wear. The rotation is ensured by a convex surface of their bottoms and a slanted surface of the cams.

The push rods transmit the force from the tappets to the rocker and they are made as steel stems with hardened tips or duralumin tubes with spherical steel tips press-fitted at both ends. The push rod tips bear against the tappet hollow at one end against the spherical surface of the rocker adjusting screw at the other.

The rockers transmit the force from the push rod to the valve. The rockers are made of steel and are installed on a hollow fulcrum. A bronze bush is press fitted into the rocker hole to reduce friction. The hollow fulcrum is supported by standards on the cylinder head. Endplay of the rocker is prevented by a coil spring. The rocker arm is a bell crank made of steel. At the middle of the rocker arm, there is a boss with a bore into which is pressed the bushing. A hardened curved pad is provided on the end of the rocker where it contacts the valve stem tip, while a threaded hole is machined in its other end to receive the adjusting screw used to set the valve clearance, the clearance between the rocker contact pad and the valve stem tip, so that the valve will be tightly pressed against its seat when hot. The rocker arm freely oscillates about the rocker-arm shaft supported by a series of pedestals or brackets, which are bolted to the top deck of the cylinder head.

An engine valve is a device designed to open a passage when moving in one direction and to close it when moving in the opposite direction. Each cylinder of a four-stroke-cycle diesel or

gasoline engine is commonly equipped with an intake valve and an exhaust valve. The purpose of the intake valve is to allow the air fuel mixture or air to enter the cylinder. After the combustion process has been completed, the burned gases are permitted to escape from the cylinder through the exhaust valve. To obtain sufficient valve area, some automobiles have two intake valves and two exhaust valves.

A valve consists of a head and stem. The valve head has a narrow chamfer of 45° or 30° referred to as valve face. The valve face fits tightly against the seat, which is achieved by grinding. The kinds of the inlet and exhaust valves are of different diameter. For better engine breathing, the inlet valve has a larger diameter than the exhaust one.

The cylindrical stem of the valve has a recess at the upper end for fastening the valve spring. The valve stems slide in the cast-iron or cerametallic valve guides.

The valve spring provides the force necessary to close the valve and hold it tightly against its seat.

Valve guide supports the valve stem and guides its movement so that the valve face remains perfectly concentric with the valve seat and fits it without any skewing. Replaceable or insert, valve guides are fabricated from cast iron or a cermet material and pressed in the cylinder head.

To decrease oil penetration along the valve stem to the combustion chambers, the seating collars are fitted with rubber rings or the seats are provided with rubber caps. More uniform heating and wear of the valve are ensured with the valves rotating during the operation of the engine. In general, there are two ways of rotating: one is free rotate and the other is positive rotate.

The valves of some automobile engines are made to rotate positively by a special mechanism during engine operation. This mechanism known as the valve rotator and consists of a stationary housing with five ramp like grooves along its circumference that contain five steel balls loaded by return spring. Freely placed on top of the balls is a flexible washer against which rests valve spring through the intermediary of a seating collar.

As the valve is opened, spring is compressed and its increasing load causes the flexible washer to flatten out and force balls down their ramps against the resistance offered by their return springs. As the balls roll down, they turn through some angle the flexible washer, seating collar and valve spring together with the valve; when the valve is closed, the valve spring load will decrease. The flexible washer deflects to acquire its initial conical shape and abutting against a shoulder in housing and releases the balls which are then forced by their coil springs to return to their starting position.

Words and Expressions

1. sprocket ['sprɔkit] *n.* 链轮齿，链齿

2. manifold ['mænifəuld] *n.* 歧管；总管；多种；复印本 *adj.* 多种的，多方面的

3. tappet ['tæpit] *n.* (凸轮)挺杆；气门推杆

4. pivot ['pivət] *n.* 枢；旋转 *v.* 装枢轴于；以……为中心旋转

5. helical ['helikəl] *adj.* 螺旋的，螺旋形的

6. retainer [ri'teinə] *n.* 止推挡圈；定位器，固位器

7. convex ['kɔn'veks] *adj.* 凸的，凸面的，凸圆的

8. duralumin [djuə'ræljumin] *n.* 硬铝，杜拉铝

9. spherical ['sferikəl] *adj.* 球的，球形的

10. fulcrum ['fʌlkrəm] *n.* 支点，支轴，支柱

11. oscillate ['ɔsileit] *v.* 摆动；振动；摇摆

12. pedestal ['pedistl] *n.* 轴承座；轴架；支座

13. circumference [sə'kʌmfərəns] *n.* 圆周；胸围

14. terminate ['tə:mineit] *v.* 终止，结束，终结

15. chamfer ['tʃæmfə] *n.* 锥角；切角面

16. concentric [kɔn'sentrik] *adj.* 同心的；同轴的

17. penetration [peni'treiʃən] *n.* 渗透；穿透；侵入

18. conical ['kɔnikəl] *adj.* 圆锥形的，圆锥的

19. cerametallic *adj.* 金属陶瓷的

20. valve clearance　气门间隙

21. valve gear　气门机构，配气机构

22. fresh charge　新鲜充量

23. communicate with　与……连通，和……互通

24. coil spring　螺旋弹簧，圈弹簧

25. camshaft play　凸轮轴端隙

26. valve stem　气门杆，阀杆

27. rocker contact pad　摇臂接触部位

28. variable coil pitch spring　变螺距弹簧

29. cam lobe　凸轮的凸角

Notes

1. The valve gear of an internal combustion engine provides timely admission of the fresh charge into the cylinders and exhaust of spent gases from them.

　　内燃机的配气机构能定时地将新鲜的混合气充入汽缸，并且将废气从汽缸中排出。

2. The push rods transmit the force from the tappets to the rocker and they are made as steel stems with hardened tips or duralumin tubes with spherical steel tips press-fitted at both ends.

　　推杆将挺杆传来的推力传给摇臂，推杆由顶部淬火的钢柱或由两端压入配合的带球形钢头的硬铝管制成。

3. The cylindrical stem of the valve has a recess at the upper end for fastening the valve spring.

气门圆柱形杆部上端有一凹槽以便紧固气门弹簧。

4. The valves of some automobile engines are made to rotate positively by a special mechanism during engine operation.

有些发动机的气门上安装有特殊的结构，这种结构可使气门在发动机工作时正向转动。

Exercises

A. Vocabulary

I. Translate the following expressions into Chinese.

1. valve gear

2. exhaust manifold

3. timing gears

4. push rod

5. rocker arm

6. valve guide

7. spring retainer

8. valve stem

9. valve clearance

10. variable coil pitch spring

II. Identify the English names of the automobile according to the picture.

1. _____   2. _____

3. _____   4. _____

5. _____   6. _____

7. _____   8. _____

9. _____   10. _____

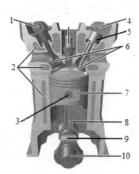

B. Comprehension

I. Discuss the following questions in groups and write down your answers.

1. What is the function of the valve gear of an internal combustion engine?

_____

2. What does the valve gear of an internal combustion engine consist of?

_____

3. Which component drives the camshaft?

_____

4. What is the function of the valve spring?

_____

II. Read the following passage carefully and fill in the blanks with the proper forms of the given words.

cause　　close　　down　　compress　　decrease
ramp　　flatten　　abut　　release　　deflect

As the valve is opened, spring is ____ and its increasing load ____ the flexible washer to ____ out and force balls down their ____ against the resistance offered by their return springs. As the balls roll ____, they turn through some angle the flexible washer, seating collar and valve spring together with the valve; when the valve is ____, the valve spring load ____. The flexible washer ____ to acquire its initial conical shape and ____ against a shoulder in housing and ____ the balls which are then forced by their coil springs to return to their starting position.

C. Translation

I. Translate the following sentences into Chinese.

1. Camshaft's function is to open the engine valves positively and timely, in a definite sequence, and to control their closing against the return action of the valve springs.

2. The valve spring provides the force necessary to close the valve and hold it tightly against its seat.

3. As the valve is opened, spring is compressed and its increasing load causes the flexible washer to flatten out and force balls down their ramps against the resistance offered by their return springs.

II. Translate the following sentences into English.

1. 配气机构由正时齿轮、凸轮轴、挺杆、气门、带有锁紧装置的气门弹簧和气门导管组成。

2. 摇臂的一端是经过淬火的圆弧形长臂，与气门杆尾端接触；而有螺纹孔的另一端安装有调整螺钉，用来调整气门长臂与气门杆尾端之间的间隙，从而保证气门在受热后紧紧地压在气门座上。

3. 发动机气门向某一个方向运动时开启一个通道；而当它向相反的方向移动时则关闭此通道。

Reading Material

Read the following passages and answer the questions according to the information given in the passages.

Passage One　The Future of Auto Development

The automotive industry has faced considerable challenges over the last couple of years such as overcapacity, ultra-competitive markets, fluctuating commodity price and rising pension coat. It's gotten to the point that some industry observers have dubbed the current situation the Perfect Storm.

To weather this storm, automakers will have to increase the innovation and reduce prices. So there will be significant change in the design content for automobiles over the next decade. The

biggest change will be in electronics or "mechatronics" as it is known in the industry. Beginning in the 1990s, electronics in automobiles have increased steadily. This trend should continue, with electronics going from 22% of total car value in 2002 to a forecasted 35% by 2015. And growth in electronics should revolve around convenience, safety and environmental requirements.

Similarly, software will play an expanding role in auto design, with the amount of money spent on software almost doubling between 2002 and 2015. The interior, power train and chassis will contribute most to this growth in software value.

The introduction of software-controlled electronics will also spur the growth of in-vehicle networks and subsystem interdependencies. Furthermore, Original Equipment Manufacturer (OEM) will rely increasingly on suppliers such as Delphi and Bosch, whose share of product development is forecasted to increase to 70% by 2015.

Future Auto Development

PTC has conducted a joint study with the center for automotive research, which looks at product development in the auto industry. Although the final study won't be available until later this year, major conclusions are already known. For example, Auto companies all over the world take roughly the same amount of time to develop a new platform, about 24 months. Innovation will increasingly come from suppliers. Math-bases design, analysis, and Computer Aided Design (CAD) will become even more important. Design for Manufacturing and Assembly (DFMA), along with design for durability and reliability, will remain the most important design criteria. With electronics success depends on engineers and IT departments having a company-wide view and closer coordination on system components. Engineers will need to know the entire life cycle of a product, from planning to after market support and disposal.

An Example of Complexity

Taking a look at the design and development of a wiring harness will demonstrate the complexity of such life-cycle approach across electronic, mechanical and software design.

Systems definition: This includes translating vehicle electrical specifications into required connections in each system; breaking down the system logically by function; creating block diagrams of designs and selecting the right components and connectors.

Topology development: This includes translating a conceptual model into an implemental topology, component placement in vehicle, partitioning the vehicle for the harness, and placing interconnects based on physical constraints and logical requirements.

Physical harness development: This includes translating topology into real-world connections, determining physical properties of the harness such as splices, wires, connectors and other attached parts, performing electronic 3D routing, and developing 2D harness manufacturing drawings from 3D routings.

Schematic release: This is usually the final step and includes the merger of system design and harness documentation into a practical format for field use, developing engineering system views for troubleshooting, and providing service drawings.

As these steps show, even harness design requires interplay between electrical and mechanical engineering and consideration of the harness' entire life cycle.

It's important to realize that software design differs from mechanical and electronic design. The differences encompass culture, process and tools. There is universal agreement that software development is often the least controlled of the design activities discussed thus far. Software revisions are increasing in number and are more loosely managed compared to those in other design domains. The frequent and long revision cycles for software are creating problems, including some downstream in configuration and connecting systems, subsystems and components.

Auto companies need to get a much better handle on software. A tool that might help is the Unified Modeling Language (UML), which is becoming a de-facto method for communicating software capabilities to suppliers and other businesses.

Automakers also need tighter teamwork between mechanical, electrical and software engineers. The major hurdle preventing better teamwork is the different culture, which includes different tools, practices, and rules for managing design and revisions, and lack of data-sharing standards preventing easy integration.

Auto companies must also have a Product Life-cycle Management (PLM) strategy that addresses all design disciplines. Tile strategy should include product-data management which gives engineers the right data at the right time. There should be a single source of product data that supports all design tools along with traceability. Cross-discipline collaboration lets engineers identify and resolve issues across all CAD domains.

Process management establishes consistent, repeatable development processes including revision and new car introductions.

Questions

1. What challenges faced by the automobile industry are included?

2. What will be the development trend of automobile industry in the future?

3. What will the "mechatronics" of automobile industry be in the future?

Passage Two   Burned Valve

A "burned valve" is a valve that has overheated and lost its ability to hold a leak-free seal. Valve burning is usually limited to exhaust valves because they run much hotter than intake valves.

The diagnosis of a burned valve is usually the result of a compression test. If a cylinder shows little or no compression, it frequently means the exhaust valve is not sealing. The valve may or may not be actually burnt (melted), but have other physical damage such as cracks or areas where pieces of metal are missing or eroded away from the valve face.

The cure for this condition is to remove the cylinder head, replace the bad valve and reface (or replace) the valve seat. As a rule, the head is usually given a complete valve job at the same time because the rest of the valves and guides probably need attention, too. If one exhaust valve has failed, the rest are probably on the verge of failure if they haven't already started to leak.

Why Valves Burn

There are several reasons why valves burn. One is normal wear. As an engine accumulates

miles, the constant pounding and thermal erosion wears away the metal on the face of the valve and seat. The exhaust valve sheds most of its heat through the seat, so when the face and seat become worn and the area of contact is reduced, the valve starts to run hot. Eventually the buildup of heat weakens the metal and pieces of it start to break or flake away. Once this happens, it forms a hot spot that accelerates the process all the more. The valve begins to leak and compression drops. The result is a weak or dead cylinder and a noticeable drop in engine power, smoothness and performance.

A bad exhaust valve will also increase exhaust emissions significantly because it allows unburned fuel to leak into the exhaust. High hydrocarbon(HC) emissions, therefore, may also be an indicator of a burned valve.

An exhaust valve can also burn if the valve lash closes up for some reasons(improper lash adjustment, cam or lifter wear, a bent push rod, worn rocker arm or cam follower, etc.). The lack of lash (clearance) in the valvetrain prevents the valve from closing fully, which causes it to leak compression and overheat.

Valve burning can also be caused by any condition that makes the engine run hot or elevates combustion temperatures. This includes cooling problems, abnormal combustion like detonation or preignition, loss of Exhaust Gas Recirculation (EGR), retarded ignition timing or lean fuel mixtures.

Valve Recession

A condition known as "valve recession" can allow the valves to recede or sink into the head because of excessive seat wear. This causes the valve lash to be lost which allows the valves to leak and burn. It occurs primarily in older engines (mostly those built prior to 1975) that were not designed to run on unleaded gasoline. When leaded gasoline was still around, lead acted like a lubricant to reduce valve seat wear. But when lead was eliminated, it meant engines had to be made with harder seats. These older engines didn't have hard seats, so many of them began to experience valve wear problems when switched to unleaded fuel. If you're driving an antique or classic car, therefore, you should either use some type of lead substitute fuel additive to protect the valves or have the seats replaced with hard seats when the engine is overhauled.

Questions

1. What is a "burned valve"?

2. Why valves burn?

3. What does valve recession mean?

Unit 5 Engine Fuel System

The fuel system has the job of supplying a combustible mixture of air and fuel to the engine. The fuel system consists of the fuel tank, fuel pump, carburetor, fuel filter and fuel lines. All automobiles have some forms of fuel supply system. The purpose of the supply system is to store and then to supply a clean, continuous, and adequate amount of fuel under sufficient pressure to the carburetor. The fuel, which can be either gasoline or diesel fuel, is stored in a fuel tank. Moreover, the system must perform these functions regardless of the outside temperature, altitude and speed of the vehicle, as shown in Figure 2-8.

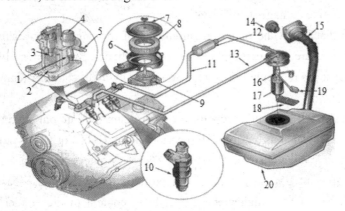

Figure 2-8 Fuel Supply System

1—fuel return 2—throttle plate 3—fuel injector nozzle 4—fuel pressure regulator 5—fuel inlet
6—air cleaner 7—cover 8—air filter 9—carburetor 10—fuel injector 11—fuel feed line
12—inline fuel filter 13—fuel return line 14—fuel cap 15—filter pipe 16—fuel level gauge sensor
17—in-take fuel pump 18—in-take fuel filter 19—float 20—fuel tank

Gasoline

Gasoline is a complex blend of carbon and hydrogen compounds. It is distilled from crude petroleum and is highly flammable. It also changes readily from a liquid to a vapor. This characteristic is called volatility. Volatility is a measurement of how easily the fuel vaporizes. If the gasoline does not vaporize completely, it will not burn properly. The most important feature of gasoline is resistance to knock (octane).

If the gasoline vaporizes too easily the mixture will be too lean to burn properly. Since high temperature increases volatility, it is desirable to have a low volatility fuel for warm temperature and a high volatility fuel for cold weather. Gasoline will turn to vapor inside the fuel tank or fuel lines. Inside the fuel line, fuel vapor may block the flow of liquid gasoline. This is called vapor lock, Which is common in fuel lines where the inlet side of the pump is exposed to high temperatures.

The flammability of gasoline varies with its quality and the additives mixed with the gasoline. The way gasoline burns inside the combustion chamber is most important. Increasing the pressure of the fuel mixture in the combustion chamber before ignition helps to increase the power of an engine. This is done by compressing the fuel mixture to a smaller volume. Higher compression ratio not only boosts power but also gives more efficient power. However, as the compression ratio goes up, knocking tendency is also increased. The octane number of a gasoline is a measure

of its antiknock quality or ability to resist detonation during combustion. Detonation is sometimes referred to as knock, can be defined as an uncontrolled explosion of the last portion of the burning fuel-air mixture due to excessive temperature and pressure condition in the combustion chamber. Since detonation creates shock pressure waves, and hence audible knock, rather than smooth combustion and expansion of the fuel-air mixture, it results in loss of power, excessive localized temperatures, and engine damage if sufficiently severe.

Other factors that affect the octane requirements of the engine are: air/fuel ratio, ignition timing, engine temperature, and carbon built up in the cylinder. Many automobile manufacturers have installed exhaust gas recirculation systems to reduce cylinder chamber temperature.

Diesel

Diesel fuel is a specific fractional distillate of petroleum fuel oil, but alternatives that are not derived from petroleum, such as biodiesel, biomass to liquid (BTL) or gas to liquid (GTL) diesel, are increasingly being developed and adopted. Diesel engines generally have a better fuel economy than equivalent gasoline engines and produce less greenhouse gas emission. Their greater economy is due to the higher energy per-liters content of diesel fuel and the intrinsic efficiency of the diesel engine. Diesel is fired by compression rather than a spark in the internal combustion engine. This is to say that the piston squeezes the fuel fast enough into a small enough space into the combustion chamber, that the fuel ignites. An explosive detonation from the friction of fuel subjected to rapid compression. Since diesel fuel vaporizes at a much higher temperature than gasoline, there is no need for a fuel evaporation control system as with gasoline. Diesel fuels are rated with a cetane number rather than an octane number, while a higher octane of gasoline indicates resistance to ignition the higher cetane rating of diesel fuel indicates the ease at which the fuel will ignite. Diesel fuel emissions are higher in sulfur and lower in carbon monoxide and hydrocarbons than gasoline and are subject to different emission testing standards.

Fuel Tank

The fuel tank is used to store the fuel of engine needed. Most automobiles have a single tank located in the rear of the vehicle. The fuel tank is designed to fit around frame and to be protected from impacts. Fuel tanks have internal baffles to prevent the fuel from sloshing back and forth. The fuel cap on the fuel tank is used to keep the fuel from splashing out, release the vacuum created by the fuel removing, and prevent vapors from escaping directly into the atmosphere. All tanks have a fuel filler pipe, a fuel outlet line to the engine and a vent system. All catalytic converter cars are equipped with a filler pipe restrictor leading fuel.

The fuel levels are measured by a fuel-metering unit. One style of the unit has a hinged float inside the tank. As the float position changes with different levels of fuel, the needle changes position on the dashboard gauge.

Fuel Pumps

Two types of fuel pumps are used in automobiles: mechanical and electric. All fuel injected cars today use electric fuel pumps, while most carbureted cars use mechanical fuel pumps.

The mechanical fuel pump is used on many vehicles with carburetors and driven by the camshaft. Mechanical fuel pumps are diaphragm pumps mounted on the engine and operated by an eccentric cam usually on the camshaft. As the camshaft turns, the lobe lifts a lever up and down, causing a pumping action. A rocker arm attached to the eccentric moves up and down flexing the diaphragm and pumping the fuel to the engine. Fuel is drawn from the tank by a vacuum and sent to the carburetor.

Electrical fuel pump can be used instead of mechanical type. The types of the electrical fuel pumps employed include the bellow and the impeller or roller vane. Because electric pumps do not depend on an eccentric for operation, they can be located anywhere on the vehicle.

Fuel system that has electrical fuel pumps and fuel injectors may use a fuel pressure regulator to keep the pressure constant.

Fuel Filters

Fuel filter are used to stop any contamination from getting into the fuel system of both gasoline and diesel engines.

The gasoline engines may have one or two filters in the fuel system. The first filter is usually placed inside the fuel tank to prevent large pieces of contaminant from damaging the fuel pump. The second one is an in-line type or an in-carburetor type used to filter out small dirt particles.

Many diesel engines used in automotive applications have only one filter, which is called the primary filter. On some engines, a secondary filter is adopted and combined with primary one to build into a single filter.

Carburetor

Carburetors used on gasoline engine are designed to mix the air and fuel at the correct ratio. The most correct air-fuel ratio is 14.6 parts of air to part of fuel.

On the intake stroke, the piston moves down and the intake valve is opened, then a vacuum is produced and causes air to be drawn or pulled into the engine. The air passes through the carburetor and venture as it goes into the engine.

A venturi is a streamlined restriction that partly closes the carburetor bore. The air entering the venturi is forced to speed up. The greater velocity of air passed through the venture, the greater the vacuum produced, and the more fuel is drawn in.

The flow of air and fuel through the carburetor is controlled with a throttle plate. The throttle plate is placed below the venturi and connected to the acceleration pedal. As the driver's foot on the pedal is depressed, the throttle plate opens, and there is very little restriction of air and fuel, the load and speed are increased.

Words and Expressions

1. combustible [kəm'bʌstəbl] *adj.* 易燃的，燃烧性的 *n.* 可燃物
2. carburetor [kɑ:bə'retə(r)] *n.* 化油器
3. altitude ['æltitju:d] *n.* 高度，海拔；高地
4. hydrogen ['haidrəudʒən] *n.* 氢

5. compound ['kɔmpaund] *n.* 混合物 *adj.* 复(混)合的，合成的 *v.* 混合；调合；妥协

6. petroleum [pi'trəuliəm] *n.* 石油

7. flammability [ˌflæmə'biləti] *n.* 易燃，可燃性

8. volatility [ˌvɔlə'tiliti] *n.* 挥发性，挥发度

9. octane ['ɔktein] *n.* 辛烷

10. cetane ['si:tein] *n.* 十六烷

11. alternative [ɔ:l'tə:nətiv] *n.* 替换物；取舍 *adj.* 两者择一的；供选择的

12. hydrocarbon ['haidrəu'ka:bən] *n.* 碳氢化合物

13. baffle ['bæfl] *n.* 挡板；隔板；障碍

14. slosh [slɔʃ] *n.* 晃动 *v.* 搅动；把……泼溅出

15. catalytic [ˌkætə'litik] *adj.* 催化的，接触反应的

16. hinge [hindʒ] *n.* 铰链；折叶；关键 *v.* 用铰链装

17. dashboard ['dæʃ,bɔ:d] *n.* 仪表盘

18. eccentric [ik'sentrik] *adj.* 偏心的，不同轴的

19. diaphragm ['daiəfræm] *n.* 膜片；膜片泵；隔板；遮光板；薄膜

20. contamination [kənˌtæmi'neiʃən] *n.* 污染，污染物

21. venturi [ven'tuəri] *n.* 文氏管，喉管

22. streamlined ['stri:mlaind] *adj.* 流线型的 streamline *v.* 使……流线化

23. detonation [ˌdetəu'neiʃən] *n.* 爆炸，爆裂，爆炸声

24. antiknock [ˌænti'nɔk] *n.* 抗爆剂，抗爆，抗爆震的

25. vapor lock 气阻

26. fuel filter 燃油滤清器

27. resistance to knock 抗爆震

28. compression ratio 压缩比

29. ignition timing 点火正时

30. carbon monoxide 一氧化碳

31. air-fuel ratio 空燃比

32. throttle plate 节气门

Notes

1. Diesel fuel is a specific fractional distillate of petroleum fuel oil, but alternatives that are not derived from petroleum, such as biodiesel, biomass to liquid (BTL) or gas to liquid (GTL) diesel, are increasingly being developed and adopted.

柴油是石油馏分中一种特别的燃料，但那些并非石油衍生产品的替代品，如生物柴油、生物质液体、天然气液化柴油，开始迅速发展并被人们接纳。

2. Diesel is fired by compression rather than a spark in the internal combustion engine. This

is to say that the piston squeezes the fuel fast enough into a small enough space into the combustion chamber, that the fuel ignites. An explosive detonation from the friction of fuel subjected to rapid compression.

柴油燃烧是压燃而不是火花塞点燃。也就是说，活塞以足够快的速度挤压燃油进入足够小的燃烧室空间，使燃料点燃。因为燃料的快速压缩产生了摩擦，从而导致燃料被引爆。

3. While a higher octane of gasoline indicates resistance to ignition, the higher cetane rating of diesel fuel indicates the ease at which the fuel will ignite.

汽油的辛烷值高意味着不易燃烧，而柴油的十六烷值较高却意味着燃油容易燃烧。

4. The greater velocity of air passed through the venturi, the greater the vacuum produced, and the more fuel is drawn in.

流经喉管的空气速度越快，产生的真空度越大，吸进的燃油就越多。

Exercises

A. Vocabulary

I. Translate the following expressions into Chinese.

1. catalytic converter
2. fuel-metering unit
3. diaphragm pump
4. acceleration pedal
5. vapor lock
6. resistance to knock
7. ignition timing
8. air-fuel ratio
9. throttle plate
10. compression ratio

II. Identify the English names of the automobile according to the picture.

1. _____ 2. _____
3. _____ 4. _____
5. _____ 6. _____
7. _____ 8. _____
9. _____ 10. _____

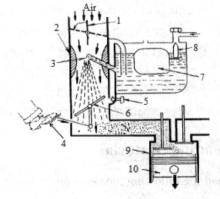

B. Comprehension

I. Discuss the following questions in groups and write down your answers.

1. What is the function of the fuel system?

_____

2. Which is diesel fuels rated with?

_____

3. In what respects does the mechanical pump differ from the electrical pump?

_____

4. How does the fuel system work?

_____

II. Read the following passage carefully and fill in the blanks with the proper forms of the given words.

additive	boost	flammability	volume	ignition
define	tendency	antiknock	chamber	detonation

The _____ of gasoline varies with its quality and the _____ mixed with the gasoline. The way gasoline burns inside the combustion _____ is most important. Increasing the pressure of the fuel mixture in the combustion chamber before _____ helps to increase the power of an engine. This is done by compression the fuel mixture to a smaller _____. Higher compression ratio not only _____ power but also give more efficient power. However, as the compression ratio goes up, knocking _____ is also increased. The octane number of a gasoline is a measure of its _____ quality or ability to resist _____ during combustion. Detonation sometimes referred to as knock, can be _____ as an uncontrolled explosion of the last portion of the burning fuel-air mixture due to excessive temperature and pressure condition in the combustion chamber.

C. Translation

I. Translate the following sentences into Chinese.

1. The flammability of gasoline varies with its quality and the additives mixed with the gasoline. The way gasoline burns inside the combustion chamber is most important.

2. Detonation is sometimes referred to as knock, can be defined as an uncontrolled explosion of the last portion of the burning fuel-air mixture due to excessive temperature and pressure condition in the combustion chamber.

3. This is to say that the piston squeezes the fuel fast enough into a small enough space into the combustion chamber, that the fuel ignites.

II. Translate the following sentences into English.

1. 使用电动燃油泵和喷油器的燃油系统通常会采用燃油压力调节器来保持油压恒定。

2. 流经喉管的空气速度越快，产生的真空度越大，吸进的燃油就越多。

3. 通过化油器的空气和燃油的量是由节气门来控制的。

Reading Material

Read the following passages and answer the questions according to the information given in the passages.

Passage One   On Board Diagnostics(OBD)

OBD, or on board diagnostics, was first introduced by General Motors in 1981. The purpose of OBD was to monitor the emission control system in the car. When the computer system of the car sees a fault in the emission control system, three things are supposed to happen. First, it would set a warning light on the dashboard, to inform the driver that a problem existed. Second, it set a code in the computer. Third, it's to record that code in the computer's memory, which can be later retrieved by a technician for diagnosis and repair.

This system worked so well, in 1986 California mandated that all cars sold in the state be equipped with OBD. This then became an industry standard throughout the nation, and all cars sold in the nation had some forms of OBD, as the following figure shown.

The first version of OBD had a lot of shortcomings. First, it only covered the engine emission system. The fuel tank vapors were not monitored. The exhaust emissions were not measured, and only devices specifically installed for emission control were monitored. Second, there was no standardization throughout the industry. Each manufacturer had a different term for the warning light that was illuminated when a fault was determined. GM called it a "check engine" light or "service engine" light, Chrysler called it a "power loss" light, Ford called it an "engine" light.

Most foreign cars called it a "check engine" light. This was not only confusing to the technician, but also to the motorist. Many motorists upon seeing the "service engine" light illuminated, brought their car to a repair facility and either asked for an oil change or tune-up, expecting the light to go out. Needless to say, this did not happen, and after spending unnecessary money on service work, the system then had to be diagnosed and repaired. The coding system for each manufacturer was also different making diagnosis much tougher.

The clean air act of 1990 mandated that beginning with the 1996 model year, all cars sold in the U.S. be equipped with a new version of on board diagnostics. This system became known as OBD II. The manufacturers beat the deadline and almost all cars were equipped with OBD II in the 1995 model year. If your car is a 1995 model or newer, chances are it is equipped with OBD II.

Among the many differences between OBD and OBD II, was the standardization of the system. All dashboard warning lights now say "check engine", usually with a picture of an engine with the word "check" across it. The coding system is now standard. There are now over 400 possible trouble codes that can be stored in the system. All causes of excessive are now monitored. If the gas cap is left loose and vapors are escaping from the gas tank, the "check engine" light will be illuminated and a code will be set.

It is extremely important now that the engine be shut off when refueling the vehicle. Another big difference between the systems is that with OBD when a fault is seen the warning light is illuminated and a code set. The warning light will then go out when the fault is no longer seen, but

the code will be set and retained in the computer's memory. In OBD II systems the light does not go out until the fault is repaired and reset by the technician.

This can create two problems for the motorist. First, if the warning light is set because of a loose gas cap, it will not go out when the cap is tightened. The car will have to be brought to a service facility to reset the light, at a cost to the motorist. Second, the danger exists that when the car is brought into a repair facility, the technician might reset the light without actually repairing the fault. In this case the light will come back on again.

It is important that the motorist be aware of the "check engine" light, as well as all other dashboard warning lights and what they mean. This knowledge will help eliminate unnecessary costs due to unnecessary repairs. When any dashboard warning light comes on, check the owners' manual before bringing the car to a repair facility.

Questions

1. What does the OBD system mean?
2. What are the differences between OBD and OBD II?
3. Why the "check engine" light is important for the motorist?

Passage Two   Leak Down Test

A leak down or "cylinder leakage" test is similar to a compression test which tells you how well your engine's cylinders are sealing. But instead of measuring pressure, it measures pressure loss.

A leak down test requires the removal of all the spark plugs. The crankshaft is then turned so that each piston is at top dead center (both valves closed) when each cylinder is tested. Most people start with cylinder number one and follow the engine's firing order.

A threaded coupling attached to a leakage gauge is screwed into a spark plug hole. Compressed air (80–90 psi) is then fed into the cylinder.

An engine in great condition should generally show only 5%–10% leakage. An engine that's still in pretty good condition may show up to 20% leakage. But more than 30% leakage indicates trouble.

The neat thing about a leakage test (as opposed to a compression test) is that it's faster and easier to figure out where the pressure is going. If you hear air coming out of the tailpipe, it indicates a leaky exhaust valve. Air coming out of the throttle body or carburetor would point to a leaky intake valve. Air coming out of the breather vent or Positive Crankcase Ventilation(PCV) valve fitting would tell you the rings and/or cylinders are worn.

A leakage test can also be used in conjunction with a compression test to diagnose other kinds of problems.

A cylinder that has poor compression, but minimal leakage, usually has a valvetrain problem such as a worn cam lobe, broken valve spring, collapsed lifter, bent push rod, etc.

If all the cylinders have low compression, but show minimal leakage, the most likely cause is incorrect valve timing. The timing belt or chain may be off a notch or two.

If compression is good and leakage is minimal, but a cylinder is misfiring or shows up weak in a power balance test, it indicates a fuel delivery (bad injector) or ignition problem (fouled spark plug or bad plug wire).

Questions

1. What does the leak down mean?

2. How to do a leak down test?

3. If compression is good and leakage is minimal, but a cylinder is misfiring or shows up weak in a power balance test, what will you do then?

Unit 6　Engine Cooling System

A typical four cylinder vehicle cruising along the highway at around 50 miles per hour, will produce 4,000 controlled explosions per minute inside the engine as the spark plugs ignite the fuel in each cylinder to propel the vehicle down the road. Obviously, these explosions produce an enormous amount of heat and, if not controlled, will destroy an engine in a matter of minutes. The purpose of the cooling system is to keep the engine at its most efficient operating temperature at all speeds under all driving conditions.

As fuel is burned in the engine, about one-third of the heat energy in the fuel is converted into power. Another third goes out through the exhaust pipe unused, and the remaining third must be handled by the cooling system. This means that the engine can work effectively only when the heat energy is equally handled so as to keep the engine temperature in balance, as shown in Figure 2-9.

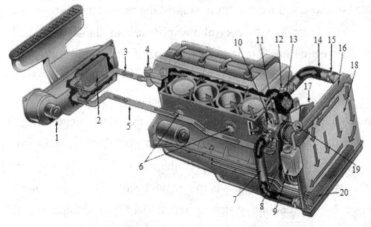

Figure 2-9　Cooling System

1—blower motor　2—heater core　3—heater supply hose　4—heater control valve　5—heater return hose

6—freeze-out plugs　7—low radiator hose　8—fan belt　9—overflow recovery tank　10—water pump

11—bypass hose　12—coolant temperature sensor　13—thermostat　14—upper radiator hose

15—hose clamp　16—radiator tank　17—fan　18—radiator corer　19—pressure cap　20—AT fluid cooler

Today's cooling system has become infinitely more reliable and efficient at doing its job. The temperature is quite essential for an engine to produce power. No engines can work well without suitable operating temperatures. If the engine runs too hot, it may suffer pre-ignition, while the air-fuel charge is ignited prematurely from excessive combustion chamber temperature. Viscosity of the oil circulating in an over heating engine is reduced. Hot oil also forms varnish and carbon deposits may be drown into the combustion chamber where it increases HC emission. This also causes poor performances, premature wear, and may even result in engine damage. What's more, the behavior of the metals at excessively high temperature also differs from that at normal temperatures and can produce a condition in which the metal deforms slowly and continuously at a constant stress. If the engine runs too cold, the fuel will not vaporize properly. If liquid fuel reaches the cylinders, it will reduce lubrication by washing the oil from the cylinder walls and diluting the engine oil. This causes a loss of performance, an increase in HC emissions and premature engine wear. For these reasons, a cooling system of some kind is necessary in any internal combustion engine.

The working principle of cooling system is liquid coolant being pumped by a mechanical water pump through the engine, then out to the radiator to be cooled by the air stream coming through the front grill of the vehicle. There are generally two different types of cooling system: water-cooling system and air-cooling system. Water-cooling system is more common. The cooling medium, or coolant, in them is either water or some low-freezing liquid, called antifreeze. A water-cooling system consists of the engine water jacket, thermostat, water pump, radiator, radiator cap, fan, fan drive belt and necessary hoses.

The cooling system is made up of the passages inside the engine block and heads, a water pump to circulate the coolant, a thermostat to control the temperature of the coolant, a radiator to cool the coolant, a radiator cap to control the pressure in the system, and some plumbing consisting of interconnecting hoses to transfer the coolant from the engine to radiator and also to the car's heater system where hot coolant is used to warm up the vehicle's interior on a cold day.

The engine is cooled mainly through heat transfer and heat dissipation. A water-cooling system means that water is used as a cooling agent to circulate through the engine to absorb the heat and carry it to the radiator for disposal. The heat generated by the mixture burned in the engine must be transferred from the iron or aluminum cylinder to the water in the water jacket. The outside of the water jacket dissipates some of the heat to the air surrounding it, but most of the heat is carried by the cooling water to the radiator for dissipation. When the coolant temperature in the system reaches 90°, the thermostat valve open fully, its slanted edge shutting off the shorter circuit so that the coolant circulates through the longer one: water-pump—cooling jacket—thermostat—radiator top—tank—radiator core—bottom tank—pump.

Water pumps have many designs, but most of them are the centrifugal type. They consist of a rotating fan, or impeller, and seldom are of the positive displacement type that uses gears or plungers. Many water pumps have a spring-loaded seal to avoid leakage of water around the pump shaft. Some V-type engines have a pump on each cylinder block.

The radiator is a device designed to dissipate the heat which the coolant has absorbed from the engine; it is constructed to hold a large amount of water in tubes or other passages which provide a large area in contact with the atmosphere.

In order to prevent the coolant from boiling, the cooling system is designed to be pressurized. Under pressure, the boiling point of the coolant is raised considerably. However, too much pressure will cause hoses and other parts to burst, so a system is needed to relieve pressure if it exceeds a certain point. The job of maintaining the pressure in the cooling system belongs to the radiator cap. The cap is designed to release pressure if it reaches the specified upper limit that the system was designed to handle. The radiator cap served not only to prevent the coolant from splashing out the filler opening, but also to prevent evaporation of the coolant.

The fan designed to draw cooling air through the radiator core. The fan is usually mounted on an extension of the water pump shaft and is driven by a V-belt from a pulley mounted on the front end of the crankshaft. Usually the same belt drives the alternator, and belt tension is adjusted by swinging the alternator on its mounting.

An air-cooling system contains a centrifugal fan, thermostat, fan drive belt, radiator fins, baffle plates, air control ring, etc. An air-cooling system means that air is used as a cooling agent to circulate through the engine to carry the heat away from the moving parts. When the engine is running, forced air is directed over and through the fins to dissipate the heat. In order to regulate the engine temperature by controlling the volume of cooling air, a thermostat is installed inside the metal housing which encloses the engine.

The thermostat unit is placed between the engine and the radiator to make sure that the coolant stays above a certain preset temperature. If the coolant temperature falls below this temperature, the thermostat blocks the coolant flow to the radiator, forcing the fluid instead through a bypass directly back to the engine. The coolant will continue to circulate like this until it reaches the design temperature, at which point, the thermostat will open a valve and allow the coolant back through the radiator.

The engine cooling system actually is a temperature-regulation system. For a late-model engine, the cooling system must maintain a temperature that is high enough for efficient combustion but not so high that the engine will be damaged. The two jobs of the cooling system are to carry excess heat away from the engine and maintain uniform temperature throughout the engine.

Words and Expressions

1. cruise　[kruːz]　*n.* 巡航，漫游　*v.* 巡航，航游于，慢速行驶于
2. efficient　[i'fiʃənt]　*adj.* 效率高的；胜任的

3. infinitely ['infinitli] *adv.* 无限地，无穷地

4. essential [i'senʃəl] *n.* 要素，要点 *adj.* 必要的；重要的；本质的

5. reliable [ri'laiəbl] *adj.* 可靠的，可信的

6. prematurely [ˌpri:mə'tjuəli] *adv.* 过早地；早熟地

7. viscosity [vis'kɔsiti] *n.* 黏度，黏性

8. varnish ['vɑ:niʃ] *n.* 油漆；(内燃机中的)漆膜；清漆 *v.* 粉饰，装饰；涂油漆于……

9. deposit [di'pɔzit] *n.* 存款，堆积物；定金 *v.* 存放；堆积；沉淀

10. deform [di:'fɔ:m] *v.* 使……残缺，使……变形

11. continuously [kən'tinjuəsli] *adv.* 不断地，连续地

12. behavior [bi'heivjə] *n.* 行为，举止

13. dilute [dai'lju:t] *adj.* 冲淡的，稀释的；微弱的 *vt.* 冲淡，稀释

14. lubrication [ˌlu:bri'keiʃən] *n.* 润滑

15. vaporize ['veipəraiz] *v.* 使……蒸发，蒸发

16. grill [gril] *n.* 烤架，铁格子 *v.* 烧，烤

17. antifreeze ['antifri:z] *n.* 防冻剂

18. thermostat ['θə:məstæt] *n.* 节温器；自动调温器；温度调节装置

19. radiator ['reidieitə] *n.* 散热器，暖气片；辐射体

20. interior [in'tiəriə] *adj.* 内部的，内地的，国内的 *n.* 内部，内在

21. disposal [dis'pəuzəl] *n.* 处理；消除，销毁

22. slant [slɑ:nt] *n.* 倾斜，斜面；个人观点或见解；倾向性 *v.* 倾斜

23. centrifugal [sen'trifjugəl] *adj.* 离心的

24. plunger ['plʌndʒə] *n.* 柱塞；冲杆；模冲；活塞

25. leakage ['li:kidʒ] *n.* 泄漏，漏损物，漏损量

26. dissipation [ˌdisi'peiʃən] *n.* 耗散，损耗，散逸；能量耗散；损耗

27. evaporation [iˌvæpə'reiʃən] *n.* 蒸发；消失；脱水，干燥

28. alternator ['ɔ:ltəneitə] *n.* 交流发电机

29. uniform ['ju:nifɔ:m] *adj.* 一致的，统一的 *n.* 制服 *v.* 穿制服

30. interconnecting 互相连接

31. centrifugal fan 离心式鼓风机，离心式风扇

32. baffle plate 挡板，缓冲板，折流板

33. water pump 水泵

34. radiator cap 散热器盖，水箱盖

35. heat transfer 热传导，传热

36. heat dissipation 热消散，热散逸

37. convert ... into　把……转变成

38. cooling jacket　冷却水套

39. positive displacement type　容积式；正排量型

Notes

1. This means that the engine can work effectively only when the heat energy is equally so as to keep the engine temperature in balance.

这意味着只有均等地处理热能以保持发动机温度的均衡，发动机才能有效地工作。

2. The behavior of metals at excessively high temperatures also differs from that at normal temperatures.

金属在过高温度中的性能与在正常温度中的性能也是有区别的。

3. This causes a loss of performance, an increase in HC emissions and premature engine wear.

这将导致工作不正常、碳氢化合物的排放增加以及发动机过早磨损。

4. The heat generated by the mixture burned in the engine must be transferred from the iron or aluminum cylinder to the water in the water jacket.

发动机中可燃混合气燃烧所产生的热量必须从铁制或铝制的汽缸中传送到冷却水套里的冷却水中。

5. They consist of a rotating fan or impeller, and seldom are the positive displacement type that uses gears or plungers.

它们(水泵)由一个旋转叶片，即叶轮组成，而很少采用由齿轮或柱塞构成的容积式水泵。

Exercises

A. Vocabulary

I. Translate the following expressions into Chinese.

1. radiator fin

2. temperature-regulation system

3. fan drive belt

4. interconnecting

5. heat transfer

6. positive displacement type

7. radiator cap

8. heat dissipation

9. centrifugal fan

10. water jacket

II. Identify the English names of the automobile according to the picture.

1. _____ 2. _____

3. _____ 4. _____

5. _____ 6. _____

7. _____ 8. _____

9. _____ 10. _____

B. Comprehension

I. Discuss the following questions in groups and write down your answers.

1. What is the purpose of the cooling system?

_____

2. What is the main function of radiator cap?

_____

3. Why does a thermostat need a liquid–cooling system?

_____

4. List the main parts of a liquid–cooling system.

_____

II. Read the following passage carefully and fill in the blanks with the proper forms of the given words.

design	place	coolant	bypass	radiator
below	circulate	point	force	preset

The thermostat unit is _____ between the engine and the _____ to make sure that the coolant stays above a certain _____ temperature. If the coolant temperature falls _____ this temperature, the thermostat blocks the _____ flow to the radiator, _____ the fluid instead through a _____ directly back to the engine. The coolant will continue to _____ like this until it reaches the _____ temperature, at which _____, the thermostat will open a valve and allow the coolant back through the radiator.

C. Translation

I. Translate the following sentences into Chinese.

1. The purpose of the cooling system is to keep the engine at its most efficient operating temperature at all speeds under all driving conditions.

2. The cooling system is made up of the passages inside the engine block and heads, a water pump to circulate the coolant, a thermostat to control the temperature of the coolant, a radiator to cool the coolant and a radiator cap to control the pressure in the system.

3. For a late-model engine, the cooling system must maintain a temperature that is high enough for efficient combustion but not so high that the engine will be damaged.

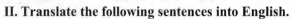

II. Translate the following sentences into English.

1. 发动机的冷却系统实际上是一个温度调节系统。

2. 水箱盖不仅可以防止冷却液从加液口溢出，也可以防止冷却液的蒸发。

3. 这意味着只有均等地处理热能以保持发动机温度的均衡，发动机才能有效地工作。

Reading Material

Read the following passages and answer the questions according to the information given in the passages.

Passage One   Cooling System Maintenance and Repair

An engine that is overheating will quickly self destruct, so proper maintenance of the cooling system is very important to the life of the engine and the trouble free operation of the cooling system in general.

The most important maintenance item is to flush and refill the coolant periodically. The reason for this important service is that antifreeze has a number of additives that are designed to prevent corrosion in the cooling system. This corrosion tends to accelerate when several different types of metal interact with each other. The corrosion causes scale that eventually builds up and begins to clog the thin flat tubes in the radiator and heater core, causing the engine to eventually overheat. The anti-corrosion chemicals in the antifreeze prevent this, but they have a limited life span.

Newer antifreeze formulations will last for 5 years or 150,000 miles before requiring replacement. These antifreezes are usually red in color and are referred to as "Extended Life" or "Long Life" antifreeze. GM has been using this type of coolant in all their vehicles since 1996. The GM product is called "Dex-Cool".

Most antifreeze used in vehicles however, is green in color and should be replaced every two years or 30,000 miles, which ever comes first. You can convert to the new long life coolant, but only if you completely flush out all of the old antifreeze. If any green coolant is allowed to mix with the red coolant, you must revert to the shorter replacement cycle.

Look for a shop that can reverse-flush the cooling system. This requires special equipment and the removal of the thermostat in order to do the job properly. This type of flush is especially important if the old coolant looks brown or has scale or debris floating around in it.

If you remove the thermostat for a reverse flush, always replace it with a new thermostat of the proper temperature. It is cheap insurance.

The National Automotive Radiator Service Association (NARSA) recommends that motorists have a seven-point preventative cooling system maintenance check at least once every two years. The seven-point program is designed to identify any areas that need attention. It consists of the following:

- A visual inspection of all cooling system components, including belts and hoses.
- A radiator pressure cap test to check for the recommended system pressure level.
- A thermostat check for proper opening and closing.

- A pressure test to identify any external leaks to the cooling system including the radiator, water pump, engine coolant passages, radiator and heater hoses and heater core.
- An internal leak test to check for combustion gas leakage into the cooling system.
- An engine fan test for proper operation.
- System powers flush and refill with car manufacturers' recommended concentration of coolant.

Let's take these items one at a time.

Visual Inspection

What you are looking for is the condition of the belts and hoses. The radiator hoses and heater hoses are easily inspected just by opening the hood and looking. You want to be sure that the hoses have no cracking or splitting and that there is no bulging or swelling at the ends. If there is any sign of problems, the hose should be replaced with the correct part number for the year, make and model of the vehicle. Never use a universal hose unless it is an emergency and a proper molded hose is not available.

Heater hoses usually run straight and are not molded, so a universal hose is fine to use and often is available. Make sure that you use the proper inside diameter for the hose being replaced. For either the radiator hoses or the heater hoses, make sure that you route the replacement hose in the same way that the original hose was running. Position the hose away from any obstruction that can possibly damage it and always use new hose clamps. After you refill the cooling system with coolant, do a pressure test to make sure that there are no leaks.

On older vehicles, the water pump is driven by a V-belt or serpentine belt on the front of the engine that is also responsible for driving the alternator, power steering pump and air conditioner compressor. These types of belts are easy to inspect and replace if they are worn. You are looking for dry cracking on the inside surface of the belt.

On later vehicles, the water pump is often driven by the timing belt. This belt usually has a specific life expectancy at which time it must be replaced to insure that it does not fail. Since the timing belt is inside the engine and will require partial engine disassembly to inspect, it is very important to replace it at the correct interval. Since the labor to replace this belt can be significant, it is a good idea to replace the water pump and the belt at the same time. This is because 90 percent of the labor to replace a water pump has already been done to replace the timing belt. It is simply good insurance to replace the pump while everything is apart.

Radiator Pressure Cap Test

A radiator pressure cap is designed to maintain pressure in the cooling system at a certain maximum pressure. If the cooling system exceeds that pressure, a valve in the cap opens to bleed the excessive pressure into the reserve tank. Once the engine has cooled off, a negative pressure begins to develop in the cooling system. When this happens, a second valve in the cap allows the coolant to be siphoned back into the radiator from the reserve tank. If the cap should fail, the engine can easily overheat. A pressure test of the radiator cap is a quick way to tell if the cap is doing its job. It should be able to hold its rated pressure for two minutes. Since radiator caps are quite inexpensive, it is highly recommended to replace it every 3 years or 36,000 miles, just for added insurance. Make absolutely sure that you replace it with one that is designed for your vehicle.

Questions

1. What are the procedures in the seven-point preventative colling system maintenance?

2. What are the procedures in visual check?

3. Please describe how to do a radiator pressure cap test.

Passage Two   PCV Valve

The blowby vapors that end up in an engine's crankcase contain moisture as well as combustion byproducts and unburned fuel vapors. The crankcase is sealed to prevent the escape of these gases into the atmosphere, but the vapors must be removed to prevent oil contamination that leads to sludge formation. The positive crankcase ventilation (PCV) system siphons these vapors from the crankcase and routes them into the intake manifold so they can be reburned in the engine.

The main component in the PCV system is the PCV valve, which is usually located in the valve cover. A hose connects the PCV valve to the intake manifold. A second hose between the air cleaner and crankcase or other valve cover (V-6 or V-8 applications) provides fresh air to help flush the vapors out of the crankcase. Some engines have a separate air filter for the PCV breather hose located inside the air cleaner.

The PCV valve is a spring-loaded valve with a specific orifice size designed to restrict the amount of air that's siphoned from the crankcase into the intake manifold. This is necessary because air drawn through the valve from the crankcase has a leaning effect on the fuel mixture much the same as a vacuum leak. So air flow through the valve must be controlled within certain limits. At idle, air flow is reduced because little blowby is produced. When the engine is cruising and vacuum is high, airflow through the PCV valve is at a maximum to purge the blowby vapors from the crankcase.

It's important to note that PCV valves are sized for specific engine applications. The wrong PCV valve for an application can flow too much or too little air causing driveability problems. Varnish deposits can clog the valve, so replacement for preventative maintenance is recommended (every 50,000 miles usually).

Not all engines have PCV valves. Some (like Ford Escort, GM FWD cars with the Quad Four engine, etc.) ventilate the crankcase with a small breather hose and calibrated orifice. There is no spring-loaded PCV valve. On these applications, no maintenance is usually necessary.

Questions

1. What is the PCV valve?

2. How does a PCV valve work?

3. Is it important to note that PCV valves are sized for specific engine applications? Why?

Unit 7　Engine Lubrication System

An automobile could not move itself without the aid of friction. However, excessive friction in the engine would mean rapid destruction. Of course, we cannot eliminate friction, but we can reduce it to a considerable degree by the use of lubrication oil so that the automobile can move smoothly with proper friction.

The engine lubrication is mainly conducted by the lubricating oil, which has several functions in the lubricating system. First of all, the oil forms a protective coating on the metal surface and prevents a metal to metal contact, thus reducing friction and minimizing wear. Secondly, as the oil is fed to the various moving parts of the engine, it absorbs and carries the heat away from the engine parts. Thirdly, as the oil circulates through the moving parts of the engine, it tends to wash off dirt away from the engine parts. Finally, the oil absorbs shocks between bearings and other engine parts, and forms a good seal between piston rings and cylinder walls.

Engine lubricating systems are divided into two types: splash and pressure feed. In the splash lubricating system, there are dippers on the lower parts of the connecting rod bearing caps. These dippers enter oil trays in the oil pan with each crankshaft revolution. The dippers splash oil to the upper part of the engine. The oil is thrown up as the oil sprays, which provides adequate lubrication to valve mechanisms, cylinder walls, piston rings and bearings.

Pressure or forced lubrication is practically used in all engines apart from simple lubrication and splash lubrication, and is characterized by the oil being fed under pressure from a pump to the majority of engine parts, especially to the main bearings and connecting rod bearings.

The lubricating system, no matter what type, has the job if supplying adequate amounts of oil to all moving engine parts so that the oil can do the various jobs. In some heavy-duty engines, where the oil has a harder and hotter job to do, oil cooler is included in the lubricating system. The oil cooler has a radiator much like the cooling system radiator, through which the oil passes; this cools the oil. All engines have some sort of lever indicator, which usually consists of a dipstick or oil lever stick, that enters the crankcase from the side of the block. To check the oil lever in the open pan, the dipstick can be pulled out and the height of the oil on the stick noted. Oil can then be added if the oil lever is too low for adequate engine protection.

In general, the lubrication system of an automotive engine apart from the lubricating also contains a reservoir (called the oil pan, sump, or crankcase) to hold the oil supply, a pump to develop pressure, and the valves for controlling flow and pressure etc.

The oil pumps are of the positive displacement type in several designs. Vanes, plungers, rotors and gears are all used to build up the necessary pressure. The pumps of gear and rotor types are always positively driven, usually from the camshaft either by means of gears or cams, as shown in Figure 2-10.

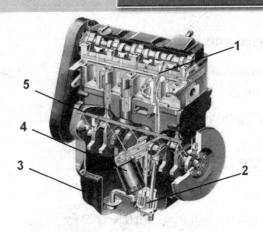

Figure 2-10   Lubrication System

1—oil gallery   2—oil pump   3—oil pan   4—oil filter   5—main oil gallery

The gear-type pumps used in engine lubrication systems may be either of duplex type or simplex type. The duplex type oil pump comprises two sections. Each pump section operates independently of the other, like a simplex pump.

The simplex type oil pump consists of an oil pick up, a housing, an end cover and a pair of gears. The driving gear of the pump is keyed to the pump drive shaft, which is supported by two bushings pressed in the housing of the pump and its end cover. The driven gear meshes with the driving gear and is free to rotate on a fixed spindle pressed in the pump housing. In operation, the oil entering the pump through the inlet port in the housing becomes trapped between the teeth of the contra-rotating gears and the surrounding wall of the pumping chamber. The oil is thus carried around the periphery of the gears (not between them) and then discharged through opposite discharge port. At this point, the action of the intermeshing teeth prevents the oil from returning to the inlet side of the pump.

To remove mechanical impurities from the oil circulating through the engine lubrication system, the oil filter is used. The oil filter can filter dirt and solids out of the oil in lubrication system. As these particles of foreign matter are prevented from entering the engine by oil filter, the rate of wear of engine parts is reduced. Engines of more recent designs use a full-flow centrifugal oil filter, that is, all oil passes through the filter before it reaches the bearings. This is a reaction-type centrifugal filter with which all of delivered by the oil pump is cleaned in the filter rotor. This filter has an oil outlet pipe fitted inside the hollow spindle of the filter rotor and connected to the oil line that distributes the oil to the various parts of the lubrication system.

The oil pressure relief valve is mainly to act both as a pressure regulator and as a safety device in lubrication system. As a pressure regulator, the valve prevents the oil pump from building up excessive pressure. When the oil passages of the engine rise too high, the relief valve will drain the excess filtered oil into the engine crankcase. As a safety device, the valve is set by the adjusting screw to secure the oil circulation through engine parts under proper pressure.

Words and Expressions

1. destruction [di'strʌkʃən] *n.* 损坏，破坏

2. feed [fi:d] *v.* 供给

3. shock [ʃɔk] *n.* 振动

4. silicone ['silikəun] *n.* 聚硅氧；硅铜；硅树脂

5. dipstick ['dipstik] *n.* 油尺，水[油]位指示器

6. periphery [pə'rifəri] *n.* 周边，周线，外围

7. intermeshing [ˌintə'meʃing] *adj.* 相互啮合的

8. impurity [im'pjuərit] *n.* 杂质；夹杂物；不纯

9. centrifugal [sen'trifjugəl] *adj.* 离心的；利用离心力的

10. spindle ['spindl] *n.* 轴，转轴

11. clog [klɔg] *v.* 阻塞

12. rotor ['rəutə] *n.* 转子；涡轮

13. regulator ['regjuleitə] *n.* 调节器

14. lubrication oil 润滑油

15. wash off 冲洗，洗去

16. relief valve 安全阀，卸压阀，溢流阀

17. main bearing cap 主轴承盖

18. contra-rotating gear 反转齿轮

19. lubrication system 润滑系

20. simplex type 单缸式

21. bypass valve 旁通阀

22. remove...from... 从……中除(消)去

23. oil pump 油泵

24. oil filter 机油滤清器

25. apart from... 除……之外

Notes

1. An automobile could not move itself without the aid of friction.
不借助于摩擦力，汽车就不能向前行驶。

2. The oil is fed to the various moving parts of the engine, it absorbs and carries the heat away from the engine parts.
当机油被供给发动机的各运动部件时，它可以吸收并带走发动机部件散发的热量。

3. As these particles of foreign matter are prevented from entering the engine by oil filter, the rate of wear of engine parts is reduced.

由于机油滤清器阻止了杂质微粒进入发动机，这就降低了发动机部件的磨损率。

4. In the event the filter gets clogged or obstructed, a bypass valve is provided so that oil will continue to reach the bearings.

如果机油滤清器被阻塞，就得用分流阀使机油继续流向各轴承。

5. The oil pressure relief valve is mainly to act both as a pressure regulator and as a safety device in lubrication system.

机油减压阀在润滑系统中主要起着一个压力调节器和安全装置的作用。

Exercises

A. Vocabulary

I. Translate the following expressions into Chinese.

1. lubrication oil

2. rotor pump

3. bypass valve

4. main bearing cap

5. rough filter

6. oil pressure sensor

7. relief valve

8. oil filter

9. contra-rotating gear

10. duplex type

II. Identify the English names of the lubrication system according to the picture.

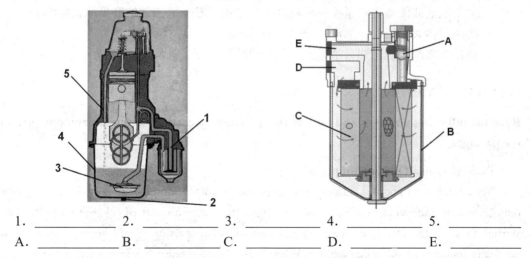

1. _____   2. _____   3. _____   4. _____   5. _____
A. _____   B. _____   C. _____   D. _____   E. _____

B. Comprehension

I. Discuss the following questions in groups and write down your answers.

1. What is the function of an oil pressure relief valve ?

_____

2. What does the lubrication system consist of?

_____

3. Besides lubrication, what else functions do the oil have?

_____

II. Read the following passage carefully and fill in the blanks with the proper forms of the given words.

filtrate   trap   routed   changed   filter   contaminants   flow   valvetrain

In today's engines, all the oil that's picked up by the oil pump is _____ through the _____ before it goes to the crankshaft bearings, cam bearings and _____. This is called "full-flow" _____. It's an efficient way of removing _____, and it assures only filtered oil is supplied to the engine. In time, though, accumulated dirt and debris _____ by the filter begin to obstruct the _____ of oil. The filter should be changed before it reaches this point, which is why the filter needs to be replaced when the oil is _____.

C. Translation

I. Translate the following sentences into Chinese.

1. Under normal driving conditions, running a quart low probably doesn't make much difference in terms of bearing temperature or overall engine lubrication.

2. As the crankshaft spins around, it can whip the oil into foam if the level is too high. This, in turn, can cause a drop in oil pressure and loss of lubrication to critical engine parts.

3. Follow your vehicle manufacturer's guidelines for the type and viscosity of oil to use in your engine.

II. Translate the following sentences into English.

1. 由于机油滤清器阻止了杂质微粒进入发动机，发动机部件的磨损率就降低了。

2. 机油有四大作用，即润滑、冷却、清洗和密封。

3. 机油进入汽缸盖，通过油道流入凸轮轴轴瓦和配气机构。

Reading Material

Read the following passages and answer the questions according to the information given in the passages.

Passage One   Oil Consumption

My engine uses about a quart of oil every 1,000 miles. Should I be concerned? Not if you plan to sell or trade your vehicle soon. An engine that uses a quart of oil every 1,000 miles is starting to show the effects of wear. The amount of oil it is using is still acceptable, but it will gradually increase as the miles add up. When it reaches the point where it's using a quart every 500 miles or less, it's time for an overhaul.

Oil consumption depends primarily on two things: the valve guides and piston rings. If the valve guides are worn, or if there's too much clearance between the valve stems and guides, or if the valve guide seals are worn, cracked, missing, broken or improperly installed, the engine will suck oil down the guides and into the cylinders. The engine may still have good compression, but will use a lot of oil.

An oil consumption problem caused by worn valve guides can usually be cured by a valve job. Knurling, sleeving or replacing the guides, or boring out the guides and installing valves with oversized stems will stop the loss of oil.

Oil can also get past the rings if the rings or cylinders are badly worn or damaged, if the cylinders were not honed properly when the engine was built (or rebuilt), or if the rings were installed improperly.

When a newly-built engine is first started, the rings require a certain amount of time to "seat" or break-in. If the rings fail to seat properly, the engine will use oil. This may be the case if somebody applied the wrong finish to the cylinders, failed to clean and lubricate the cylinders properly before the engine was fired up, or didn't use the proper break-in procedure.

If the rings and/or cylinders are at fault, the engine will have lower than normal compression readings.

In some instances, worn rod bearings, excessive bearing clearances and/or excessive oil pressure can splash too much oil on the cylinders causing oil to get past the rings.

The cure for worn rings and cylinders is to overhaul the engine block. The cylinders have to be refinished and new rings installed to regain good oil control.

Questions

1. My engine uses about a quart of oil every 1,000 miles. Should I be concerned?

2. What does oil consumption depend on?

3. When a newly-built engine is first started, the rings require a certain amount of time to "seat" or break-in.What does this mean?

Passage Two　Oil Change

How often should I change my oil? Most vehicle manufacturers recommend changing the oil once a year or every 7,500 miles in passenger car and light truck gasoline engines. For diesel engines and turbocharged gasoline engines, the usual recommendation is every 3,000 miles or six months.

If you read the fine print, however, you'll discover that the once a year, 7,500 mile oil change is for vehicles that are driven under ideal circumstances. What most of us think of as "normal" driving is actually "severe service" driving. This includes frequent short trips (less than 10 miles, especially during cold weather), stop-and-go city traffic driving, driving in dusty conditions (gravel roads, etc.), and driving at sustained highway speeds during hot weather. For this type of driving, which is actually "severe service" driving, the recommendation is to change the oil every 3,000 miles or six months.

For maximum protection, most oil companies say to change the oil every 3,000 miles or three to six months regardless of what type of driving you do.

A new engine with little or no wear can probably get by on 7,500 mile oil changes. But as an

engine accumulates miles, blowby increases. This dumps unburned more fuel into the crankcase which dilutes the oil. This causes the oil to break down. So if the oil isn't changed often enough, you can end up with accelerated wear and all the engine problems that come with it (loss of performance and fuel economy, and increased emissions and oil consumption).

Oil Analysis

Truck fleets often monitor the condition of the oil in their vehicles by having samples analyzed periodically. Oil samples are sent to a laboratory that then analyzes the oil's viscosity and acid content. Oil is then burned in a device called a spectrometer that reveals various impurities in the oil. From all of this, a detailed report is generated that reveals the true condition of the oil.

Oil analysis is a great idea for fleets and trucks that hold a lot of oil. But most consumers would have a hard time justifying the cost. Having an oil sample analyzed typically costs $12 to $20 for the lab work and report. Most quick lube shops charge $16.95 to $19.95 for an oil change. So why spend your money on a report that will probably tell you your oil needs changing? Just change the oil every 3,000 miles and don't worry about it.

Regular oil changes for preventative maintenance are cheap insurance against engine wear, and will always save you money in the long run if you keep a car for more than three or four years. It's very uncommon to see an engine that has been well maintained with regular oil changes develop major bearing, ring, cam or valve problems under 100,000 miles.

What about the Oil Filter?

To reduce the costs of vehicle ownership and maintenance, many car makers say the oil filter only needs to be replaced at every other oil change. Most mechanics will tell you this is false economy.

The oil filters on most engines today have been downsized to save weight, cost and space. The "standard" quart-sized filter that was once common on most engines has been replaced by a pint-sized (or smaller) filter. You don't have to be a rocket scientist to figure out that a smaller filter has less total filtering capacity. Even so, the little filters should be adequate for a 3,000 mile oil change intervals—but may run out of capacity long before a second oil change at 6,000 or 15,000 miles.

Replacing the oil filter every time the oil is changed, therefore, is highly recommended.

An engine's main line of defense against abrasion and the premature wear it causes is the oil filter. The filter's job is to remove solid contaminants such as dirt, carbon and metal particles from the oil before they can damage bearing, journal and cylinder wall surfaces in the engine. The more dirt and other contaminants the filter can trap and hold, the better.

In today's engines, all the oil that's picked up by the oil pump is routed through the filter before it goes to the crankshaft bearings, cam bearings and valvetrain. This is called "full-flow" filtration. It's an efficient way of removing contaminants, and it assures only filtered oil is supplied to the engine. In time, though, accumulated dirt and debris trapped by the filter begin to obstruct the flow of oil. The filter should be changed before it reaches this point, which is why the filter needs to be replaced when the oil is changed.

If you wait too long to change the filter, there's a danger that it might become plugged. To prevent this from causing a catastrophic engine failure due to loss of lubrication, oil filters have a built-in safety device called a "bypass valve". When the pressure drop across the filter exceeds a predetermined value (which varies depending on the engine application), the bypass valve opens so oil can continue to flow to the engine. But this allows unfiltered oil to enter the engine. Any contaminants that find their way into the crankcase will be pumped through the engine and accelerate wear.

Filter Replacement

If you do your own oil changes, make sure you get the correct filter for your engine. Follow the filter manufacturer's listings in its catalog. Many filters that look the same on the outside have different internal valving. Many overhead cam engines, for example, require an "anti-drainback" valve in the filter to prevent oil from draining out of the filter when the engine is shut off. This allows oil pressure to reach critical engine parts more quickly when the engine is restarted. Filters that are mounted sideways on the engine typically require an anti-drainback valve.

CAUTION: The threads on a spin-on filter must also be the correct diameter and thread pitch (SAE or metric) for your engine. If you install a filter with SAE threads on an engine that requires metric threads (or vice versa), you can damage the threads that hold the oil filter in place. Mismatched threads can also allow the filter to work loose, which causes a sudden loss of oil pressure that may ruin your engine!

Some people say it's best to change the oil when the oil is hot (like right after driving), while others say it makes no difference.

CAUTION: Hot oil is thinner and runs out faster but can also burn you if you're not careful. In any event, avoid unnecessary skin contact with oil because oil is a suspected carcinogen (causes cancer).

Changing the oil when it is cold may take a bit longer because the oil will drain more slowly from the engine, but there's no danger of being burned. Also, most of the oil will have drained down into the oil pan when the engine has sat for a period of time, which means you'll actually get a little more of the old oil out of the engine than if you attempt to drain it while it is still hot.

Used motor oil should be disposed of properly. The Environmental Protection Agency does not consider used motor oil to be a hazardous chemical, but it can foul ground water and does contain traces of lead. The best way to dispose of used motor oil is to take it to a service station, quick lube shop, parts store or other facility for recycling. Your old oil will either be refined into other lubricants or petroleum products, or burned as fuel.

Do not dump used motor oil on the ground, down a drain, into a storm sewer or place it in the trash. Many landfills will not accept used motor oil even if it is in a sealed container because it will eventually leak out into the ground. If you can't find an environmentally-acceptable way to dispose of the stuff, maybe you shouldn't be changing your own oil. All the service facilities that

do oil changes have storage tanks and recycling programs to dispose of used oil.

Questions

1. How often should I change my oil?

2. How to do the oil analysis?

3. If you do your own oil changes, make sure you get the correct filter for your engine. What does it mean?

Unit 8　Electronic Fuel Injection System

Automobile engineers are continually striving towards minimal fuel consumption and cleaner exhaust emissions. The application of electronic control, once too complex and expensive, is becoming more and more a remarkably straight-forward economical solution.

Engine power, fuel consumption and exhaust emission all depend on the accuracy of the air-fuel ratio. With petrol engines there are many operating conditions under which it is difficult to ensure the correct air-fuel ratio will always be delivered to the engine's cylinders for combustion.

Electronic fuel injection systems can be broken down to three subsystems, which are as follows:

1. Fuel-supply system includes the fuel pump, lines, and filters that feed clean fuel to the fuel-metering system.

2. Fuel-metering system includes all parts that control the correct amount of fuel entering the engine.

3. Air-intake system includes air filters, ducts and valves that control how much clean air enters the engine, as shown in Figure 2-11.

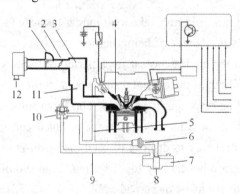

Figure 2-11　The Electronic Fuel Injection System

1—air flow meter　2—throttle valve　3—air intake chamber　4—injector valve　5—flue delivery pipe

6—fuel filter　7—fuel tank　8—fuel pump　9—flue return pipe　10—fuel pressure regulator

11—intake runner　12—air cleaner

The Fuel Delivery System

The fuel delivery system consists of the fuel tank, fuel pump, fuel filter, fuel delivery pipe (fuel rail), fuel injector, fuel pressure regulator, and fuel return pipe.

Fuel is delivered from the tank to the injector by means of an electric fuel pump. The pump is typically located in or near the fuel tank. Contaminants are filtered out by a high capacity in line fuel filter.

Fuel is maintained at a constant pressure by means of a fuel pressure regulator. Any fuel which is not delivered to the intake manifold by the injector is returned to the tank through a fuel return pipe.

The Air Induction System

The air induction system consists of the air cleaner, air flow meter, throttle valve, air intake chamber, intake manifold runner and intake valve.

When the throttle valve is opened, air flows through the air cleaner, through the air flow meter (on L type systems), past the throttle valve, and through a well tuned intake manifold runner to the intake valve. Air delivered to the engine is a function of driver demand. As the throttle valve is opened further, more air is allowed to enter the engine cylinder.

Toyota engines use two different methods to measure intake air volume. The L type Electronic Fuel Injection(EFI) system measures air flowing directly by using an air flow meter. The D type EFI system measures air flowing indirectly by monitoring the pressure in the intake manifold.

The Electronic Control System

The electronic control system consists of various engine sensors, Electronic Control Unit (ECU), fuel injector assemblies, and related wiring.

The ECU determines precisely how much fuel needs to be delivered by the injector by monitoring the engine sensors. The ECU turns the injectors on for a precise amount of time, which is referred to as injection pulse width or injection duration, to deliver the proper air/fuel ratio to the engine.

Multi-port Fuel Injections

This is the most common type of fuel injection system found today. Regardless of the manufacturer, they all function in the same basic way. On these systems an equal amount of fuel is delivered to each cylinder.

These systems all use sensors which transmit operating conditions to the computer. Information from these sensors is processed by the computer which then determines the proper air/fuel mixture. The signal is sent to fuel injectors which open and inject fuel into their ports. The longer the injector is held open, the richer the fuel mixture is. Most fuel injection systems need the following information to operate properly.

Temperature Sensors

This includes both air and coolant temperature. The computer uses this information to determine how rich or lean the mixture should be. The colder the temperature is, the richer the

mixture is.

Throttle Position Sensors or Switches

The computer uses this information to determine the position of the throttle valve(s). Some vehicles use sensors which relay the exact position of the throttle valve(s) at all times. Others use switches which only relay closed and wide-open throttle positions (some may also use a mid-throttle switch). These switches and sensors help determine engine load.

Airflow Sensors

These sensors also help the computer determine engine load by indicating the amount of air entering the engine. There are several different types of airflow sensors，but in the end，they all do the same job.

Manifold Pressure Sensors

If a vehicle is not equipped with an airflow sensor, it uses a manifold pressure sensor to determine engine load. Note that some vehicles with an airflow sensor may also have a manifold pressure sensor. This is used as fail-safe if the airflow sensor fails. As engine load increases, so does intake manifold air pressure.

Engine Speed and Position Sensors

Engine speed/position sensors can be referenced from the crankshaft，camshaft or both. In addition to helping determine engine load，these sensors also tell the computer when the injectors should be fired.

These systems operate at a relatively high pressure (usually at least 30 psi). To control the fuel pressure, a fuel pressure regulator is used. As engine load increases, more fuel pressure is needed. This is due to the richer mixture (more fuel needed) and to overcome the increased air pressure in the ports. Any unused fuel is diverted back to the fuel tank by using a return line.

Words and Expressions

1. strive [straiv] *v.* 努力，争取；斗争，奋斗

2. induce [in'dju:s] *v.* 诱导，诱发，引起，导致

3. equivalence [i'kwivələns] *n.* 等效(性)，等值(性)

4. theoretical [θiə'retikəl] *adj.* 理论(上)的

5. ideal [ai'diəl] *adj.* 理想的；观念的

6. lag [læg] *v.* 走得慢 *n.* 落后

7. puddle ['pʌdl] *v.* 搅拌 *n.* 搅泥浆；水坑，胶土

8. microprocessor ['maɪkrəʊ'prɑsesə] *n.* 微信息处理机，微处理器

9. optimum ['ɔptiməm] *n.* 最适条件，最适度

10. intermittent [ˌintə'mitənt] *adj.* 间歇的

11. evaluate [i'væljueit] *vt.* 评价，估……的价

12. fuel injection system 燃油喷射系统

13. throttle valve　节流阀

14. air flow meter　空气流量计

15. thermo-time switch　热限时开关

16. air/fuel mixture　混合气

17. temperature sensor　温度传感器

18. throttle position sensor　节流阀位置传感器

19. airflow sensor　空气流量传感器

20. manifold pressure sensor　歧管压力传感器

21. engine speed and position sensor　发动机转速和位置传感器

22. air-fuel ratio　空燃比

23. excess air ratio　过量空气系数

24. rich mixture　浓混合气

25. lean mixture　稀混合气

26. fuel injection　燃油喷射

27. intake manifold　进气歧管

28. the manifold runner　歧管通道

29. the fuel pump　燃油泵

30. fuel-metering system　燃油计量系统

31. single point fuel injection　单点喷射

32. multipoint fuel injection　多点喷射

Notes

1. Automobile engineers are continually striving towards minimal fuel consumption and cleaner exhaust emissions.

汽车工程师们不断朝着最少的燃油消耗量和更干净的排放这一目标努力。

2. The air induction system consists of the air cleaner, air flow meter, throttle valve, air intake chamber, intake manifold runner and intake valve.

进气系统由空气滤清器、空气流量计、节流阀、空气进气室、进气歧管管道和进气阀组成。

3. Information from these sensors is processed by the computer which then determines the proper air/fuel mixture.

计算机处理来自这些传感器的信息，然后确定适合的混合气。

4. These sensors also help the computer determine engine load by indicating the amount of air entering the engine.

这些传感器也通过指出进入发动机的空气总量来帮助计算机确定发动机负荷。

5. Engine speed/position sensors can be referenced from the crankshaft，camshaft or both.

发动机速度 / 位置传感器是可以通过曲轴、凸轮轴或者二者一起进行工作的。

Exercises

A. Vocabulary

I. Translate the following expressions into Chinese.

1. intake manifold

2. throttle position sensor

3. fuel injection system

4. crankshaft position sensor

5. exhaust gas oxygen sensor

6. fuel pressure regulator

7. intake manifold runner

8. multipoint fuel injection

9. pulsation damper

10. idle control valve

II. Identify the English names of the EFI system according to the picture.

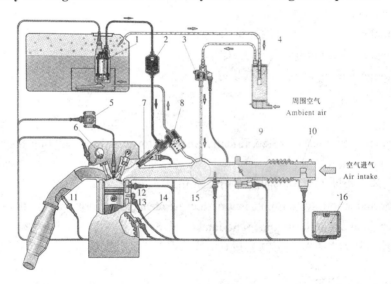

周围空气
Ambient air

空气进气
Air intake

1. _____ 2. _____ 3. _____ 4. _____

5. _____ 6. _____ 7. _____ 8. _____

9. _____ 10. _____ 11. _____ 12. _____

13. _____ 14. _____ 15. _____ 16. _____

B. Comprehension

I. Discuss the following questions in groups and write down your answers.

1. What subsystems can electronic fuel injection systems be broken down?

_____

_____

2. What does the single point fuel injection mean?

_____

_____

3. How does EFI system operate?

_____

_____

II. Read the following passage carefully and fill in the blanks with the proper forms of the given words.

intake valve   air cleaner   output actuator   input sensor
demand   air   throttle valve   spark advance system

When the throttle valve is opened, air flows through the ____, through the air flow meter (on L type systems), past the ____, and through a well tuned intake manifold runner to the ____.

Air delivered to the engine is a function of driver ____. As the throttle valve is opened further, more ____ is allowed to enter the engine cylinders.

The input phase of electronic control allow the Electronic Control Unit (ECU) to monitor engine operating conditions, utilizing information from the ____.

The process phase of electronic control requires the ECU to use this input information to make operating decisions about the fuel and ____.

The output phase of electronic control requires the ECU to control the ____, the fuel injectors, and igniter to achieve the desired fuel metering and spark timing.

C. Translation

I. Translate the following sentences into Chinese.

1. The computer uses this information to determine how rich or lean the mixture should be.

2. In addition to helping determine engine load, these sensors also tell the computer when the injectors should be fired.

3. If a vehicle is not equipped with an airflow sensor, it uses a manifold pressure sensor to determine engine load. Note that some vehicles with an airflow sensor may also have a manifold pressure sensor.

II. Translate the following sentences into English.

1. 燃油供给系统包括燃油箱、燃油泵、燃油滤清器、供油管、喷油器、燃油压力调节器和回油管。

2. 燃油被电动燃油泵从燃油箱输送到喷油器，典型的燃油泵被固定在燃油箱里面或其附近。杂质通过燃油管上串接的高容量滤清器过滤。

3. 燃油压力调节器将燃油维持在恒定压力，没有被喷油器喷射到进气歧管的燃油将通过回油管返回到燃油箱。

Reading Material

Read the following passages and answer the questions according to the information given in the passages.

Passage One   Common Rail Diesel Injection

Common rail diesel injection is a modern variant of direct injection system for diesel engines. It features a high-pressure (1000+ bar) fuel rail feeding individual solenoid valves, as opposed to low-pressure fuel pump feeding pump nozzles or high-pressure fuel line to mechanical valves controlled by cams on the camshaft. The third generation common rail diesels now feature piezoelectric injectors for even greater accuracy, with fuel pressures up to 180 MPa/1800 bar.

The common rail system accumulates high-pressure fuel in the common rail and injects the fuel into the engine cylinder at timing controlled by the engine ECU, allowing high-pressure injection independent from the engine speed. As a result, the common rail system can reduce harmful materials such as nitrogen oxides (NO_X) and particulate matter (PM) in emissions and generates more engine power.

Today the common rail system has brought about a revolution in diesel engine technology. Robert Bosch GmbH, Denso Corporation, Siemens VDO and Delphi Automotive Systems are the main suppliers of modern common rail systems. Different car makers refer to their common rail engines by different names.

Questions

1. What are the advantages of the common rail system?

2. How does the common rail system work?

3. How many main suppliers of modern common rail systems are there in the world?

Passage Two   The Injectors

My mechanic says my injectors are dirty and need to be cleaned. What does that mean? "Dirty" is actually a misnomer. Rarely are injectors clogged with dirt. Rather, they are usually clogged or restricted by a buildup of fuel varnish deposits. This reduces the amount of fuel that the injector sprays, which in turn may cause the engine to run lean and misfire, hesitate or stall.

A fuel injector is nothing more than spray nozzle. With mechanical injectors, a spring loaded valve allows fuel to squirt out of the nozzle when line pressure overcomes spring tension that holds the valve shut. With electronic injectors, a spring-loaded solenoid pulls open a pintle valve or ball type valve when the injector is energized by the computer. This allows the pressurized fuel in the fuel rail to flow through the injector and squirt out the nozzle.

Injectors come in a variety of styles. Early Bosch style injectors have a pintle valve and are the ones most prone to clogging. In 1989, General Motors introduced its new "Multec" style injectors which have a ball valve design and are claimed to be more resistant to clogging. Other injectors have a disc-valve design that is also said to resist clogging.

The truth is any injector can clog. Nobody's injectors are immune to this kind of problem, but some are obviously better than others.

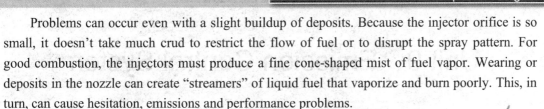

Problems can occur even with a slight buildup of deposits. Because the injector orifice is so small, it doesn't take much crud to restrict the flow of fuel or to disrupt the spray pattern. For good combustion, the injectors must produce a fine cone-shaped mist of fuel vapor. Wearing or deposits in the nozzle can create "streamers" of liquid fuel that vaporize and burn poorly. This, in turn, can cause hesitation, emissions and performance problems.

Injector Cleaning

The cure for a set of clogged injectors is cleaning or replacement if they're too badly clogged to respond to cleaning. Injectors are expensive to replace. New domestic injectors sell for $60 to $100 each, with new import injectors fetching $125 to $175 each. Injectors should only be replaced as a last resort.

If your injectors are clogged, they can be cleaned with pressurized solvent, or removed for off-car cleaning. There are also fuel tank additives that claim to clean clogged injectors, but the cleaning efficiency of such products is usually minimal. So save your money and put it towards a professional cleaning.

There are do-it-yourself on-car injector pressure cleaning kits that are similar to the equipment professionals use. But some of these kits can be tricky or even dangerous to use. Our advice is to let a professional do it.

On-car injector cleaning involves feeding solvent under pressure into the injector fuel rail or supply line. The concentrated solvent passes through the injectors, loosens and washes away the accumulated varnish deposits. The results are usually good, and make a noticeable difference in idle smoothness, emissions and fuel economy.

If your injectors are really clogged and fail to respond well to on-car cleaning, off-car cleaning using special fuel injection cleaning equipment would be the next logical option. Some of this equipment is designed to "reverse" flush the injectors, so any debris that's trapped inside the injector or above the inlet screen will also be removed. Off-car cleaning also allows a mechanic to observe the spray pattern of the injectors to make sure there aren't any streamers or problems. Off-car cleaning is more expensive because of the labor involved to remove the injectors, but the results are usually better.

Keeping Injectors Clean

The best way to minimize or eliminate the need for injector cleaning is to use a quality brand of gasoline that contains sufficient detergent to prevent varnish buildup. Most brand name gasolines today have enough detergent to do this. As a rule, premium grades usually contain a somewhat higher concentration of cleaners.

You can also use fuel tank additives to keep your injectors clean. Such products really aren't necessary if you're using quality gasoline. But if you're buying the cheapest gas you can find, using an additive might be good insurance.

Questions

1. My mechanic says my injectors are dirty and need to be cleaned. What does this mean?
2. How to do the injectors cleaning?
3. How to keep injectors clean?

Unit 9　Emission Control System

The vehicle components are responsible for reducing air pollution. This includes crankcase emissions, evaporative emission and tailpipe exhaust emissions. Crankcase emissions consist of unburned fuel and combustion byproducts. These gases are recirculated back into the engine for reburning by the positive crankcase ventilation (PCV) system. Evaporative emissions are the fuel vapors that seep out of the fuel tank. They are prevented from escaping into the atmosphere by sealing the fuel system and storing the vapors in a vapor canister for later reburning. Tailpipe exhaust emissions consist of carbon monoxide (CO), unburned hydrocarbons (HC) and oxides of nitrogen (NO_X). This formation of these pollutants is minimized by various ways. Engine design features control over fuel calibration and ignition timing, and the Exhaust Gas Recirculation (EGR) system. The pollutants that make it into the exhaust are "reburned" before they exit the tailpipe by the catalytic converter. The emission control system is an integral part of the engine, and should not be tampered or disconnected. Devices related to the emission control system installed on the automobile are tailpipe, muffler, EGR valve, catalytic converter, air pump, PCV valve and charcoal canister.

Catalytic Converter

Automotive emissions are controlled in three ways. One is to promote more complete combustion so that there are less byproducts. The second is to reintroduce excessive hydrocarbons back into the engine for combustion and the third is to provide an additional area for oxidation or combustion to occur. This additional area is called a catalytic converter. The catalytic converter looks like a muffler. It is located in the exhaust system ahead of the muffler. Inside the converter are pellets or a honeycomb made of platinum or palladium. The platinum or palladium is used as a catalyst (a catalyst is a substance used to speed up a chemical process). As hydrocarbons or carbon monoxide in the exhaust is passed over the catalyst, it is chemically oxidized or converted to carbon dioxide and water. As the converter works to clean the exhaust, it develops heat. The dirtier the exhaust, the harder the converter works and the more heat is developed. In some cases the converter can be seen to glow from excessive heat. If the converter works too hard to clean a dirty exhaust it will destroy itself. Also leaded fuel will put a coating on the platinum or palladium and render the converter ineffective.

PCV Valve

The purpose of the Positive Crankcase Ventilation (PCV) system is to take the vapors produced in the crankcase during the normal combustion process and redirect them into the air/fuel intake system to burn during combustion. These vapors dilute the air/fuel mixture so they have to be carefully controlled and metered so as not to affect the performance of the engine. This is the job of the Positive Crankcase Ventilation (PCV) valve. At idle, when the air/fuel mixture is very critical, just a few vapors are allowed into the intake system. At high speed when the mixture is less critical and the pressure in the engine is greater, more of the vapors are allowed into the intake system when the valve or the system is clogged vapors will back up into the filter housing or at worst, the excess pressure will push past seals and create engine oil leaks. If the wrong valve is used or the system has air leaks, the engine will idle rough or at worst engine oil will be sucked out of the engine, as shown in Figure 2-12.

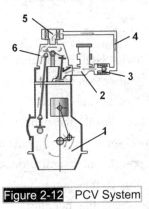

Figure 2-12　PCV System

1—crankcase　2—intake manifold　3—PCV　4—ventilation pipe

5—ventilation outlet filter　6—cylinder head cover

EGR Valve

The purpose of the Exhaust Gas Recirculation (EGR) valve is to meter a small amount of exhaust gas into the intake system. This dilutes the air/fuel mixture so as to lower the combustion chamber temperature. Excessive combustion chamber temperature creates oxides of nitrogen, which is a major pollutant. While the EGR valve is the most effective method of controlling oxides of nitrogen, it adversely affects engine performance. The engine was not designed to run on exhaust gas. For this reason, the amount of exhaust entering the intake system has to be carefully monitored. Since EGR action reduces performance by diluting the air/fuel mixture, the system does not allow EGR action when the engine is cold or when the engine needs full power.

Evaporative Controls

Gasoline evaporates quite easily. In the past, these evaporative emissions were vented into the atmosphere and 20% of all HC emissions from the automobile are from the gas tank. In 1970 a legislation was passed prohibiting venting of gas tank fumes into the atmosphere. An evaporative control system was developed to eliminate this source of pollution. The function of tile fuel evaporative control system is to trap and store evaporative emissions from the gas tank and carburetor. A charcoal canister is used to trap the fuel vapors. The fuel vapors adhere to the charcoal. Until the engine is started, the engine vacuum can be used to draw the vapors into the engine so that they can be burned along with the fuel air mixture. This system requires the use of a sealed gas tank, filler cap. Tin's cap is so important to the operation of the system that a test of the cap is now being integrated into many state emission inspection programs. Pre-1970 car released fuel vapors into the atmosphere through the use of a vented gas cap. Today with the use of sealed caps redesigned, gas tanks are used. The tank has to have the space for the vapors to collect so that they can then be vented to the charcoal canister. A purge valve is used to control the vapor flow into the enginc. The purge valve is operated by engine vacuum. One common

problem with this system is that the purge valve goes bad and engine vacuum draws fuel directly into the intake system. This enriches the fuel mixture and will foul the spark plugs. Most charcoal canisters have a filter that should be replaced periodically. This system should be checked when fuel mileage drops.

Air Injection

Since no internal combustion engine is 100% efficient, there will always be some unburned fuel in the exhaust. This increases hydrocarbon emissions. To eliminate this source of emissions, an air injection system was created. Combustion requires fuel, oxygen and heat. Without any one of the three, combustion cannot occur. Inside the exhaust manifold there is sufficient heat to support combustion. If we introduce some oxygen, then any unburned fuel will ignite. This combustion will not produce any power, but it will reduce excessive hydrocarbon emissions. Unlike in the combustion chamber, this combustion in uncontrolled, so if the fuel content of the exhaust is excessive, explosions that sound like popping will occur. There are times when under normal conditions, such as decoration, the fuel content is excessive. Under these conditions we would want to shut off the the air injection system. This is accomplished through the use of a diverter valve, which instead of shutting the air pump off, diverts the away from the exhaust manifold. Since all of this is done after the combustion process is complete, this is one emission control that has no effect on engine performance. The only maintenance that is required is a careful inspection of the air pump drive belt.

Taking Aim at Polluters

Advanced technologies should be incorporated into auto design to reduce exhaust emissions, according to an article in *China Economic Times*. An excerpt is as follows:

The State Environmental Protection Administration estimates that by 2005 about 79 percent of all air pollution will come from automobile exhaust emissions. And urban air pollution will shift from the current combination of coal smoke and auto exhaust to mainly auto exhaust.

The country's large-scale auto emission pollution can be attributed to the backward standard of controls. In 2001 China adopted the first standard of exhaust emission, equivalent to the Euro I, twenty years later than developed countries. And the second standard, equivalent to the Euro II, was instituted in 2003, eight years later than developed nations. The current schedule calls for adopting the Euro III standard between 2008 and 2010, still eight years late. The delay in adopting international emission standards has led to high fuel consumption, the low fuel utilization and rampant emissions from made-in-China autos.

There is a huge gap between the technologies of emission control and engine production in China and those of the developed countries.

In addition, due to lack of strict supervision in the management of obsolete autos, many of these vehicles have entered the market and continue to run on the road.

For controlling exhaust emission pollution effectively, China should try to master advanced technologies as quickly as possible. The Euro III and IV standards adhere to an advanced system.

Taking into account fuel quality, road condition, transportation management, driving technique and habit and daily car maintenance, some joint ventures have already mastered such technology. Domestic enterprises should speed up the pace of their research in this aspect.

Measures should also be taken to accelerate the discard of old cars. Meanwhile, preferential tax policies should be allowed to encourage consumers to purchase low polluters.

Exhaust pollution should not be an obstacle to the growth of China's auto industry, once effective measures and advanced technologies are implemented.

Words and Expressions

1. tailpipe　[teilpaɪp]　*n.* 排气管

2. byproduct　['bai,prɔdʌkt]　*n.* 副产品

3. seep　[si:p]　*v.* (液体等)渗漏

4. canister　['kænistə]　*n.* (放咖啡、茶叶、烟等的)小罐，筒，(防毒面具的)滤毒罐

5. reburn　['ri:'bə:n]　*v.* 再燃烧，复燃

6. pollutant　[pə'lu:tənt]　*n.* 污染物

7. feature　[fi:tʃə]　*n.* 外貌，特征

8. hydrocarbon　['haidrəu'kɑ:bən]　*n.* 烃，碳氢化合物

9. incorporate　[in'kɔ:pəreit]　*v.* 合并，并入

10. equivalent　[i'kwivələnt]　*adj.* 等价的

11. institute　['institju:t]　*v.* 创立，开始；制定

12. rampant　['ræmpənt]　*adj.* 蔓生的；猖獗的

13. gap　[gæp]　*n.* 差距，隔阂

14. obsolete　['ɔbsəli:t]　*adj.* 过时的

15. supervision　[,sju:pə'viʒən]　*n.* 监督

16. import　[im'pɔ:t]　*v.* 调入

17. preferential　[,prefə'renʃəl]　*adj.* 优先的，特惠的

18. obstacle　['ɔbstəkl]　*n.* 障碍(物)

19. implement　['implimənt]　*v.* 实现，实施

20. PVC　曲轴箱正压通风装置

21. carbon monoxide　一氧化碳

22. ignition timing　点火定时

23. Exhaust Gas Recirculation (EGR)　废气再循环；排气再循环

24. catalytic converter　(汽车等的)催化式排气净化器

25. speed up　加速

26. back up　倒退

27. at worst　在最坏的情况下

28. run on　涉及

29. exhaust gas　排气，废气

30. gas tank　汽油箱

31. adhere to　黏附，黏着

32. filler cap　(汽油箱)加油口盖

33. purge valve　排气阀

34. air injection　空气喷射，(特指废气净化系中的)二次空气喷射

35. exhaust manifold　排气歧管

36. diverter valve　分流阀

37. drive belt　传动皮带

38. attribute...to　把……归因于，把……归咎于

Notes

1. The dirtier the exhaust, the harder the converter works and the more heat is developed.
尾气越脏，净化器工作的难度就越大，并且产生更多的热量。

2. These vapors dilute the air/fuel mixture, so they have to be carefully controlled and metered so as not to affect the performance of the engine.
曲轴箱里的蒸汽可稀释/可燃混合物，因此蒸汽的量必须要认真控制和测定，以免影响发动机的性能。

3. 20% of all HC emissions from the automobile are from the gas tank.
汽车排放的碳氢化合物的20%来自汽油油箱。

4. The only maintenance that is required is a careful inspection of the air pump drive belt.
唯一要做的检修是认真检查空气泵的传动皮带。

5. In addition, air injection system can be used to reduce the amount of hydrocarbons (HC) and carbon monoxide (CO) in the exhaust is by forcing fresh air into the exhaust system after combustion.
除此之外，通过将新鲜的空气充入燃烧后的排气系统中，空气喷射系统能够降低废气中碳氢化合物和一氧化碳的数量。

6. The method used to reduce oxides of nitrogen is to cool down the combustion process by using an exhaust gas recirculation (EGR) valve.
用来降低氮氧化物产生的方法是利用废气再循环阀来使燃烧过程中的温度降低。

Exercises

A. Vocabulary

I. Translate the following expressions into Chinese.

1. catalytic converter

2. EGR valve

3. gas tank

4. exhaust gas

5. evaporative emission control

6. exhaust gas recirculation system

7. carbon monoxide

8. positive crankcase ventilation

9. State Environmental Protection Administration

10. Emission Control System

II. Identify the English names of the emission control system according to the picture.

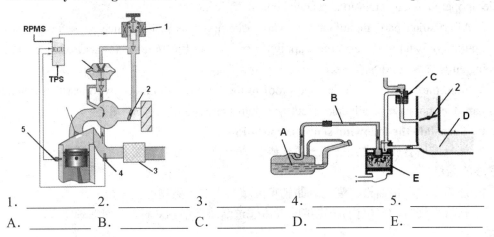

1. _____ 2. _____ 3. _____ 4. _____ 5. _____

A. _____ B. _____ C. _____ D. _____ E. _____

B. Comprehension

I. Discuss the following questions in groups and write down your answers.

1. How does EGR work?

_____

2. What is the composition of PCV?

_____

3. What is the purpose of air injection ?

_____

II. Read the following passage carefully and fill in the blanks with the proper forms of the given words.

emission　legal　full-time　drive　plug　revision

exhaust system　equip with　aftermarket　disconnect

The federal anti-tampering law does not, however, apply to race cars that are not operated on the street, other _____ off-road vehicles, show cars that are not street _____, or vehicles not factory _____ emission controls (most 1967 and earlier vehicles). So that exempts all antique cars, and most classic cars and muscle cars.

_____ to the Clean Air Act in 1990 further broadened the definition of _____ tampering to include virtually ANY type of engine or _____ modification that alters what comes out the tailpipe. That means any nonstock _____ part that is installed on your engine must be

EPA-approved and _____(except on the exempt vehicles previously noted).

Before the law was revised in 1990, it was only illegal for professional mechanics to remove or _____ emission control devices. There was nothing to prevent a motorist from tampering with their own vehicles. That loophole has since been _____.

C. Translation

I. Translate the following sentences into Chinese.

1. Federal law makes it illegal for Anyone to tamper with, disconnect, remove or other wise render inoperative Any emissions-related control device.

2. Aftermarket parts manufacturers who make nonstock performance parts for engines, the fuel, ignition or exhaust systems must apply for special certification for any parts they want to sell as being emissions-legal.

3. First, they must submit detailed proof in the form of laboratory dyno test that documents their part does not have an adverse effect on exhaust emissions.

II. Translate the following sentences into English.

1. 尾气中所含碳氢化合物和一氧化碳的成分越多，净化器工作的难度就越大，并且产生更多的热量。

2. 通常是汽车中油箱、废气、曲轴箱区域产生的污染物占大多数。

3. 每次燃烧时，(气缸内)一定量的气体通过活塞环漏到曲轴箱，使曲轴箱里的压力稍有增加。

Reading Material

Read the following passages and answer the questions according to the information given in the passages.

Passage One　Emissions Test

You try to figure out why it failed the test, get the problem fixed and then try to pass the test again. This may or may not be an ordeal depending on what's wrong with your engine, how easily the problem is to diagnose and repair, and whether or not you flunk a retest.

The worst case scenario is spending a lot of money on repairs only to find that they didn't solve your emissions problem. You bounce back and forth between the repair facility and test station, wasting time and money all the while cursing the incompetent mechanics who tried to fix your car and the bureaucrats who created the clean air emissions testing program.

But in states or municipalities where periodic emissions testing is required, you cannot get your vehicle registration or emissions compliance sticker unless you either pass the test or meet the "waiver" requirements.

A "waiver" is a kind of loophole that allows some vehicles to pass an emissions test even when they can't meet the applicable emission requirements. Some would argue this isn't fair to those whose vehicles meet the requirements and pass the test, but nobody said emissions testing was fair.

Waivers were created by politicians who recognized the fact that many people (voters) can't afford to pay for all the repairs that might be required to pass an emissions test. So credit is given for a good faith effort and for spending a fixed dollar amount on repairs. Once you've spent up to the limit, you get an automatic pass.

Waiver limits vary from one state to another, and some vary by the model year of vehicle. Waiver limits typically range from $75 up to $150, but may be as much as $450 on new vehicles in some states. So if you don't know what the applicable waiver limit is on your vehicle, ask. Unless you're a real zealot about clean air, there's no legal reason to spend a dime more than the waiver limit on emission repairs.

How to Improve Your Odds of Passing an Emissions Test

The best way to improve the odds of passing an emissions test is to maintain your vehicle. A well-maintained engine is usually a clean engine as far as emissions are concerned.

Changing the spark plugs, air filter, fuel filter, PCV valve and oil regularly (or just before an emissions test), checking ignition timing and adjusting the carburetor (if you have an older vehicle) can reduce emissions and greatly improve your chance of passing.

Also, filling up your fuel tank with gasoline that contains 10% ethanol alcohol (many premium grade fuels use alcohol as an octane booster.) may help lower your emissions even more. Many areas now have "reformulated" gasoline that contains alcohol or MTBE(methyl tert-butyl ether) that adds oxygen to the fuel to reduce carbon monoxide and hydrocarbon emissions.

Just before the test, make sure your vehicle is at normal operating temperature. Take it out for a short spin down the expressway. This will heat up the oxygen sensor and catalytic converter to minimize emissions.

Questions

1. My car failed an emissions test. Now what can I do?

2. What is the emission system composed of?

3. How should you improve your odds of passing an emissions test?

Passage Two   Emissions Be Concerned

If you're serious about clean air—or at least worried, you won't pass an emissions test. Most emission testing programs to date only check for only two pollutants: carbon monoxide (CO) and hydrocarbons (HC). In areas that have the new "enhanced" I/M 240 emissions testing program, they also check for oxides of nitrogen (NO_X) and the operation of your "evaporative emissions" control system (the system that captures and holds vapors from your fuel tank).

Carbon Monoxide (CO)

Of the three main pollutants, carbon monoxide is the deadliest because you can't see it or smell it. A concentration of only 0.5% CO in the air can render a person unconscious—and kill within 10 to 15 minutes! Even concentrations as small as 0.04% can cause headaches and be life—threatening after several hours exposure.

WARNING: Never run an engine inside an enclosed garage, not even for a few minutes. The fumes can build up quickly and overcome you before you realize what's happening. Carbon monoxide is invisible and odorless, so you can't really tell when it's around.

Carbon monoxide is formed when the fuel mixture is rich and there is insufficient oxygen to burn all the fuel completely. The richer the fuel mixture, the greater the quantity of CO produced. So high CO emissions indicate incomplete combustion typically caused by carburetor maladjustment, a clogged air filter, sticking choke, defective heated air intake system, plugged PCV valve, faulty oxygen sensor, excessive fuel pressure or a fuel injection metering problem.

Carbon monoxide production is the highest when the engine is first started because the fuel mixture is richer than normal during this time and the catalytic converter has not yet reached operating temperature.

Carbon monoxide emissions are minimized by maintaining a balanced to slightly lean fuel mixture. This requires careful adjustment of the carburetor idle mixture screws, which may have "limiter caps" to limit the amount of adjustment or are covered with plugs to prevent tampering. On some fuel injected engines, there is also an adjustment for the idle mixture, but it is usually factory sealed to prevent tampering. The fuel mixture is further balanced by the oxygen sensor and computer system. Most of the carbon monoxide that is produced by the engine is converted into carbon dioxide (CO_2) by the catalytic converter.

Hydrocarbons (HC)

Hydrocarbon emissions are unburned gasoline and oil vapors. Though not directly harmful, they are a major contributor to smog and ozone pollution, which are toxic. Hydrocarbons in the atmosphere react with sunlight and break down to form other chemical compounds that irritate the eyes, nasal passages, throat and lungs.

HC emissions, which are usually measured in parts per million (PPM), can go up as a result of ignition misfiring (a fouled plug or bad plug wire), "lean" misfiring (incorrect carburetor, idle adjustment or vacuum leaks that creates a lean mixture that misfires), loss of compression (such as a burned or leaky exhaust valve), or engine wear that causes the engine to burn oil (worn valve guides, rings and/or cylinders).

Hydrocarbon emissions are controlled by maintaining the fuel mixture so it is neither too lean nor too rich to ignite, by keeping the combustion chamber tightly sealed (good rings and valves), and by maintaining the ignition system (changing the plugs periodically). The HC produced in the engine is reburned in the catalytic converter and changed into water vapor and carbon dioxide.

Oxides of Nitrogen (NO_X)

Nitrogen makes up about 78% of the air we breathe. Though normally inert and not directly involved in the combustion process, combustion temperatures above 2,500 degrees Fahrenheit cause nitrogen and oxygen to combine and form various compounds called "oxides of nitrogen", which is abbreviated NO_X. This mostly occurs when the engine is under load and the throttle is open wide.

NO_X is a nasty pollutant both directly and indirectly. In concentrations as small as a few parts per million, it can cause eye, nose and lung irritations, headaches and irritability. Higher

concentrations can cause bronchitis and aggravate other lung disorders. Once in the atmosphere, it reacts with oxygen to form ozone (which is also toxic to breathe) and smog.

To reduce the formation of NO_X, Exhaust Gas Recirculation (EGR) is used. By recirculating a small amount of exhaust gas back into the intake manifold to dilute the air/fuel mixture, EGR has a "cooling" effect on combustion, thus keeping temperatures below the NO_X formation threshold.

On 1981 and later engines with computerized engine controls, a special "three-way" catalytic converter is used to reduce NO_X in the exhaust. The first chamber of the converter contains a special "reduction" catalyst that breaks NO_X down into oxygen and nitrogen. The second chamber contains the "oxidation" catalyst that reburns CO and HC.

High NO_X emissions are almost always due to a defective EGR valve or some component that controls the operation of the EGR valve. A related symptom that usually occurs when EGR is lost is spark knock (detonation) during acceleration.

Evaporative Emissions

The fuel vapors that evaporate from your fuel tank can be another source of smog and ozone pollution. So fuel systems for the past twenty years have been sealed to prevent the loss of vapors.

Some venting of the tank must be provided so it can "breathe" during temperature changes and when the engine is running, so this is provided by hoses connected to a charcoal filled canister usually located in the engine compartment. The charcoal particles in the canister soak up and store fuel vapors when the engine is not running. Then, when the engine is started, a "purge valve" opens to siphon the vapors into the engine where they are burned.

If the canister or any of its hose connections leak or the gas cap does not seal tightly, fuel vapors can escape into the atmosphere around the clock. The amount of pollution can really add up, especially during hot weather, so it's important to make sure the system is functioning properly. The new OBD II test program includes a pressure check of the fuel tank system as well as a flow test of the purge valve.

Questions

1. What kinds of emissions should one be concerned about?
2. What is the emissions system composed of?
3. How do the emissions generate?

Unit 10　Intake and Exhaust Systems

The intake air system used on the engine has the following features:

1. Mass air flow sensor with integrated intake air temperature sensor.
2. Intake manifold runner control (IMRC).
3. Variable tumble (Swirl Plate) control system.

The intake system is a part of the fuel system. The air intake systems include air filter, ducting, manifolds and air temperature sensor. Some engines have supercharger in the intake system.

The air filter is used in the engine to trap contaminants, yet provide a free flow of air into the engine. A dirty air filter can cause large restrictions to the air. This condition will cause the engine to run excessively rich. Fuel mileage can be substantially reduced and exhaust emissions will also be increased.

Air filters which are usually used in cars are made of paper element. These filters permit air to flow into the engine with little resistance. They trap and hold contaminants inside the paper. When becoming plugged with dirt, they are replaced with new ones.

The intake manifold made of hard plastic for weight reduction, contains the Intake Manifold Runner Control (IMRC) valves and swirl control valves. Each manifold runner is fitted with both an IMRC valve and swirl control valve.

Many engines today use an intake air temperature sensor to sense or measure the temperature of the air entering the engine. The sensor is located on the top of the intake manifold.

A turbocharger is a device used to supercharge an engine. The turbocharger usually consists of a turbine and a compressor. High-velocity exhaust gases pass out of the exhaust ports and then through a turbine. Here the exhaust gases cause the turbine to rotate very rapidly. The turbine causes the compressor to turn very rapidly as well. As the compressor turns, it draws in a large amount of fresh air. The intake air is pressurized and forced into the intake manifold and then into the cylinders. If a corresponding amount of fuel is added, a large increase in power will obtain, as shown in Figure 2-13.

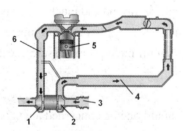

Figure 2-13 Intake and Exhaust Systems

1—compressor 2—turbine 3—fresh air 4—intake ducting 5—piston 6—exhaust ducting

The purpose of the emission control system is to control the emissions and exhaust from your vehicle. The idea is to turn the harmful gases your car manufactures into harmless ones that don't ruin the environment. Some of the problem gases are: hydrocarbons(HC), carbon monoxide(CO), carbon dioxide(CO_2), nitrogen oxides(NO_X).

The exhaust system collects the high-temperature gases from each combustion chamber and sends them through an exhaust manifold, exhaust pipe, catalytic converters, muffler and tailpipe.

Exhaust Manifold

The exhaust manifold, usually constructed of cast iron, is a pipe that conducts the exhaust

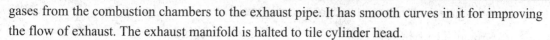
gases from the combustion chambers to the exhaust pipe. It has smooth curves in it for improving the flow of exhaust. The exhaust manifold is halted to tile cylinder head.

Exhaust Pipe

The exhaust pipe is attached to the exhaust manifold. It takes the gases away through the catalytic converter, then through the muffler system to the outside environment.

Muffler

The muffler is employed to reduce the exhaust sound of the engine. Two types are primarily used. One uses a series of baffled chambers to reduce the sound. The other uses a perforated straight pipe enclosed in fiberglass and shell. The straight pipe reduces exhaust back pressure, but it does not reduce the sound as much as the baffle type.

Catalytic Converter

Catalytic converters are emission control devices that contain chemically treated substances that convert harmful emissions into harmless carbon dioxide and water vapor. The catalytic converter is installed to reduce hydrocarbons (HC), carbon monoxide (CO), and nitrous oxides (NO_X). The catalytic converter does this by operating at high temperature, which burns the unwanted byproducts of combustion.

Tailpipe

The tailpipe is a long metal tube attached to the muffler. It discharges the exhaust gases from the muffler of your engine into the air outside the car.

Dual Exhaust System

The advantage of a dual exhaust system is that the engine exhausts more freely, by lowering the back pressure which is inherent in an exhaust system. With a dual exhaust system, a sizable increase in engine horse power can be obtained because the "breathing" capacity of the engine is improved, leaving less exhaust gases in the engine at the end of each exhaust stroke.

Words and Expressions

1. restriction [ris'trikʃən]   *n.* 限制，约束

2. supercharger ['sju:pətʃɑ:dʒə]   *n.* 增压器

3. mass [mæs]   *n.* 质量

4. manifold ['mænifəuld]   *n.* 歧管

5. swirl [swə:l]   *n.* 旋涡(漩涡)，涡状

6. resonance ['rezənəns]   *n.* 谐振，共振

7. servo ['sə:vəu]   *n.* 伺服，伺服系统

8. accelerator [æk'seləreitə]   *n.* 加速者，加速器

9. conventional [kən'venʃənl]   *adj.* 惯例的，常规的

10. trap [træp]   *n.* 诱捕，捕捉

11. mileage ['mailidʒ]   *n.* 英里数，英里里程

12. emission [i'miʃən]   *n.* 排放物

13. turbocharger ['tə:bəu,tʃa:dʒə] n. 涡轮增压器

14. turbine ['tə:bin] n. 涡轮

15. compressor [kəm'presə] n. 压缩机

16. muffler ['mʌflə] n. 消声器

17. hydrocarbon ['haidrəu'ka:bən] n. 烃，碳氢化合物

18. monoxide [mə'nɔksaid] n. 一氧化物

19. fiberglass ['faibəgla:s] n. 玻璃纤维，玻璃丝

20. exhaust [ig'zɔ:st] v. 排气 n. 排气；排气装置

21. nitrogen ['naitrədʒen] n. [化]氮

22. phosphorus ['fɔsfərəs] n. 磷

23. goal [gəul] n. 目的，目标；守门员；球门，(球赛等的)得分

24. emit [i'mit] vt. 发出，放射，吐露；散发；发表，发行

25. vaporization [,veipərai'zeiʃne] n. 汽化器，喷雾器，蒸馏器

26. computerization [kəm,pju:tərai'zeiʃən; -ri'z-] n. 计算机化

27. diagnose ['daiəgnəuz] v. 诊断

28. convolute ['kɔnvəlju:t] v. 回旋，卷绕，盘旋 adj. 旋绕的

29. discharge [dis'tʃa:dʒ] v. 放出，流出，排出

30. noxious ['nɔkʃəs] adj. 有害的

31. platinum ['plætinəm] n. 白金，铂

32. air flow sensor 空气流量传感器

33. intake air temperature sensor 进气空气温度传感器

34. throttle body 节流阀体

35. throttle position sensor 节流阀位置传感器

36. exhaust manifold 排气歧管

37. catalytic converter 催化转化器

38. air filter 空气滤清器

39. intake ducting 进气管

40. intake manifold 进气歧管

41. intake air temperature sensor 进气温度传感器

Notes

1. The air filter is used in the engine to trap contaminants, yet provide a free flow of air into the engine.

空气滤清器在发动机上用于滤清杂质，从而使顺畅的空气流进入发动机。

2. Many engines today use an intake air temperature sensor to sense or measure the temperature of the air entering the engine.

今天的很多发动机使用进气温度传感器来感知或者测量进入发动机的空气温度。

3. When becoming plugged with dirt, they are replaced with new ones.

当被杂质堵塞时，它们被新的部件所代替。

4. The exhaust manifold，usually constructed of cast iron，is a pipe that conducts the exhaust gases from the combustion chambers to the exhaust pipe.

排气歧管通常由铸铁铸造，是将废气由燃烧室导入排气管的管路。

5. The advantage of a dual exhaust system is that the engine exhausts more freely, by lowering the back pressure which is inherent in an exhaust system.

双排气系统的好处是通过降低排气系统原来固有的背压，使发动机排放废气时更顺畅。

Exercises

A. Vocabulary

Ⅰ. Translate the following expressions into Chinese.

1. air filter

2. air flow sensor

3. exhaust pipe

4. baffle type

5. turbocharger

6. tailpipe

7. exhaust ducting

8. muffler

9. intake manifold

10. back pressure

II. Identify the English names of the intake and exhaust systems according to the picture.

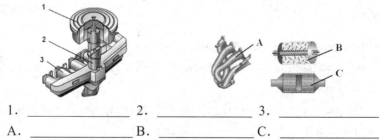

1. _____　2. _____　3. _____

A. _____　B. _____　C. _____

B. Comprehension

I. Discuss the following questions in groups and write down your answers.

1. What is the composition of air intake system?

_____

2. What is the function of the muffler?

_____

3. What is the purpose of catalytic converters?

_____

II. Read the following passage carefully and fill in the blanks with the proper forms of the given words.

> *deposit   ring   overhaul   burning oil   exceed   quart*
> *sooner or later   pollution   excessive   emission testing*

I see blue smoke in my exhaust when I start my engine. Is this anything I should worry about? Yes, because your engine is _____. That, in turn, means your engine has worn valve guides, piston rings. An engine that burns a lot of oil (more than a quart in 500 miles) is an engine that needs to be _____. Normal oil consumption should be a quart or less in 1,500 miles. Most newer engines consume less than half a _____ of oil between oil changes (every 3,000 miles). So if your engine is burning oil, it's essentially worn out and needs to be repaired.

Because the cost of overhauling or replacing an engine often _____ the value of an older car or truck, many people will just keep on driving a "mosquito fogger" in spite of the blue clouds of smoke it leaves behind. Never mind the _____ it causes, oil is cheaper than a new or rebuilt engine they reason. That philosophy may be okay if you live out in the sticks somewhere. But in urban areas that require periodic vehicle _____, an engine that's burning oil usually won't pass the test because of _____ hydrocarbon (HC) emissions. You may get by on a waiver after you've spent some money (in vain) on a tune-up, but the fact remains you're still a polluter.

An engine that burns a lot of oil will also eventually foul the spark plugs. Thick, black oily _____ build up on the plugs until they cease to fire. Then the engine misfires and loses power. Cleaning or changing the plugs may temporarily solve the problem, but _____ they'll foul out again.

Forget about "miracle" oil additives or pills that claim to stop oil burning. They don't. Better to save your money and put it towards a valve job and new set of _____.

C. Translation

I. Translate the following sentences into Chinese.

1. The intake manifold made of hard plastic for weight reduction, contains the IMRC valves and swirl control valves.

2. It takes the gases away through the catalytic converter, then through the muffler system to the outside environment.

3. With a dual exhaust system. a sizable increase in engine horse power can be obtained because the "breathing" capacity of the engine is improved，leaving less exhaust gases in the engine at the end of each exhaust stroke.

II. Translate the following sentences into English.

1. 当前很多发动机应用进气温度传感器来感知或者测量进入发动机的空气温度。

2. 三元催化转化器是一种排放控制装置，它可以通过内部的化学物质将有害的排放物转化成无害的二氧化碳和水蒸气。

3. 进气系统包括空气滤清器、进气管、进气歧管和进气温度传感器。

Reading Material

Read the following passages and answer the questions according to the information given in the passages.

Passage One　Wiper Blades

Wiper blades are one of the most neglected components on vehicles today. Many blades are cracked, split, torn, brittle, worn or otherwise in obvious need of replacement. Others may look okay, but do a lousy job of wiping when put to the test.

Ninety percent of all driving decisions are based on a clear unobstructed view of the road, which means good visibility is absolutely essential—especially during wet weather when vision may be obscured by water, road splash, sleet or snow on the windshield. But good visibility requires wipers that are in good condition. If the wipers are chattering, streaking or otherwise failing to wipe cleanly and consistently, you need new blades—NOW!

Most experts say wiper blades should be replaced every six to twelve months for optimum performance and driving visibility. That's because wiper blades don't last forever. Natural rubber deteriorates over time. Halogen-hardened rubber as well as synthetic rubber provides longer life. But eventually all blade materials fall victim to environmental factors. Exposure to sunlight and ozone causes the rubber to age, even if the wipers aren't used much.

As a set of blades age, they lose much of their flip-over flexibility and they're less able to wipe cleanly. They may develop a permanent set (called "parked" rubber) or curvature which prevents full contact with the windshield. This tends to be more of a problem on vehicles that are parked outside in the hot sun all day. The sun bakes and hardens the rubber. Then when the wipers are needed, they streak and chatter because they've taken a set and won't follow the curvature of the windshield. It can be very annoying as well as dangerous.

Cold weather can affect blade life, too. Freezing temperature makes rubber hard and brittle, which increases the tendency to crack and split. The holders can also become clogged with ice and snow, preventing the holder from distributing spring tension evenly over the blade. The blade "freezes up" and leaves streaks as it skips across the glass.

Heavy use can be hard on wiper blades, too, because dust, abrasives, road grime and even bug juice wear away the edge that the blades need to wipe cleanly. As the blade loses its edge, which is precision cut square to maximize the squeegee effect, water gets under the blade and remains on the glass. The result is reduced visibility and poor wiping action.

Any blade that's chattering, streaking or doing a lousy job of wiping, therefore, is a blade that's overdue for replacement. The same goes for any blade that is cracked, torn, nicked or otherwise damaged.

Checking Your Blades

A simple check is to try your windshield washers. If the blades are not in good condition, you'll see why when they attempt to wipe the washer solvent off the glass. Streaking, chattering or any other problems will be clearly obvious.

This test also gives you the opportunity to check your windshield washer system. Do both squirters work? If not, a nozzle may be plugged with dirt or a hose may be kinked or loose. Does the spray hit the windshield where it is supposed to? If not, the nozzles need adjusting. Does the washer pump deliver an adequate stream of solvent? If not, the vehicle may have a weak washer pump, or a clogged, kinked or loose hose. Most washer reservoirs have a screen to filter out debris that could clog or damage the pump. If this screen itself is buried under debris, it can choke off the flow of solvent to the washers.

After you've checked the windshield wipers, check the rear wiper too if your vehicle has a rear wiper system. Many sport utility vehicles, vans, minivans, station wagons, hatchbacks and fastbacks do. After all, it's just as important to see what's behind you when backing up in the rain as it is to see what's ahead. You can use the same test (try the rear windshield washer, if so equipped), or simply spray some water onto the glass with a squeeze bottle and see how the wiper performs.

Other Factors that Affect Your Wipers

How well the wiper blades perform also depends on the condition of the wiper arms and holders. A blade's wiping ability is affected by the amount of spring tension on the wiper arm, the number of pressure points or claws that hold the blade, and the design of the blade itself. If the springs in the arms are weak, which is more apt to be a problem in older vehicles, the wipers may not be pressed against the glass firmly enough to wipe cleanly. Replacing the blades won't make any difference because the problem is weak arms, not bad blades.

If the blades can be pulled away from the glass with little resistance, it's time for new arms. Most vehicle manufacturers publish tension specs for their arms. If the arm doesn't meet the specs, it needs to be replaced.

Remember to check the tension on the rear wiper arm, too, because rear wiper arms are often damaged by drive-through car wash rollers.

Wind lift is another factor that can interfere with good wiping action at highway speeds. Many windshields are steeply sloped to improve aerodynamics. But steeply raked windshields with a lot of glass area direct more wind against the wipers. This can lift the blades away from the glass at high speed unless the wiper system and blades are designed to counter the aerodynamic forces. Some blades have specially designed vents and airfoils to minimize lift and/or generate downforce to keep the blades in constant contact with the glass as speed increases. If your original equipment blade holders need to be replaced, be sure that the replacements have the same anti-wind lift design.

Another factor to keep in mind is the design of the blade holder. A blade holder needs to distribute the tension of the wiper arm evenly over the blade while also allowing the blade to flex as it follows the changing curvature of the glass. The better quality replacement blade holders typically have six to eight claws to spread the pressure of the wiper arm over the blade. More claws also increase flexibility so the blades don't lose contact at the sides of the glass.

Replacement Blades

You can usually replace wiper blades yourself, and can replace just the blade with a refill or the entire blade assembly. Refills will save you money. If you're installing a blade assembly, most come with some type of adapter to fit the arms on your vehicle. The old blades pull or push off the arm by pressing a release button or pin on the wiper holder.

If you are replacing the blade only with a refill, the old blade can be removed by squeezing the locking tags in at the end of the blade so it will slip out of the holder. Make sure the replacement blade is the same length and claw width as the original. A blade that is too long may create interference problems, while one that is too short may not fit the holder.

For cold weather driving, you might consider installing a set of "winter blades" on your vehicle. These have an enclosed holder that prevents ice and snow from building up and interfering with the wiper's ability to do its job.

Questions

1. How often should one replace his/her wiper blades?

2. What are the factors that affect your wipers?

3. How to check the wiper blades?

Passage Two　The Tires Service

Is it still necessary to rotate the tires every so often? There are two schools of thought on this subject. Rotating the tires, which is recommended by all tire manufacturers, involves changing their position on the vehicle from one wheel location to another. This helps to even out tire wear between all the tires so the tires last longer and do not develop abnormal wear patterns. This may be recommended every 8,000 to 15,000 miles.

On front-wheel drive cars and minivans, the front wheels tend to wear at a much faster rate than those on the rear. After 50,000 or 60,000 miles of driving, the front tires may be worn out while the ones on the back may still have half or more of their tread life remaining. By rotating the tires front to rear and side to side, differences in wear patterns between the wheel locations spread the wear out and more or less wear the tires evenly—just as the theory goes. Consequently, tires that would have lasted only 50,000 or 60,000 miles on the front of a front-wheel drive car may last 70,000 or 80,000 miles. But on the other hand, the tires on the rear that may well have gone 100,000 miles only last 70,000 or 80,000 miles.

Those who say rotating tires is a waste of time argue that it makes more sense to replace the front tires on a front-wheel drive car or minivan when they wear out, but to leave the back tires alone—especially if you're putting a lot of miles on the vehicle or plan to keep it a long time. The back tires will probably last as long as two sets of front tires, so in the long run you end up buying the same number or possibly even fewer tires by not rotating. Plus, you've saved the time and money that would have been spent on rotating the tires.

This argument doesn't fly in the case of certain low profile performance tires that have a tendency to develop a heel-and-toe wear pattern if left in the same wheel position too long.

For rear-wheel drive cars and trucks, the recommended tire rotation pattern is to rotate the

front wheels to the opposite side on the rear, and move the rear wheels to the same side on the front.

For front-wheel drive cars and minivans, the recommended tire rotation pattern is to rotate the rear wheels to the front on the opposite side, and move the front wheels to the rear on the same side.

If your vehicle has "directional" tires (small arrows or triangles indicating the direction of travel), the wheels must not be switched side to side. They can, however, be rotated front to rear on the same side.

If the front and rear wheels and/or tires on your vehicle are of different size, then rotation is out of the question.

I'm buying a new set of tires. Should I have them balanced?

Yes. Balancing helps to guarantee a smooth ride at highway speeds, and it helps to maximize tire life. An out-of-balance tire can be very annoying because it produces a shake that increases in intensity The faster you go, the harder on the suspension of the up-and-down shaking of the wheel, not to mention your nerves, and also increases tread wear. An out-of-balance tire can develop a cupped wear pattern. So do yourself and your tires a favor and have them balanced.

Nowadays almost all service facilities and tire stores use an off-car electronic spin balancer to balance the wheels. The tire and wheel are mounted on the balancer, then spun to find any heavy spots on the wheel. The balancer then indicates where weights (and how much weight) need to be placed to counterbalance the heavy spot.

Off-car spin balancers actually check two kinds of balance—"static" and "dynamic". Static imbalance causes a wheel to shake up and down as it spins, so static balance is achieved when both halves of the tire wheel assembly weigh exactly the same. Dynamic imbalance causes a tire and wheel to shake back and forth or sideways as it spins. Dynamic balance is achieved when the front and back sides of the wheel and tire weigh the same.

Questions

1. Is it still necessary to rotate the tires every so often?
2. What is the heel-and-toe wear pattern?
3. I'm buying a new set of tires. Should I have them balanced? Why?

Chapter 3　Chassis

Unit 1　Power Train

The power developed inside the engine cylinder is ultimately aimed to turn the wheels so that the motor vehicle can move on the road. The reciprocating motion of the piston turns a crankshaft to rotate the flywheel through the connecting rod. The circular motion of the crankshaft is now to be transmitted to the driving wheels. It is transmitted through the clutch for manual transmission or torque converter for automatic transmission, a transmission, universal joints, propeller shaft or drive shaft, final drive, differential and halfshaft extending to the wheels. The application of engine power to the driving wheels through all these parts is called power train. The power train is usually the same on all modern passenger cars and trucks, but its arrangement may vary according to the method of drive and type of transmission units.

The power train serves two functions: it transmits power from the engine to the drive wheels, and it varies the amount of torque. The power train includes: ①clutch: that is used only on manual transmission, or torque converter and used only on automatic transmission; ②transmission: that is either manual or automatic; ③universal joint: that permits movement between the final drive and transmission; ④drive shaft: that transmits the power from transmission to differential; ⑤final drive: that turns the drive through 90° and reduces the speed of the drive; ⑥differential: that carries the power to the two wheel axles; ⑦axle shaft: that carries the power to the two wheels, as shown in Figure 3-1.

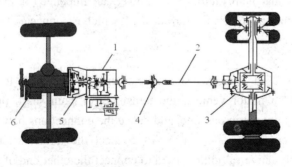

Figure 3-1　The Power Train

1—transmission　2—drive shaft　3—differential　4—universal joint　5—clutch　6—engine

Clutch

The clutch is a device used to provide smooth engagement and disengagement of engine and transmission. The engagement of engine and transmission means the linkup between engine and power train and transfer the engine power to the driving axle and wheels, and their disengagement

means to halt the power transfer that allows the engine to operate while the transmission does not. Three types of clutch are coil spring type, diaphragm spring type and semi-centrifugal type.

In conjunction with electronic control unit, automatic clutches provide automatic drive-away, or, together with servo-operated manual transmission, they provide a fully automatic transmission. Electronic transaction control as well as power interruption during braking are likewise possible.

Transmission

There are two types of transmission—manual transmission (MT) and automatic transmission (AT). In a car with a manual transmission, a driver shifts the gears manually. In a car with an automatic transmission, the gears shift automatically.

A manual transmission requires use of a clutch to apply and remove engine torque to the transmission input shaft. The clutch allows this to happen gradually so that the car can be started from a complete stop.

Manual transmissions usually have four or five speeds, and often have "overdrive", which means that the output shaft can turn faster than the input shaft for fuel economy on the highway. When you use it, it will reduce the engine speed by one-third, while maintaining the same road speed.

An automatic transmission is a device that provides gear reduction, with resulting multiplication of torque. The gear ranges are automatically selected to provide the most efficient operation and the best torque output.

Automatic transmission have three basic systems—a torque converter, a gear system and a hydraulic system.

The gear system changes the ratio in the automatic transmission. The planetary gear system has three parts—the sun gear, the planet gears and carrier, and the internal gear or ring gear.

The torque converter is like the clutch in a manual transmission. It is the coupling between the engine and power train that transmits power to the drive wheels.

It has three parts that help multiply the power: an impeller (or pump) connected to the engine's crankshaft, a turbine to turn the turbine shaft which is connected to the gears, and a stator (or guide wheel) between the two.

Universal Joint

A universal joint is used where two shafts are connected at an angle to transmit torque. In the transmission system of a motor vehicle, the transmission main shaft, propeller shaft and the differential pinion shaft are not in one line, and hence the connections between them are made by universal joint. One universal joint is used to connect the transmission main shaft and the propeller shaft; the other universal joint is used to connect the other end of the propeller shaft and the differential pinion shaft. Thus, the connections between the three shafts are flexible and at an angle with each other. The universal joint permits the torque transmission not only at angle, but also while this angle is changing constantly.

Drive Shaft

The drive shaft transmits the drive from the transmission mainshaft to the final drive pinion. The drive shaft is not solidly bolted to the transmission and the final drive. There must be some allowance for motion between the final drive and transmission. The universal joints provides this

coupling.

Final Drive

The final drive transfers power from the engine and transmission to the wheels that drive the car. The final drive takes power from the spinning drive shaft and transfers it 90° to make the drive wheels turn. The final drive assembly also provides gear reduction so that the drive wheel spins more slowly than the drive shaft. The gear reduction varies, depending on engine size and power, engine torque, and vehicle size and weight.

The final drive works fine as long as both drive wheels turn at the same speed, however, this system cannot provide different rates of speed for different wheels. A differential system is needed to allow for speed differences. This gear system is the heart of the final drive assembly.

Differential

When a car moves straight ahead, the drive wheels have an equal amount of transaction. When a car goes around a corner, power can no longer be divided evenly between the two side gears.

When it reaches the differential pinion, the outside wheel turns faster than the inside wheel.

Torsen differential is a new pattern differential mechanism, and is used on FWD vehicle widely. Audi 80 and Audi 90 (Audi Quattro) full wheel drive saloon cars adopt this new pattern Torsen differential between front axle and rear axle.

Axle Shaft

The axle shaft (half shaft) connects the differential sun wheel to the road wheel.

Words and Expressions

1. reciprocate [ri'siprəkeit] *v.* 互给，酬答；互换；报答

2. torque [tɔːk] *n.* 转矩，扭转力矩

3. differential [ˌdifə'renʃəl] *adj.* 差动(的)；(有)差别的 *n.* (传动系)差速器

4. linkup ['liŋkʌp] *n.* 连接，联系，会合

5. halt [hɔːlt] *n.* 停止，暂停，中断 *v.* 立定，停止

6. diaphragm ['daiəfræm] *n.* 膜(片)

7. shift [ʃift] *vt.* 替换，转移，变速 *vi.* 转换，移动，转变；推托；变速

8. overdrive ['əuvə'draiv] *v.* 超速传动

9. carrier ['kæriə] *n.* (货运)运载工具；托架底盘；行车装置

10. impeller [im'pelə] *n.* 叶轮，转子

11. turbine ['təːbin,-bain] *n.* 涡轮，涡轮机

12. stator ['steitə] *n.* 定子，固定片

13. universal joint 万向节

14. propeller shaft 传动轴；螺旋轴

15. drive shaft 传动轴；主动轴

16. final drive 主减速器

Notes

1. Final drive: that turns the drive through 90° and reduces the speed of the drive.
主减速器：用来把动力传动路线改变 90°，并且降低转速。

2. An automatic transmission is a device that provides gear reduction, with resulting multiplication of torque.
自动变速器是用来减速增扭的装置。

3. A universal joint is used where two shafts are connected at an angle to transmit torque.
当两个轴以一定的角度连接起来来传递动力的时候就需要用万向节。

4. There must be some allowance for motion between the final drive and transmission.
主减速器和变速器之间必须能够相对运动。

5. Torsen differential is a new pattern differential mechanism, and is used on Four-wheel drive(FWD) vehicle widely.
托森差速器是一种广泛用在四轮驱动车辆上的新型差速器。

Exercises

A. Vocabulary

I. Translate the following expressions into Chinese.

1. drive line

2. propeller shaft

3. halfshaft

4. transaxle

5. side gear

6. universal joint

7. final drive

8. driving wheel

9. driving axle

10. rear wheel drive

II. Identify the English names of the power train according to the picture.

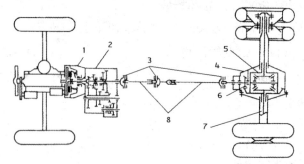

1. _____ 2. _____ 3. _____ 4. _____

5. _____ 6. _____ 7. _____ 8. _____

B. Comprehension

I. Discuss the following questions in groups and write down your answers.

1. What is the power train composed of ?

_____

2. What's the function of the power train?

_____

3. What's the function of the differential?

_____

II. Read the following passage carefully and fill in the blanks with the proper forms of the given words.

> *the clutch*   *the power train*   *a drive shaft*   *final drive*   *torque converter*

1. If you've read about _____, you know that an engine is connected to a transmission by way of a clutch.

2. One important function of _____ is to transmit the power of the engine to the wheels.

3. A conventional vehicle with the engine at the front and driving wheels at the rear uses _____, or called a propeller shaft, to transmit torque from the transmission to the _____.

4. The automatic transmission uses a _____, which acts as a hydraulic coupling to transfer the drive.

C. Translation

I. Translate the following sentences into Chinese.

1. The drive line consists of the parts from the back of the flywheel to the wheels. These parts include the clutch, the transmission, the drive shaft and the final drive assembly.

2. When the car is turning, the inside wheels travel a shorter distance than the outside wheels and also the front wheels travel a different distance than the rear wheels.

3. If your car did not have a differential, the wheels would have to be locked together, forced to spin at the same speed.

II. Translate the following sentences into English.

1. 动力通过传动系从发动机传递到车轮，进而带动汽车前进。
2. 离合器位于发动机和变速器之间。
3. 装有自动变速器的汽车没有离合器，它们用的是液力变矩器。

Reading Material

Read the following passages and answer the questions according to the information given in the passages.

Passage One   Automatic Transmission (AT) and Continuously Variable Transmission (CVT)

With the development of automatic transmission car, people are afraid of China's traditional

clutch industry's prospects increasingly, many enterprises are seeking ways to continue to develop. The three major factors are China's auto production continued to grow, the increase in car ownership and export market demand expansion. This drives China's auto clutch industry's development. In particular, dual clutch transmission(DCT) technology's development in China will bring China's friction clutch to gain new opportunities for development.

The future development of transmission can be said to be uncompromising, but compared to the AT, CVT is an obvious advantage and will become Chinese Transmission mainstream development in the next period of time due to the following reasons: First, CVT has an obvious advantage on the energy consumption. Second, CVT transmission and the engine achieved the best match.

Of course, CVT also has its own drawbacks, such as the torque of transmission is limited, power is low; the cost of research and development(R&D) and the use is high. And at present the cars equipped with CVT is rare in domestic market. The two most common models are the Audi A6, the Honda Fit, ect. Localization of CVT is lagging behind the pace. But it does not mean that CVT has no market. Its unique advantages determine that CVT will eventually replace AT, and become the development direction of transmission.

Questions

1. Why can China's auto production continued to grow?

2. What's the future development of transmission?

3. What are CVT's drawbacks?

Passage Two "Part-time" and "Full-time" Four-Wheel Drive

Part-time four-wheel drive(FWD or 4WD) allows a vehicle to be driven in the two-wheel drive mode for ordinary highway and everyday driving, which reduces drivetrain friction and tire wear for improved fuel economy and tire life, and allows it to be switched to four-wheel drive when extra traction is needed when driving off-road, on gravel, snow, ice or mud.

Vehicles with part-time four-wheel drive may have manual or automatic locking hubs on the front wheels that must be engaged to change from two-wheel to four-wheel drive. With manual locking hubs, you have to get out of the vehicle and twist a knob on both hubs to engage the front wheels. On some vehicles, the hubs engage and lock when the vehicle is driven backwards momentarily. This saves getting in and out of the car but prevents you from shifting to 4WD on the "fly" (on the go). On other applications, the front hubs do not disengage and turn the front driveshafts at all times.

Vehicles with part-time 4WD also have a "transfer case" that splits drive torque between the front and rear axles. On some vehicles, the vehicle must be stopped or going slower than 2 mph before the transfer case can be shifted from 2WD into 4WD. On others, the transfer case can be shifted on the go regardless of speed.

On Jeeps and similar vehicles, you can also select 4WD low range (4L) or 4WD high range (4H). The low range is for creeping along at slow speeds while driving on rough off-road terrain. The high range is for driving at faster speeds on snow covered pavement or gravel or mud roads.

Full-time four wheel drive, on the other hand, is just what the name implies. All four wheels are constantly driven by the engine to provide maximum traction. This type of setup is used on some performance cars to enhance handling traction. Most such vehicles have a "viscous coupling" in the drivetrain or transfer case that allows a certain amount of "give" in the drive torque between the front and rear wheels. This is necessary to compensate for the different speeds at which the front and rear wheels rotate when turning a tight corner.

NOTE: Four wheel drive does not necessary mean that all four wheels will provide constant drive traction. Unless a vehicle has limited slip differentials, it's possible that either wheel on the front and/or rear axle may lose its grip and spin while its companion just sits there. That's the way standard differentials work. Even so, with four-wheel drive, you will always have at least one front and one rear wheel turning at all times—which should be enough to pull you through.

Questions

1. What's the meaning of "part-time" and "full-time" four-wheel drive?

2. What's the difference between "part-time" and "full-time" four-wheel drive?

3. Four wheel drive does not necessary mean that all four wheels will provide constant drive traction. Please make a further explanation.

Unit 2　Clutch

The reason why you need a clutch in a car is that the engine spins all the time, but the cars' wheels don't. In order for a car to stop without stalling the engine, the wheels need to be disconnected from the engine somehow. The clutch allows us to smoothly engage a rotating engine to a non-rotating transmission by controlling the slippage between them, as shown in Figure 3-2.

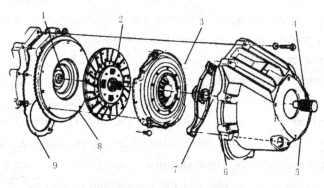

Figure 3-2　Clutch Assembly

1—pilot bearing　2—clutch lining　3—pressure and cover　4—input shaft　5—clutch housing
6—release lever　7—release bearing　8—flywheel　9—cover plate

The clutch is a device that you can connect and disconnect the engine and the transmission. When you depress the clutch pedal, the engine and the transmission are disconnected so the engine can run even if the car is standing still. When you release the clutch pedal, the engine and the input shaft are directly connected to one another. The input shaft and gear turn at the same rotational speed (the unit is rpm) as the engine.

The clutch works on the principles of friction. When two friction surfaces are brought in contact with each other and pressed, they are united due to the friction between them. If now one is revolved, the other will also be revolved. The friction between the two surfaces depends upon the area of the surfaces, pressure applied upon them and coefficient of friction of the surface materials. The two surfaces can be separated and brought into contact when required. One surface is considered as driving member and the other as driven member. The driving member is kept rotating. When the driven member is brought in contact with the driving member, it also starts rotating. When the driven member is separated from the driving member, it does not revolve. This is the principle on which a clutch operates.

The dry clutch mechanism includes three basic parts: driving member, driven member and operating members.

The Driving Member

The driving member consists of two parts: the flywheel and the pressure plate. The flywheel is a major part of the clutch. The flywheel is bolted directly to the engine crankshaft, when coupled with the clutch disc and pressure plate transfer the flow of the engine to the transmission.

The flywheel provides a mounting location for the clutch assembly as well. When the clutch is applied, the flywheel transfer engine torque to the clutch disc, Because of its weight, the flywheel helps to smooth engine operation. The flywheel also has a large ring gear at its outer edge, which engages with a pinion gear on the starter motor during engine cranking.

The pressure plate is bolted to the flywheel. One side of the pressure plate is machined smooth. This side will press the clutch disc facing are against the flywheel. The outer side has various shapes to facilitate attachment of spring and release mechanism. The two primary types of pressure plate assemblies are coil spring assembly and diaphragm spring.

The Driven Member

The driven member, or clutch disc, is located between the flywheel and pressure pate. The clutch disc consists of a circular metal plate attached to a reinforced splined hub. The hub is often mounted on coil springs to provide cushioned engagements. The splined hub is free to slide lengthwise along the splines of the transmission input shaft. When engaged, the clutch disc drives the input shaft through these splines. The clutch disc operates in conjunction with a pressure plate or clutch cover. In its operating position in the engine/transmission linkup, the clutch disc is sandwiched between the engine flywheel and clutch pressure plate.

The Operating Members

The operating members consist of the clutch pedal, clutch return spring, clutch linkage, clutch fork and throwout bearing. The clutch linkage includes the clutch pedal and a mechanical or hydraulic system to move the other operating members.

The clutch fork and linkage provide the means of converting the up-and-down movement of the clutch pedal to the back-and-forth movement of the clutch release bearing assembly. The clutch release bearing, in most cases, is a ball bearing assembly with a machined face on one side that is designed to contact the pressure plate diaphragm release fingers during disengagement.

When the clutch pedal is depressed, the linkage moves the release bearing lever. The release lever is attached at the opposite end to a release bearing which straddles the transmission clutch shaft, and presses inward on the pressure plate fingers or the diaphragm spring. This inward pressure acts upon the fingers and internal linkage of the pressure plate and allows the clutch plate to move away from the flywheel, interrupting the flow of power . The transmission can be shifted into any gear. The clutch pedal is slowly released gradually to move the clutch plate toward the flywheels under pressure of the pressure plate springs. The friction between the clutch plate and the flywheel becomes greater as the pedal is released and the engine speed increased. Once the vehicle is moving, the need for clutch slippage is lessened , and the clutch pedal can be fully released .

Cars equipped with automatic transmissions don't have a clutch. On those cars, the transmission operates automatically so that the driver is not required to use a clutch to shift gears.

Words and Expressions

1. clutch　[klʌtʃ]　 n. [机]离合器；离合器踏板

2. spin　[spin]　 v. 旋转；纺，纺纱　 n. 旋转

3. stall　[stɔːl]　 n. 货摊；畜栏，厩；出售摊　 v. (使)停转，(使)停止，迟延

4. engage　[in'geidʒ]　 vt. 使忙碌；雇用，预定；使从事于，使参加　 vi. 答应；从事；交战　[机]接合，啮合

5. friction　['frikʃən]　 n. 摩擦，摩擦力

6. coefficient　[kəui'fiʃənt]　 n. [数]系数

7. bolt　[bəult]　 n. 门闩；螺栓；闪电；跑掉　 v. 上门闩；囫囵吞下；逃跑

8. pinion　['pinjən]　 n. 小齿轮

9. starter　['staːtə]　 n. 起动器，起动钮

10. motor　['məutən]　 n. 发动机；电动机

11. straddle　['strædl]　 v. 跨骑

12. finger　['fiŋgə]　 n. 手指；指状物；钩爪；机械手；指针；箭头；塞尺

13. dry clutch　干摩擦离合器

14. splined hub　花键毂；花键套节

15. coil spring　螺旋弹簧

16. clutch pedal　离合器踏板

17. clutch linkage　离合器操纵杠杆机构

18. clutch fork　离合器分离叉

19. throwout bearing　分离轴承

20. release lever　分离杠杆

21. ring gear　齿圈

Notes

1. In order for a car to stop without stalling the engine, the wheels need to be disconnected from the engine somehow.

为了使汽车停止而使发动机继续转动，要断开车轮和发动机之间的连接。

2. The clutch works on the principles of friction. When two friction surfaces are brought in contact with each other and pressed, they are united due to the friction between them.

离合器是利用摩擦原理来工作的，当将两个摩擦表面压到一块的时候，它们因为二者之间的摩擦力而结合为一体。

3. The friction between the two surfaces depends upon the area of the surfaces, pressure applied upon them and coefficient of friction of the surface materials.

两个摩擦面之间的摩擦力取决于它们之间的接触面积、作用在接触面上的压力以及表面材料的摩擦系数。

4. In its operating position in the engine/transmission linkup, the clutch disc is sandwiched between the engine flywheel and clutch pressure plate.

在发动机和变速器相互衔接的闭合位置，离合器盘被夹在发动机飞轮和离合器压盘之间。

5. This inward pressure acts upon the fingers and internal linkage of the pressure plate and allows the clutch plate to move away from the flywheel, interrupting the flow of power .

向内部的压力作用在弹簧指和压盘的内部传动机构上，使离合器盘离开飞轮，从而中断了动力传动。

Exercises

A. Vocabulary

I. Translate the following expressions into Chinese.

1. clutch pedal

2. release fork

3. release bearing

4. pressure plate

5. flywheel

6. return spring

7. clutch disc

8. release lever

9. driving member

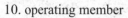
10. operating member

II. Identify the English names of the clutch according to the picture.

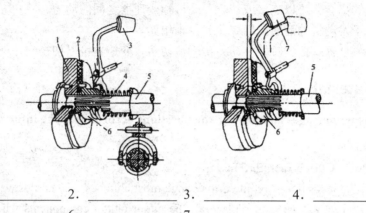

1. _____ 2. _____ 3. _____ 4. _____
5. _____ 6. _____ 7. _____

B. Comprehension

I. Discuss the following questions in groups and write down your answers.

1. What is the clutch composed of?

_____

2. What's the function of the clutch?

_____

3. How is a clutch engaged and disengaged?

_____

II. Read the following passage carefully and fill in the blanks with the proper forms of the given words.

engage   start   pressure plate   driven member   flywheel   input shaft

The clutch is a device to ____ and disengage power from the engine, allowing the vehicle to be stopped and ____.

A ____ or driving member is bolted to the engine flywheel and a clutch plate or ____ is located between the flywheel and the pressure plate. The clutch plate is splined to the shaft extending from the transmission to the ____, commonly called a clutch shaft or ____.

C. Translation

I. Translate the following sentences into Chinese.

1. However, if a rapidly rotating engine is suddenly connected to the drive line of a stationary vehicle, a violent shock will result.

2. Although there are many types of clutch, the dry single plate type of friction clutch is used almost exclusively in passenger cars.

3. The release levers are mounted on splines attached to housing.

4. Housing is attached to engine flywheel.

5. The pressure on driven disk fitted onto the splined portion of shaft is provided by spring

installed between the housing and pressure driving disks.

II. Translate the following sentences into English.

1. 汽车中的离合器可以连接或切断发动机和变速器之间的动力。

2. 飞轮位于发动机的后面，用螺栓和曲轴相连。

3. 当踩下离合器踏板的时候，动力传动被切断，变速器可以切换到任何挡位。

Reading Material

Read the following passages and answer the questions according to the information given in the passages.

Passage One   Clutch Installation Tips

Because of the labor that is required to change most clutches, you do not want to have to do the job over. The best advice is to replace all the major clutch components when servicing the clutch, not just the part or parts that are obviously worn out or broken.

Most experts recommend installing a new clutch disc, pressure plate assembly, release bearing, and pilot bearing/bushing (if one is used), and resurfacing the flywheel.

The clutch is a system, so it is important to use parts that are properly matched and meet original equipment manufacturer (OEM) specifications for quality and performance. Installing a complete clutch kit from a quality supplier is your best insurance against installation problems or problems down the road.

Another item that should also be replaced is the release cable on older vehicles with this type of linkage. If a vehicle has a hydraulic linkage with a lot of miles on it, it would be wise to replace the master and slave cylinders, too, even if they are not leaking. Why? The slave cylinder is the lowest point in the hydraulic linkage, so most of the rust and sediment that has been accumulating over the years ends up in the slave cylinder. Common sense tells you this will eventually cause problems, so replacing the slave cylinder now will give your customer many more miles of trouble-free driving. At the very least, you should flush the hydraulics and refill the system with fresh fluid.

If the old clutch has seen a lot of abuse, or the vehicle has been modified for more power, a performance clutch set designed to deliver higher torque capacity should be installed to beef up the drivetrain. But avoid performance clutches that are overly aggressive and sacrifice derivability to achieve more bite.

The flywheel should always be resurfaced or replaced. Oil, dirt, grease, warpage, cracks or grooves on a flywheel will cause clutch problems. So too will excessive runout. Remember to mark the index position of the flywheel before you remove it so that it can be reinstalled in the same position as before. If a flywheel is cracked or damaged or cannot be resurfaced, replacement is required.

With stepped flywheels, equal amounts of metal must be machined off both steps to maintain the same relative height difference between the two. If only the wear surface is machined, it will reduce the pressure exerted by the pressure plate against the clutch disc.

With dual-mass flywheels, resurfacing is not recommended on BMW or Porsche models. If the flywheel is worn, it must be replaced.

Use a pilot tool to align the clutch disc to the flywheel when the clutch is bolted in place. Eyeballing it is not good enough because the transmission input shaft may not slide into place when you try to maneuver it into position. Tighten the pressure plate bolts gradually in a star pattern to avoid distorting the clutch. Never use an air ratchet.

On vehicles with hydraulic linkages, you may need a bleeder tool to get the air out of the lines if you have replaced the master or slave cylinder, or flushed and replaced the fluid in the system.

Lightly lubricate the splines on the transaxle input shaft and the release fork pivot, and make sure the new release bearing is properly installed in the release fork.

When reinstalling the transmission, support the weight of the tranny until it is bolted in place. If you let it hang while the input shaft is engaged with the clutch, it may bend or distort the hub in the clutch disc and prevent it from releasing.

Proper adjustment of the clutch linkage also is a must after replacing a clutch. Follow the procedure in the manual and make sure you have the right play.

Finally, do a short test drive to make sure the clutch is operating properly, meaning normal pedal travel and feel, no noise, and smooth engagement and shifts.

Questions

1. Why is it necessary to replace all the major clutch components when servicing the clutch?

2. What does OEM mean?

3. Please describe the clutch installation tips.

Passage Two Clutch Slip

I have a manual transmission. Lately the clutch has started to slip. Does this mean I need a new clutch? It depends. If your clutch has low miles on it (40,000 or less), the slippage is due to one of the two things: oil contamination or misadjusted clutch linkage. If your clutch has a lot of miles on it (60,000 or more), it's worn out and you need to replace it.

To rule out oil contamination as a possible cause of slippage, check under the rear of the engine and the bellhousing for oil leaks. If you see oil on the oil pan, the rear main oil seal is probably leaking. Other leak points include manifold and valve cover gaskets at the back of the engine, and the transmission input shaft seal.

If you've got an oil leak, don't replace the clutch until you've fixed the leak. Once the clutch linings have been contaminated by oil, there's no way to clean them. Replacing the clutch disk is the only way to restore proper clutch operation.

If you don't have a leak, check the linkage adjustment. Most cars with a cable linkage have an automatic adjusting mechanism that's supposed to maintain proper clearances. If anything is wrong, the cable would be too loose rather than too tight. But if someone has been playing around with the linkage adjustment, they may have gotten it too tight. The same goes for vehicles with hydraulic linkages. There's no way that this type of linkage can cause slippage unless it is

misadjusted by someone.

That leaves the clutch itself. Slippage can be caused by two things: worn facings or loss of spring tension in the pressure plate. Unless the clutch really has been abused or has a lot of miles on it, it's unlikely the pressure plate is weak. Normal wear reduces the thickness of the facings on the clutch disk, which in turn reduces the clamping force the pressure plate can apply to squeeze the disk against the flywheel. Replacing the clutch disk should cure the problem.

Even so, the clutch and flywheel should be carefully inspected when the parts are removed. If the pressure plate is worn or damaged, you'll need to replace that, too. Most experts recommend having the flywheel refaced to restore the friction surface. You can probably get by without refacing the flywheel—but only if the flywheel is flat, smooth, clean and uncracked. Any grooves, heat discoloration, cracking or other damage would call for resurfacing or replacing the flywheel.

Questions

1. I have a manual transmission. Lately the clutch has started to slip. Does that mean I need a new clutch?

2. How should we check the clutch slip?

3. The clutch and flywheel should be carefully inspected when the parts are removed. Why?

Unit 3　Manual Transmission

A transmission is a speed and power converting device installed between the engine and the driving wheels of the vehicle.

The transmission is designed for changing the torque transmitted from the engine crankshaft to the propeller shaft, reversing the vehicle movement and disengaging the engine from the drive line for a long time at parking or coasting. A higher torque should be applied to the wheels to set an automobile in motion or move uphill with full load rather than keep it rolling after it gets under way on levels stretches of the road, when inertial is high and tractive resistance is low. To meet these variable torque requirement, special gear box are used. Such gear boxes are called fixed-ratio transmissions. The transmission with two sliding gears or synchronizer sleeves is called two-range; with three gears, three-range. Depending on the number of forward speeds, there are three, four and five-speed trans, as shown in Figure 3-3.

There are four shafts in the transmission: input shaft(primary shafts), countershaft(layshaft), mainshaft and reverse shaft.

Input Shaft (Primary Shafts)

The input, or clutch, shaft is turned through its connection to the center of the turning clutch disc. At the transmission end of the input shaft is a gear. As the input shaft turns, two constant gears transfer engine torque to the countershaft drive gear.

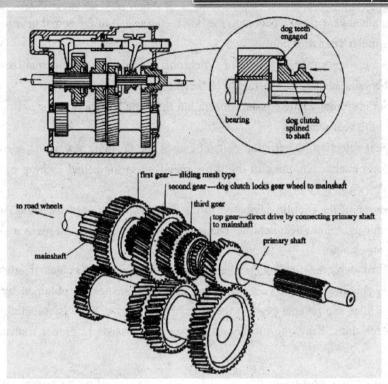

Figure 3-3　Constant-mesh Transmission

Countershaft (Layshaft)

The countershaft consists of a solid metal shaft with several gears . The countershaft gears, or "cluster gears", are part of the solid countershaft. Thus, when the countershaft turns, all these gears turn.

Mainshaft

The mainshaft also consists of a solid metal shaft with several gears, and these gears remain in constant mesh with the gears on the countershaft.

Each set of meshed gears transmits a different amount of torque and speed to the mainshaft. Thus, you can choose more speed and less torque (higher gear) or less speed and more torque (lower gear) to suit driving condition.

Reverse Shaft

There is one reverse gear on the reverse shaft, the reverse gear on the reverse gear remain in constant mesh with the reverse gear on the countershaft.

There are two types of manual transmission: constant-mesh and synchro-mesh transmission.

Constant-mesh Transmission

Figure 3-3 illustrates the flow of torque through a typical constant-mesh transmission . This type uses helical or double helical gears which are always in mesh. The mainshaft gear wheel are mounted on bearings and when a gear is required, the mainshaft gear is locked to the shaft by a dog clutch.

Although the mechanical efficiency is lower, the helical gears are quieter and any damage

resulting from a bad gear change occurs to the dog teeth instead of the actual gear teeth.

Synchro-mesh Transmission

As the name suggests, this type has a synchronization device which equalizes the speeds of the two members that have to be meshed to obtain the gear.

The layout is similar to the constant-mesh, but this type has friction cones fitted between the dog clutch and the gear wheel.

During gear selection, the friction contact causes the layshaft to vary its speed so that both parts of the dog clutch are moving at the same speed when the actual locking of the gear takes place.

The operation of the friction device performs a duty which, in older designs, was carried out by the driver during double-declutching. The synchro-mesh transmission gives a simpler, quieter and quicker gear change.

On some models, the first-second gear synchronizer sleeve has gear teeth on its outside circumference, enabling it to serve as reverse gear. Reverse gear is obtained by engaging the sliding reverse idler and reverse gear on the counter gear. Power flow is essentially the same for different transmissions. Knowing mechanical power flow assists in proper transmission trouble diagnosis.

Words and Expressions

1. convert [kən'və:t] *vt.* 使转变；转换；使……改变信仰

2. install [in'stɔ:l] *vt.* 安装；安置；使就职

3. coast [kəust] *vi.* 惯性滑行，滑[溜]下

4. synchronizer ['siŋkrənaizə] *n.* 同步装置

5. sleeve [sli:v] *n.* 衬[轴，护]套，套筒，空心轴；管接头，外[套]盒；(发动机)缸套

6. layshaft ['leiʃa:ft] *n.* 中间轴

7. countershaft ['kauntəʃa:ft] *n.* 中间轴

8. mesh [meʃ] *n.* 网孔，网丝，网眼；圈套，陷阱，[机]啮合 *vt.* 以网捕捉；啮合；编织 *vi.* 落网，相啮合

9. helical ['helikəl] *adj.* 螺旋状的

10. diagnosis [daiəg'nəusis] *n.* 诊断

11. double helical 人字齿轮；双斜齿轮

12. dog clutch 牙嵌[爪式]离合器

Notes

1. The input, or clutch, shaft is turned through its connection to the center of the turning clutch disc.

输入轴和离合器盘的中心相连，由离合器盘带动旋转。

2. The counter shaft gears, or "cluster gears", are part of the solid countershaft.

中间轴齿轮或者说是齿轮组是中间轴的一部分。

3. This type uses helical or double helical gears which are always in mesh.

这种齿变速器使用的总是处于啮合状态斜齿轮或人字形齿轮。

4. Although the mechanical efficiency is lower, the helical gears are quieter and any damage resulting from a bad gear change occurs to the dog teeth instead of the actual gear teeth.

虽然斜齿轮的机械效率有点低，但是噪音小，而且由于换挡不当引起的损坏作用在结合齿圈上而不是作用在实际的齿轮上。

5. As the name suggests, this type has a synchronization device which equalizes the speeds of the two members that have to be meshed to obtain the gear.

顾名思义，这种变速器里有一个同步装置来平衡换挡时两个相啮合部分的速度。

Exercises

A. Vocabulary

I. Translate the following expressions into Chinese.

1. reverse gear

2. second gear

3. transmission case

4. dog clutch

5. output shaft

6. clutch sleeve/synchronized sleeve

7. gear lever

8. constant-mesh transmission

9. countershaft

10. selector mechanism

II. Identify the English names of the manual transmission according to the picture.

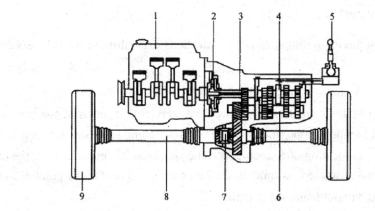

1. _____　2. _____　3. _____　4. _____

5. _____　6. _____　7. _____　8. _____

9. _____

B. Comprehension

I. Discuss the following questions in groups and write down your answers.

1. What kinds of manual transmission are used in automobile?

_____

2. There are four shafts mounted in a manual transmission. What are they called?

_____

3. Why is a transmission needed in an automobile ?

_____

II. Read the following passage carefully and fill in the blanks with the proper forms of the given words.

climbing   acceleration   traction   consumption   convert

The main goal when developing a vehicle transmission is to _____ the power from the engine into vehicle _____ as efficiently as possible, over a wide rang of road speeds. This has to be done ensuring a good compromise between the number of speeds, _____ performance, _____ and fuel _____ of the vehicle.

C. Translation

I. Translate the following sentences into Chinese.

1. Depending on the number of forward speeds there are three, four and five-speed transmissions.

2. The gearbox of this car always jumps out of gear.

3. A gearbox changes the speed and torque of the output shaft by meshing different gears.

II. Translate the following sentences into English.

1. 发动机的转矩通过离合器的从动盘向变速器第一轴传递。

2. 现在汽车的变速器里装的是斜齿轮和同步装置。

3. 卡车或公共汽车的变速器一般有四个或五个前进挡和一个倒挡。

Reading Material

Read the following passages and answer the questions according to the information given in the passages.

Passage One   Transmission Service

As a first step in any transmission or overdrive service, diagnosis of the trouble should be made in an attempt to pinpoint the trouble in the malfunctioning unit. Sometimes it is not possible to determine the exact location of a trouble, and the unit must be removed from the car so that it can be torn down and examined. At other times，diagnosis will lead to the point of trouble so that it can be eliminated without major disassembly.

Because of the variations in construction of transmissions of different automobiles, different procedures must be followed in the removal, disassembly, repair, assembly, and installation of their transmissions. These operations require about 5 to 7 hours. The difference in time is due to variations in the procedures. Basically, the procedures are similar. However, refer to the manufacturer's shop manual before attempting such work.

The overhaul procedures differ for each model of transmission. Thus, before disassembling, servicing, and reassembling a transmission, always refer to the shop manual that covers the specific model being repaired. Follow the instructions step by step.

Questions

1. What is the first step in any service?

2. Are the removal procedures the same for different automobiles?

3. What should you refer to before disassembling, servicing and reassembling a transmission?

Passage Two　Manual Transmission Fluid Change

I have a manual transmission. Does the fluid in it ever need to be changed?

Not usually. Some older import vehicles (like Volkswagen Beetles) recommended periodic lube changes for their gearboxes, but no modern car or light truck requires it. The reason why is that the oil stays relatively clean and runs fairly cool. Unlike the fluid in an automatic transmission that is being constantly churned (which generates heat) and contaminated by particles worn off the clutch plates, the fluid in a manual transmission or transaxle has life pretty easy. So it usually lasts the life of the transmission.

The only reason you might have for changing that would be that you were experiencing hard shifting problems during cold weather. Most older rear-wheel drive transmissions use a heavy gear oil like 75W, 80W or 90W, which can get pretty stiff at subzero temperatures. Changing to a lighter oil may improve shifting.

Most manual transaxles in front-wheel drive cars today use Dexron II automatic transmission fluid (ATF) to keep the gears lubed. ATF works well because it stays much more fluid at low temperatures. But ATF should not be substituted for gear oil. Always use the type of lubricant specified by the vehicle manufacturer.

Adding Oil

The only time you should have to add oil to a manual transmission or transaxle is when the tranny is leaking oil. If you see any grease or wetness around the tailshaft or driveshaft seals, the oil level in the transmission or transaxle should be checked because it may be low.

WARNING: Allowing the transmission or transaxle to run too low on lubricant can ruin it.

Questions

1. The oil usually lasts the life of the transmission. What does this mean?

2. I have a manual transmission. Does the fluid in it ever need to be changed?

3. How should one add transmission or transaxle oil?

Unit 4　Automatic Transmission

The transmission is a sort of speed and power changing device needed between the engine of the automobile and its driving wheels. It provides means of varying the gear ratio between the engine and rear wheels. An automatic transmission contains mechanical system, hydraulic system, electrical systems and computer controls, all working together in perfect harmony.

The transmission is connected to the back of the engine and sends the power from the engine to the drive wheels. An automobile engine runs at its best at a certain RPM (Revolutions Per Minute) range and it is the transmission's job to make sure that the power is delivered to the wheels while keeping the engine within that range. It does this through various gear combinations.

There are two basic types of automatic transmissions based on whether the vehicle is rear wheel drive or front wheel drive. On a rear wheel drive car, the transmission is usually mounted to the back of the engine and is located under the hump in the center of the floor board alongside the gas pedal position. A drive shaft connects the rear of the transmission to the final drive, which is located in the rear axle and is used to send power to the rear wheels. On a front wheel drive car, the transmission is usually combined with the final drive to form what is called a transaxle. The engine on a front wheel car is usually mounted sideways in the car with the transaxle tucked under it on the side of the engine facing the rear of the car. Front axles are connected directly to the transaxle and provide power to the front wheels.

Transmission Components

The main components that make up an automatic transmission include the following:

Planetary Gear Sets which are the mechanical systems that provide the various forward gear ratios as well as reverse.

The Hydraulic System which uses a special transmission fluid sent under pressure by an Oil Pump through the Valve Body to control the Clutches and the Bands in order to control the planetary gear sets.

Seals and Gaskets are used to keep the oil where it is supposed to be and prevent it from leaking out.

The Torque Converter which acts like a clutch to allow the vehicle to come to a stop in gear while the engine is still running.

The Governor and the Modulator or Throttle Cable that monitor speed and throttle position in order to determine when to shift.

On newer vehicles, shift points are controlled by **Computer** which directs electrical solenoids to shift oil flow to the appropriate component at the right instant.

Planetary Gear Sets

Automatic transmissions contain many gears in various combinations, as shown in Figure 3-4.

In a manual transmission, gears slide along shafts as you move the shift lever from one position to another, engaging various sized gears as required in order to provide the correct gear ratio. In an automatic transmission, however, the gears are never physically moved and are always engaged to the same gears. This is accomplished through the use of planetary gear sets.

Figure 3-4   Planetary Gear Sets

The basic planetary gear set consists of a sun gear. a ring gear and two or more planet gears, all remaining in constant mesh. The planet gears are connected to each other through a common carrier.

The input shaft is connected to the ring gear. The output shaft is connected to the planet carrier which is also connected to a "Multi-disk" clutch pack. The sun gear is connected to a drum which is also connected to the other half of the clutch pack. Surrounding the outside of the drum is a band that can be tightened around the drum when required to prevent the drum with the attached sun gear from turning.

The clutch pack is used, in this instance, to lock the planet carrier with the sun gear forcing both to turn at the same speed. If both the clutch pack and the band were released, the system would be in neutral. Turning the input shaft would turn the planet gears against the sun gear, but since nothing is holding the sun gear, it will just spin free and have to effect on the output shaft. To place the unit in first gear, the band is applied to hold the sun gear from moving. To shift from first to high gear, the band is released and the clutch is applied causing the output shaft to turn at the same speed as the input shaft. Many more combinations are possible using two or more planetary sets connected in various ways to provide the different forward speeds and reverse that are found in modern automatic transmissions.

Clutch Pack

A clutch pack consists of alternating disks that fit inside a clutch drum. Half of the disks are steel and have splines that fit into groves on the inside of the drum. The other half have a friction material bonded to their surface and have splines on the inside edge that fit groves on the outer surface of the adjoining hub. There is a piston inside the drum that is activated by oil pressure at the appropriate time to squeeze the clutch pack together, so that the two components become locked and turn as one.

One-Way Clutch

A one-way clutch is a device that will allow a component such as ring gear to turn freely in one direction but not in the other. A common place where a one-way clutch is used is in first gear

when the shifter is in the drive position.

Band

A band is a steel strap with friction material bonded to the inside surface, as shown in Figure 3-5. One end of the band is anchored against the transmission case while the other end is connected to a servo. At the appropriate time hydraulic oil is sent to the servo under pressure to tighten the band around the drum to stop it from turning.

Figure 3-5　Bands

Torque Converter

On automatic transmission, the torque converter takes the place of the clutch found on standard shift vehicles. It is there to allow the engine to continue running when the vehicle comes to a stop. A torque converter is a large doughnut shaped device that is mounted between the engine and the transmission. It consists of three internal elements that work together to transmit power to the transmission. The three elements of the torque converter are the pump, the turbine, and the stator. The pump is mounted directly to the converter housing which in turn is bolted directly to the engine's crankshaft and turns at engine speed. The turbine is inside the housing and is connected directly to the input shaft of the transmission providing power to move the vehicle. The stator is mounted to a one-way clutch so that it can spin freely in one direction but not in the other. Each of the three elements has fins mounted in them to precisely direct the flow of oil through the converter.

Hydraulic System

The hydraulic system is a complex maze of passages and tubes that sends transmission fluid under pressure to all parts of the transmission and torque converter. Transmission fluid serves a number of purposes including: shift control, general lubrication and transmission cooling. Unlike the engine, which uses oil primarily for lubrication, every aspect of a transmission's functions are dependant on a constant supply of fluid under pressure. This is like the human circulatory system (the fluid is even red) where even a few minutes of operation when there is a lack of pressure can be harmful or even fatal to the life of the transmission. In order to keep the transmission at normal operating temperature, a portion of the fluid is sent through one of two steel tubes to a special chamber that is submerged in anti-freeze in the radiator. Fluid passing through this chamber is cooled and then returned to the transmission through the other steel tube. In fact, most of the components of a transmission are constantly submerged in fluid including the clutch packs and bands. The friction surfaces on these parts are designed to operate properly only when they are submerged in oil.

Oil Pump

The transmission oil pump is responsible for producing all the oil pressure that is required in the transmission. The oil pump is mounted to the front of the transmission case and is directly connected to a flange on the torque converter housing.

Valve Body

The valve body is the brain of the automatic transmission. It contains a maze of channels and passages that direct hydraulic fluid to the numerous valves which then activate the appropriate clutch pack or band servo to smoothly shift to the appropriate gear for each driving situation.

Computer Control

The computer uses sensors on the engine and transmission to detect such things as throttle position, vehicle speed, engine load, stop light switch position, etc. to control exact shift points as well as how soft or firm the shift should be. Some computerized transmission even learn your driving style and constantly adapt to it so that every shift is timed precisely when you need it.

Governor, Vacuum Modulator and Throttle Cable

These three components are important in the non-computerized transmissions. They provide the inputs that tell the transmission when to shift. The Governor is connected to the output shaft and regulates hydraulic pressure based on vehicle speed.

There are two types of devices that serve the purpose of monitoring the engine load: the Throttle Cable and the Vacuum Modulator. A transmission will use one or the other but generally not both of these devices. Each works in a different way to monitor engine load. The Throttle Cable simply monitors the position of the gas pedal through a cable that runs from the gas pedal to the throttle valve in the valve body. The Vacuum Modulator monitors engine vacuum by a rubber vacuum hose which is connected to the engine.

Seals and Gasket

An automatic transmission has many seals and gaskets to control the flow of hydraulic fluid and to keep it from leaking out. There are two main external seals: the front seal and the rear seal. The front seal seals the point where the torque converter mounts to the transmission case. This seal allows fluid to freely move from the converter to the transmission but keeps the fluid from leaking out. The rear seal keeps fluid from leaking past the output shaft. A seal is usually made of rubber and is used to keep oil from leaking past a moving part such as a spinning shaft. A gasket is a type of seal used to seal two stationary parts that are fastened together. Common gasket materials include: paper, cork, rubber, silicone and soft metal.

Words and Expressions

1. neutral ['nju:trəl] *n.* [机]空挡

2. reverse [ri'və:s] *n.* 倒挡；倒退，倒转；反向

3. mount [maunt] *vt.* 设置，安放，固定在……上

4. hump [hʌmp] *n.* 小圆丘，小丘；*vt.* (使)隆起，弓起

5. axle ['æksl] *n*. 轮轴，车轴

6. transaxle [træns'æksl] *n*. 变速驱动桥

7. tuck [tʌk] *n*. (衣服等的)褶裥；打褶

8. clutch [klʌtʃ] *n*. [机]离合器；离合器踏板

9. band [bænd] *n*. [机]传送带，传动带

10. modulator ['mɔdjuleitə] *n*. 调节器

11. slide [slaid] *vi*. 滑动，滑落 *vt*. 使滑动，使滑行

12. engage [in'geidʒ] *vi*. 结合，啮合

13. mesh [meʃ] *vt*. [机]使啮合

14. alternating [ɔ:l'tə:nitiŋ] *adj*. 交互的，交替的

15. spline [splain] *vt*. 用花键连接 *n*. [机]花键，键槽，齿条

16. grove [grəuv] *n*. 树丛，小树林

17. hub [hʌb] *n*. (轮)毂；(兴趣、活动的)中心

18. strap [stræp] *n*. 带子；皮带；布带；金属带

19. anchor ['æŋkə] *vt*. 使固定，锚定

20. doughnut ['dəunʌt] *n*. 油炸圈饼；圆环图

21. fin [fin] *n*. 鳍；鳍状物

22. maze [meiz] *n*. 曲径；迷宫，迷津

23. flange [flændʒ] *n*. [机]凸缘，法兰

24. solenoid ['səulinɔid] *n*. [电]螺线管；电磁线圈

25. governor ['gʌvənə] *n*. [机]调节器，调速器；节速器

26. fasten ['fæsn] *vt*. 拴紧，使固定

27. cork [kɔ:k] *n*. 软木塞，软木制品

28. silicone ['silikəun] *n*. 硅树脂

29. drive wheel   驱动轮

30. gear combination   齿轮啮合

31. rear wheel drive   后轮驱动

32. torque converter   液力变矩器

33. planetary gear set   行星齿轮系统

34. valve body   阀体

35. planet carrier   行星齿轮架

36. clutch pack   离合器压盘

37. one-way clutch   单向离合器

38. stick shift   换挡杆换挡

39. multi-disk clutch   多片式离合器

Notes

1. The transmission is a sort of speed and power changing device needed between the engine of the automobile and its driving wheels.

变速器是一种汽车发动机和汽车驱动轮之间需要的速度、扭矩变换装置。

2. The torque converter which acts like a clutch to allow the vehicle to come to a stop in gear while the engine is still running.

同离合器一样，当液力变矩器挂入挡后，可以允许汽车在发动机仍运转时停车。

3. This is like the human circulatory system (the fluid is even red) where even a few minutes of operation when there is a lack of pressure can be harmful or even fatal to the life of the transmission.

就像人体循环系统一样(甚至液体也是红色的)，自动变速器在工作时，若传动液缺乏压力，即使只是几分钟，也会对变速器的寿命产生危害，甚至将变速器毁坏。

4. The clutch pack is used, in this instance, to lock the planet carrier with the sun gear forcing both to turn at the same speed.

在这种情况下，离合器压盘被用来将行星轮支架与太阳轮锁在一起，使得两者以同样的速度转动。

5. There is a piston inside the drum that is activated by oil pressure at the appropriate time to squeeze the clutch pack together, so that the two components become locked and turn as one.

在合适的时刻，离合器鼓中的活塞被油压推动，活塞挤压离合器压盘，使得两个元件锁在一起并作整体转动。

6. It contains a maze of channels and passages that direct hydraulic fluid to the numerous valves which then activate the appropriate clutch pack or band servo to smoothly shift to the appropriate gear for each driving situation.

它有错综复杂的通道，通道引导着传动液流向无数的阀门，这些阀门又驱动着对应的离合器压盘或伺服带子平稳地转换到适合每种行驶工况的挡位。

7. The computer uses sensors on the engine and transmission to detect such things as throttle position, vehicle speed, engine speed, engine load, stop light switch position, etc.

计算机运用发动机和变速器上的传感器来探测诸如节气门位置、车速、发动机转速、发动机负荷、停车灯开关位置等情况。

8. An automatic transmission has many seals and gaskets to control the flow of hydraulic fluid and to keep it from leaking out.

自动变速器上有很多密封件和密封垫圈，用来控制传动液体的流动，防止其泄漏。

Exercises

A. Vocabulary

I. Translate the following expressions into Chinese.

1. transaxle

2. modulator

3. hydraulic system

4. gear combination

5. torque converter

6. final drive

7. solenoid

8. planetary gear set

9. one-way clutch

10. final drive

II. Identify the English names of the automatic transmission according to the picture.

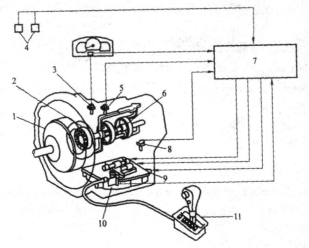

1. _____ 2. _____ 3. _____ 4. _____

5. _____ 6. _____ 7. _____ 8. _____

9. _____ 10. _____ 11. _____ .

B. Comprehension

I. Discuss the following questions in groups and write down your answers.

1. What are the components that make up the automatic transmission?

_____

2. What's the function of the one-way clutch?

_____

3. Why is the torque converter used?

_____

II. Read the following passage carefully and fill in the blanks with the proper forms of the given words.

| whether | on | or | to | alongside | connect |
| which | rear | on | usually | with | |

There are two basic types of automatic transmissions based _____ whether the vehicle is rear wheel drive _____ front wheel drive. On a rear wheel drive car, the transmission is usually mounted _____ the back of the engine and is located under the hump in the center of the floor board _____ the gas pedal position. A drive shaft _____ the rear of the transmission to the final drive, _____ is located in the rear axle and is used to send power to the _____ wheels. _____ a front wheel drive car, the transmission is _____ combined _____ the final drive to form what is called a transaxle.

C. Translation

I. Translate the following sentences into Chinese.

1. An automobile engine runs at its best at a certain RPM (Revolutions Per Minute) range and it is the transmission's job to make sure that the power is delivered to the wheels while keeping the engine within that range.

2. The clutch pack is used, in this instance, to lock the planet carrier with the sun gear forcing both to turn at the same speed.

3. On automatic transmission, the torque converter takes the place of the clutch found on standard shift vehicles.

II. Translate the following sentences into English.

1. 变速器是一种汽车发动机和汽车驱动轮之间需要的速度、扭矩变换装置。

2. 在这种情况下，离合器压盘被用来将行星轮支架与太阳轮锁在一起，使得两者以同样的速度转动。

3. 计算机运用发动机和变速器上的传感器来探测诸如节气门位置、车速、发动机转速、发动机负荷、停车灯开关位置等情况。

Reading Material

Read the following passages and answer the questions according to the information given in the passages.

Passage One   Automatic Transmission Service

How to serve an automatic transmission? The following points should be paid more attention to.

1. Watch for leaks or stains under the car.

If there is a persistent red oil leak that you are sure is coming from your car, you should have your shop check to see if it is coming from your transmission or possibly from your power steering system (some power steering systems also use transmission fluid and leaks can appear on the ground in roughly the same areas as transmission leaks). If all you see is a few drops on the ground, you may be able to postpone repairs as long as you check your fluid level often (but check with your technician to conform). If transmission fluid levels go down below minimum levels serious transmission damage can occur (the same advice goes for power steering leaks as well).

2. Check fluid for color and odor.

Most manufacturers require that you check transmission fluid levels when the vehicle is

running and on level ground. Pull the transmission dipstick out and check the fluid for color and odor. Transmission fluid is a transparent red oil that looks something like cherry cough syrup. If the fluid is cloudy or muddy, or it has a burned odor, you should have it checked by your technician who will most likely advise you to have a transmission drain and refill or a transmission flush. Ask the Wright Import for more details on this service.

3. Be sensitive to new noises, vibrations, and shift behavior.

A modern transmission should shift smoothly and quietly under light acceleration. Heavier acceleration should produce firmer shifts at higher speeds. If shift points are erratic or you hear noises when shifting, you should have it checked out immediately. Whining noises coming from the floorboard are also a cause for concern. If caught early, many problems can be resolved without costly transmission overhauls. Even if you feel that you can't afford repairs at this time, you should at least have it checked. The technician may be able to give you some hints on what to do and not do to prolong the transmission life until you can afford the repair. Ask the Wright Import any questions you have about your transmission.

Questions

1. What should you do if there is a persistent red oil leak under your car?

2. How should you check the fluid of the automatic transmission?

3. Under what situation should you have your automatic transmission checked out immediately?

Passage Two Automatic Transmission Fluid (ATF)

Most owner's manuals say it isn't necessary. Yeah, right. That's why transmission shops are making a fortune replacing burned out automatic transmissions.

For optimum protection, change the fluid and filter every 30,000 miles unless you have a new vehicle that is filled with Dexron III ATF which is supposed to be good for 100,000 miles.

Why ATF Wears out

An automatic transmission creates a lot of internal heat through friction: the friction of the fluid churning inside the torque converter, friction created when the clutch plates engage, and the normal friction created by gears and bearings carrying their loads.

It doesn't take long for the ATF to heat up once the vehicle is in motion. Normal driving will raise fluid temperatures to 175 degrees Fahrenheit(F.), which is the usual temperature range at which most fluids are designed to operate. If fluid temperatures can be held to 175 degrees F., ATF will last almost indefinitely—say up to 100,000 miles. But if the fluid temperature goes much higher, the life of the fluid begins to plummet. The problem is even normal driving can push fluid temperatures well beyond safe limits. And once that happens, the trouble begins.

At elevated operating temperatures, ATF oxidizes, turns brown and takes on a smell like burnt toast. As heat destroys the fluid's lubricating qualities and friction characteristics, varnish begins to form on internal parts, such as the valve body which interferes with the operation of the transmission. If the temperature gets above 250 degrees F., rubber seals begin to harden, which leads to leaks and pressure losses. At higher temperatures the transmission begins to slip, which only aggravates overheating even more. Eventually the clutches burn out and the transmission calls it quits. The only way to repair the damage now is with an overhaul—a job which can easily run upwards of $1,500 on a late model front-wheel drive car or minivan.

As a rule of thumb, every 20 degree increase in operating temperature above 175 degrees F. cuts the life of the fluid in half!

At 195 degrees F., for instance, fluid life is reduced to 50,000 miles. At 220 degrees F., which is commonly encountered in many transmissions, the fluid is only good for about 25,000 miles. At 240 degrees F., the fluid won't go much over 10,000 miles. Add another 20 degrees, and life expectancy drops to 5,000 miles. Go to 295 or 300 degrees F., and 1,000 to 1,500 miles is about all you'll get before the transmission burns up.

If you think this is propaganda put forth by the suppliers of ATF to sell more fluid, think again. According to the Automatic Transmission Rebuilders Association, 90% of all transmission failures are caused by overheating. And most of these can be blamed on worn out fluid that should have been replaced.

On most vehicles, the automatic transmission fluid is cooled by a small heat exchanger inside the bottom or end tank of the radiator. Hot ATF from the transmission circulates through a short loop of pipe and is thus "cooled". Cooling is a relative term here, however, because the radiator itself may be running at anywhere from 180 to 220 degrees F.!

Tests have shown that the typical original equipment oil cooler is marginal at best. ATF that enters the radiator cooler at 300 degrees F. leaves at 240 to 270 degrees F., which is only a 10% to 20% drop in temperature, and is nowhere good enough for extended fluid life.

Any number of things can push ATF temperatures beyond the system's ability to maintain safe limits: towing a trailer, mountain driving, driving at sustained high speeds during hot weather, stop-and-go driving in city traffic, "rocking" an automatic transmission from drive to reverse to free a tire from mud or snow, etc. Problems in the cooling system itself such as a low coolant level, a defective cooling fan, fan clutch, thermostat or water pump, an obstructed radiator, etc., will also diminish ATF cooling efficiency. In some cases, transmission overheating can even lead to engine coolant overheating! That's why there's a good demand for auxiliary add-on transmission coolers.

Auxiliary Cooling

An auxiliary transmission fluid cooler is easy to install and can substantially lower fluid operating temperatures. The plate/fin type cooler is somewhat more efficient than the tube and fin design, but either can lower fluid temperatures anywhere from 80 to 140 degrees when installed in series with the stock unit. Typical cooling efficiencies run in the 35%–50% range.

ATF Fluid Types

What kind of automatic transmission fluid should you use in your transmission? The type specified in your owner's manual or printed on the transmission dipstick.

For older Ford automatics and certain imports, Type "F" is usually required. Most Fords since the 1980s require "Mercon" fluid, which is Ford's equivalent of Dexron II.

For General Motors, Chrysler and other imports, Dexron II is usually specified.

NOTE: Some newer vehicles with electronically-controlled transmissions require Dexron II or Dexron III fluid. GM says its new long-life Dexron III fluid can be substituted for Dexron II in older vehicle applications.

CAUTION: Using the wrong type of fluid can affect the way the transmission shifts and feels. Using Type F fluid in an application that calls for Dexron II may make the transmission shift too harshly. Using Dexron II in a transmission that requires Type F may allow the transmission to slip under heavy load, which can accelerate clutch wear.

Changing the Fluid

It's a messy job because there's no drain plug to change the fluid, but you can do it yourself if you're so inclined. To change the fluid, you have to get under your vehicle and remove the pan from the bottom of the transmission.

When you loosen the pan, fluid will start to dribble out in all directions so you need a fairly large catch pan. You should also know that removing the pan doesn't drain all of the old fluid out of the transmission. Approximately a third of the old fluid will still be in the torque converter. There's no drain plug on the converter so you're really only doing a partial fluid change. Even so, a partial fluid change is better than no fluid change at all.

A typical fluid change will require anywhere from 3 to 6 quarts of ATF depending on the application, a new filter and a pan gasket (or RTV sealer) for the transmission pan. The pan must be thoroughly cleaned prior to reinstallation. This includes wiping all fluid residue from the inside of the pan and scraping all traces of the old gasket from the pan's sealing surface. Don't forget to clean the mounting flange on the transmission, too.

When the new filter is installed, be sure it is mounted in the exact same position as the original and that any O-rings or other gaskets have been properly positioned prior to tightening the bolts. Then tighten the bolts to the manufacturer's recommended specs.

When refilling the transmission with fresh fluid, be careful not to allow any dirt or debris to enter the dipstick tube. Using a long-neck funnel with a built-in screen is recommended.

CAUTION: Do not overfill the transmission. Too much fluid can cause the fluid to foam, which in turn can lead to erratic shifting, oil starvation and transmission damage. Too much fluid may also force ATF to leak past the transmission seals.

Add half a quart at a time until the dipstick shows full. The transmission really isn't full yet because the dipstick should be checked when the fluid is hot, and the engine is idling with the gear selector in Park. So start the engine, drive the vehicle around the block, then recheck the fluid level while the engine is idling and add fluid as needed until the dipstick reads full.

Questions

1. Why ATF wears out?

2. What kind of automatic transmission fluid should you use in your transmission?

3. How often should the automatic transmission fluid be changed?

Unit 5　The Steering System

The steering system must deliver precise directional control, and it must do so requiring little driver effort at the steering wheel. Truck steering systems are either manual or power assisted, with power assist units using either hydraulic or air assist setups to make steering effort easier.

In addition to its vital role in vehicle control, the steering system is closely related to front suspension, axle and wheel/tire components. Improper steering adjustment can lead to alignment and tire wear problems. Suspension, axle and wheel problem can affect steering and handling.

The key components that make up the steering system are the steering wheel, steering column, steering shaft, steering gear, pitman arm, drag link, steering arm, ball joints, and tie-rod assembly, as shown in Figure 3-6.

Steering Wheel

This is the driver's link to the entire system. The wheel is formed of a strong steel rod shaped into a wheel. Spokes extend from the wheel to the wheel hub, which is fastened securely at the top of the steering column. The wheel assembly is covered with rubber or plastic. The steering column transfers driver input to the steering gear. In other words, driver effort applied to the steering wheel at the rim becomes torque in the steering shaft. The larger the steering wheel diameter, the more torque is generated from the same amount of drive effort.

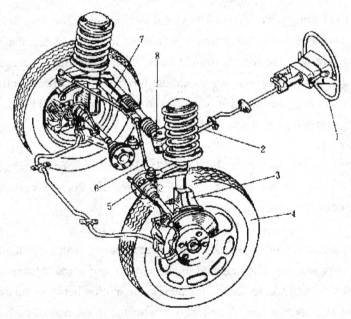

Figure 3-6　Steering System

1—steering wheel　2—steering shaft　3—steering knuckle　4—steerable wheel
5—steerable knuckle arm　6—tie rod　7—steering gear　8—steering damper

Steering Column

This is a hollow tube that extends from the steering wheel through the floorboard. It is fastened to the cab at or under the instrument panel and contains bearings to support the steering shaft.

Steering Shaft

The steering shaft is basically a rod, usually jointed, that runs from the top of the steering column to the steering gear. U-joints in the shaft accommodate any angular variations between the steering shaft and the steering gear input shaft. Usually found at one or both ends of the steering shaft, U-joints may also be used in the middle to route a multipiece shaft around the engine or accessories.

Steering Gear

This gearbox multiplies steering torque and changes its direction as received through the steering shaft from the steering wheel. There are two widely used types of gears: worm and roller, and recirculating ball.

Pitman Arm

The pitman arm is a steel arm clamped to the output shaft of the steering gear. The outer end of the pitman arm moves through an arc in order to change the rotary motion of the steering gear output shaft into linear motion. The length of the pitman arm affects steering quickness. A longer pitman arm will generate more steering motion at the front wheels for a given amount of steering wheel movement.

Drag Link

This forged rod connects the pitman arm to the steering arm. The drag link can be a one or two-piece component. The two-piece design is adjustable in length, a fact that makes it easy to center the steering gear with the wheels straight ahead. One-piece drag links are used in systems with very close tolerances. Other components are used to make adjustments to the system when a one-piece drag link is used. The drag link is connected at each end by ball joints. These ball joints isolate the steering gear and pitman arm from axle motion.

Steering Arm

Sometimes called a steering lever, this forged steel component connects the drag link to the top portion of the driver's side steering knuckle and spindle. As the steering arm moves, it changes the angle of the steering knuckle.

Ball Joints

This ball-and-socket assembly consists of a forged steel ball with a threaded stud attached to it. A socket shell grips the ball. The ball stud moves around to provide the freedom of movement needed for various steering links to accommodate relative motion between the axle and the frame rail when the front axle springs flex. A ball stud is mounted in the end of each steering arm and provides the link between the drag link and the steering arm.

Tie-Rod Assembly

The steering arm or lever controls the movement of the driver's side steering knuckle. There must be some method of transferring this steering motion to the opposite, passenger side steering knuckle. This is done through the use of a tie-rod assembly that links the two steering knuckles together and forces them to act in unison. The tie-rod assembly is also called a cross tube.

Words and Expressions

1. suspension [səs'penʃən] *n.* 悬架，悬挂装置
2. spoke [spəuk] *n.* 轮辐
3. cab [kæb] *n.* (机车、卡车等的)驾驶室
4. angular ['æŋgjulə] *adj.* 有角的
5. gearbox ['giəbɔks] *n.* (汽车的)齿轮箱，变速器
6. worm [wə:m] *n.* 蜗杆
7. roller ['rəulə] *n.* 蜗轮
8. tolerance ['tɔlərəns] *n.* [机]公差，容限
9. stud [stʌd] *n.* 柱头螺栓，螺柱
10. unison ['ju:nizn] *n.* 和谐，一致
11. steering system 转向系；转向系统
12. steering wheel 转向盘
13. steering column 转向管柱
14. steering shaft 转向轴
15. steering gear 转向齿轮，转向器
16. pitman arm 转向摇臂
17. drag link 转向直拉杆
18. steering arm 转向节臂
19. ball joint 球形接头
20. tie-rod 转向横拉杆
21. steering knuckle 转向节

Notes

1. In addition to its vital role in vehicle control, the steering system is closely related to front suspension, axle and wheel/tire components.

转向系统除了对车辆控制有着重要的作用外，还与前悬架、车桥、车轮、轮胎等部件有着密切的联系。

2. Spokes extend from the wheel to the wheel hub, which is fastened securely at the top of steering column.

转向盘辐条从转向盘轮缘延伸到转向盘的轮毂，而轮毂则被紧紧地安装在转向管柱的顶端。

3. The outer end of the pitman arm moves through an arc in order to change the rotary motion of the steering gear output shaft into linear motion.

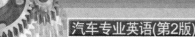

转向摇臂的外端沿着弧向运动，以便将转向器输出轴的旋转运动变成直线运动。

4. Sometimes called a steering lever, this forged steel component connects the drag link to the top portion of the driver's side steering knuckle and spindle.

由钢铁铸造的转向节臂有时又称为转向杆，它将转向直拉杆与驾驶员一侧的转向节和转向轮轴的上端部分连接在一起。

Exercises

A. Vocabulary

I. Translate the following expressions into Chinese.

1. cab

2. worm

3. roller

4. steering system

5. steering wheel

6. tie-rod

II. Identify the English names of the steering system according to the picture.

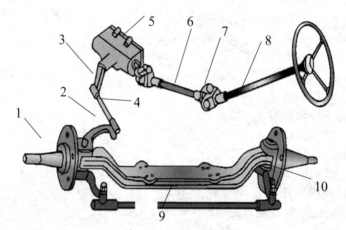

1. _____ 2. _____ 3. _____ 4. _____ 5. _____

6. _____ 7. _____ 8. _____ 9. _____ 10. _____

B. Comprehension

I. Discuss the following questions in groups and write down your answers.

1. List the components that compose the steering system.

_____

_____

2. What is the purpose of the steering system?

_____

_____

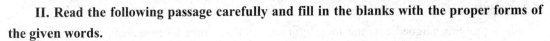
II. Read the following passage carefully and fill in the blanks with the proper forms of the given words.

form   into   from   which   with   transfer   steering   in   large   from

This is the driver's link to the entire system. The wheel is _____ of a strong steel rod shaped _____ a wheel. Spokes extend _____ the wheel to the wheel hub, _____ is fastened securely at the top of the steering column. The wheel assembly is covered _____ rubber or plastic. The steering column _____ driver input to the steering gear. In other words, driver effort applied to the _____ wheel at the rim becomes torque _____ the steering shaft. The _____ the steering wheel diameter, the more torque is generated _____ the same amount of drive effort.

C. Translation

I. Translate the following sentences into Chinese.

1. Truck steering systems are either manual or power assisted, with power assist units using either hydraulic or air assist setups to make steering effort easier.

2. The larger the steering wheel diameter, the more torque is generated from the same amount of drive effort.

3. This ball-and-socket assembly consists of a forged steel ball with a threaded stud attached to it.

II. Translate the following sentences into English.

1. 转向系统除了对车辆控制有着重要的作用外，还与前悬架、车桥、车轮、轮胎等部件有着密切的联系。

2. 转向盘辐条从转向盘轮缘延伸到转向盘的轮毂，而轮毂则被紧紧地安装在转向管柱的顶端。

3. 由钢铁铸造的转向节臂有时又称为转向杆，它将转向直拉杆与驾驶员侧的转向节和转向轮轴的上端部分连接在一起。

Reading Material

Read the following passages and answer the questions according to the information given in the passages.

Passage One   Bump Steer

When I hit a bump, my car suddenly jerks to one side. Is anything wrong?

Yes. The condition is called bump steer, and it means your steering linkage is not mounted parallel in the chassis possibly as a result of collision or frame damage, a bent steering arm, misalignment in the chassis, or an improperly mounted steering rack.

Bump steer is not a very common condition, but it can be a very unnerving thing to experience if you're unfortunate enough to encounter it. It is usually most noticeable when crossing a major dip or bump at speed, as when crossing a railroad crossing or passing through an intersection with a lot of road crown. As the suspension bounces over the bump, it suddenly feels as if someone tugged on the steering wheel. The car twitches or jerks to one side as if it has a mind of its own. This occurs because of unequal toe changes that occur as the suspension extends and compresses.

In a properly aligned car, the toe alignment of both front wheels changes equally as the suspension moves up and down. But if something causes more of a toe change in one wheel than the other, it will jerk the steering towards the side with the greatest toe change.

The thing that needs to be checked is the parallelism of the steering rack and linkage with respect to the ground. This can be done by simply measuring the distance between both ends of the rack and the ground. If one end of the rack is sitting higher than the other, the rack is misaligned in the chassis. If it can't be corrected by loosening and retightening the rack mounts, the sub frame or cross member on which the rack is mounted may be bent or damaged. This will require special straightening equipment or replacement to correct.

The height of the outer ends of the tie rods with respect to the ground should also be measured. If one tie rod is higher than the other, one of the steering arms is probably bent. The cure here is to replace the steering knuckle.

CAUTION: Bending a steering arm to correct a bump steer condition is not recommended because doing so may weaken the arm and increase the danger of breaking.

Questions

1. What is a bump steer?

2. How does a bump steer occur?

3. How to deal with a bump steer?

Passage Two   Steering System Service

My steering is loose. Any ideas why? The most common causes of steering looseness include worn tie rod ends, a worn idler arm or center link (on vehicles without rack and pinion steering), a worn steering gear or a worn steering rack.

Normally, your steering wheel should have no more than about a quarter inch of play. Any more means something is worn or loose and needs to be fixed.

WARNING: Don't put off having your steering looked at because a failure of a critical component could cause loss of steering control!

The inner and outer tie rod ends should have no perceptible looseness. Worn or loose tie rod ends are especially dangerous because if one pulls apart, you'll lose steering control. Worn tie rod ends can also cause rapid tire wear.

If you have a rear-wheel drive vehicle with conventional steering (not rack and pinion steering), the idler arm should have no more than the specified amount of maximum play. Refer to a manual for the specs and recommended procedure for checking it. Checking idler arm play usually involves pulling on the arm with a specified force and measuring how much the arm deflects.

If your vehicle has a lot of miles on it, the steering gear or rack itself may be worn. On conventional steering boxes, there's usually an adjustment screw that can be used to take some of the slack out of the system. With rack and pinion steering, adjustment is usually of little help because the rack develops center wear. If the pinion is adjusted to compensate, the rack may bind when turned to either side. The only cure for a center wear condition is to replace the rack with a new one (an entire new rack assembly).

Other Causes

Sometimes the steering will feel loose because of a worn U-joint coupling in the steering column. Loose or worn wheel bearings can also make the steering wander and feel loose.

Questions

1. My steering is loose. Any ideas why?

2. Don't put off having your steering looked at. Why?

3. What are the other causes that the steering feel lose?

Unit 6   Automobile Braking System

The most vital factor in the running and control of the modern vehicles is the braking system. In order to bring the moving motor vehicle to rest or slow down in a shortest possible time, the energy of motion possessed by the vehicle must be converted into some other form of energy. The rate of slowing down or retardation is governed by the speed of conversion of energy. Kinetic energy is the energy of motion which is converted into heat given up to air flowing over the braking system.

For realizing the full potentialities of the engine and road-holding in safety, it is necessary to bring the car rapidly to rest from any speed by some means. The means of slowing down or bringing to rest a moving vehicle in a shortest possible distance is called brakes. They are vitally important in the running and control of the motor vehicle. Lives of not only the driver and the passengers but also those of the other road users are saved. The brakes provided by the manufacturers should be effective, safe in operation, progressive and consistent in response to brake pedal as well as reasonably easy to adjust.

Modem cars can travel very fast, so good brakes are essential for safety. Practically most modern cars have disc brakes on the front wheels, and drum brakes on the rear wheels.

Brake is a friction device for converting the power of the moving vehicle into heat by means of friction. It is the main factor governing even if sufficient effort is available to lock the wheels. This amount of friction developed between two surfaces in contact is independent of the area of the surface in contact. The braking heat energy should be got rid of as early as possible.

Disc Brakes

The most common type of disc brake on modem cars is the single-piston floating caliper, as shown in Figure 3-7.

The main components of a disc brake are as follows:

(1) The brake pads;

(2) The caliper, which contains a piston;

(3) The rotor, which is mounted to the hub.

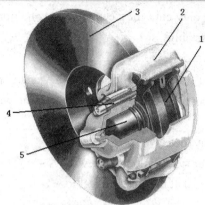

Figure 3-7　Disk Brake

1—brake slippers　2—brake caliper block　3—brake disk　4—brake clamp guiding pin　5—piston

The disc brake is like the brakes on a bicycle a lot. Bicycle brakes have a caliper, which squeezes the brake pads against the wheel. In a disc brake, the brake pads squeeze the rotor instead of the wheel, and the force is transmitted hydraulically instead of through a cable. Friction between the pads and the disc slows the disc down. A moving car has a certain amount of kinetic energy, and the brakes have to remove this energy from the car in order to stop it. How do the brakes do this? Each time you stop your car, your brakes convert the kinetic energy to heat generated by the friction between the pads and the disc. Most car disc brakes are vented. Vented disc brakes have a set of vanes, between the two sides of the disc, that pumps air through the disc to provide cooling.

Drum Brakes

Drum brakes work on the same principle as disc brakes: shoes press against a spinning surface. In this system, that surface is called a drum, as shown in Figure 3-8.

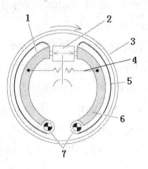

Figure 3-8　Drum brake

1—trailing shoe　2—brake cylinder　3—brake drum　4—returning spring
5—brake lining　6—leading shoe　7—eccentric anchor pin

In the drum-and-shoe type, there is a wheel brake cylinder with two pistons. When brake pedal is pushed by the driver, brake fluid is forced into the brake cylinder by the action at the master cylinder, and the two pistons are forced outward. This causes the curved brake shoes to move into contact with the brake drum. The brake shoes apply friction to the brake drum, forcing it and the wheel to slow or stop.

Many cars have drum brakes on the rear wheels and disc brakes on the front. Drum brakes have more parts than disc brakes and are harder to service, but they are less expensive to manufacture, and they easily incorporate an emergency brake mechanism.

Power Brakes

Back in the day, when most cars had drum brakes, power brakes were not really necessary drum brakes naturally provide some of their own power assist. Since most cars today have disc brakes, at least on the front wheels, they need power brakes. Without this device, a lot of drivers would have very tired legs.

The brake booster uses vacuum from the engine to multiply the force that your foot applies to the master cylinder.

Words and Expressions

1. vital ['vaitl] *adj.* 重大的；生命的；生机的；至关重要的，所必需的

2. retardation [,ri:tɑ:'deiʃən] *n.* 延迟

3. conversion [kən'və:ʃən] *n.* 变换，转化

4. potentiality [pə,tenʃi'æliti] *n.* 可能；(用复数)潜能，潜力，可能性

5. progressive [prə'gresiv] *adj.* 前进的；(税收)累进的，进步的

6. consistent [kən'sistənt] *adj.* 一致的；调和的；坚固的；相容的

7. squeeze [skwi:z] *v.* 压榨，挤，挤榨

8. emergency [i'mə:dʒənsi] *n.* 紧急情况，突然事件，非常时刻，紧急事件

9. reasonably ['ri:zənəbli] *adv.* 适度地，相当地

10. pad [pæd] *n.* 衬垫，垫块

11. caliper ['kæləpə] *n.* 卡钳

12. canister ['kænistə] *n.* 罐

13. cable ['keibl] *n.* 电缆，钢索，索缆

14. booster ['bu:stə] *n.* 助力器，加力器；附加装置，辅助装置

15. vacuum ['vækjuəm] *n.* 真空，空间；真空吸尘器 *v.* 造成真空，吸尘

16. rust [rʌst] *n.* 锈 *vi.* 生锈 *vt.* 生锈，使……生锈

17. plate [pleit] *n.* 板材，电容器板，(蓄电池)极板

18. shoe [ʃu:] *n.* (汽车轮的)制动器

19. disc brake 盘式制动器

20. rear-wheel drive 后轮驱动

21. single-piston floating caliper 单活塞，浮钳盘式制动器

22. kinetic energy　动能

23. brake booster　制动助力器

24. brake band　制动带

25. brake fluid　制动液

26. master cylinder　制动主缸

27. wheel cylinder　制动轮缸

Notes

1. In order to bring the moving motor vehicle to rest or slow down in a shortest possible time, the energy of motion possessed by the vehicle must be converted into some other form of energy.

为了使行驶的汽车在最短的时间内停车或减速，车辆所具有的动能必须转化为其他某种能量。

2. This amount of friction developed between two surfaces in contact is independent of the area of the surface in contact.

接触表面所产生的摩擦力的大小与接触面积的大小无关。

3. Practically most modern cars have disc brakes on the front wheels, and drum brakes on the rear wheels.

实际上，大多数现代的汽车的前轮采用盘式制动，后轮采用鼓式制动。

4. Drum brakes have more parts than disc brakes and are harder to service, but they are less expensive to manufacture, and they easily incorporate an emergency brake mechanism.

鼓式制动比盘式制动的零件多，维护也更困难，但鼓式制动造价便宜，且易于与紧急制动机构配合。

5. Since most cars today have disc brakes, at least on the front wheels, they need power brakes. Without this device, a lot of drivers would have very tired legs.

因为现在大多数汽车采用盘式制动，至少前轮采用盘式制动，那就需要动力制动了。没有制动助力器，很多司机的腿会非常疲劳。

Exercises

A. Vocabulary

I. Translate the following expressions into Chinese.

1. road-holding

2. single-piston

3. brake slipper

4. brake clamp guiding pin

5. returning spring

6. leading shoe

7. eccentric anchor pin

8. trailing shoe

9. brake drum

10. brake cylinder

II. Identify the English names of the battery according to the picture.

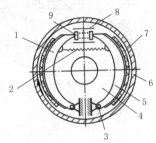

1. _____ 2. _____ 3. _____ 4. _____

5. _____ 6. _____ 7. _____ 8. _____

9. _____

B. Comprehension

I. Discuss the following questions in groups and write down your answers.

1. What are the main components of disk brakes?

_____

_____

2. What are the advantages of the floating caliper?

_____

_____

3. How does the disc brake operate?

_____

_____

II. Read the following passage carefully and fill in the blanks with the proper forms of the given words.

convert	brake	stop	kinetic	disc
pad	carvenet	generate	energy	

A moving car has a certain amount of _____ energy, and the _____ have to remove this _____ from the car in order to _____ it. How do the brakes do this? Each time you stop your _____, your brakes _____ the kinetic energy to heat _____ by the friction between the _____ and the _____. Most car disc brakes are _____.

C. Translation

I. Translate the following sentences into Chinese.

1. In the drum-and-shoe type, there is a wheel brake cylinder with two pistons.

2. Brake is a friction device for converting the power of the moving vehicle into heat by means of friction.

3. The means of slowing down or bringing to rest a moving vehicle in a shortest possible distance is called brakes.

II. Translate the following sentences into English.

1. 当驾驶员踩下制动踏板时，制动液由于主缸的作用进入轮缸，推动两个活塞向外侧移动。

2. 鼓式制动比盘式制动的零件多，维护也更困难，但鼓式制动造价便宜，且易于与紧急制动机构配合。

3. 因为现在大多数汽车采用盘式制动，至少前轮采用盘式制动，那就需要动力制动了。没有制动助力器，很多司机的腿会非常疲劳。

Reading Material

Read the following passages and answer the questions according to the information given in the passages.

Passage One   The Brake

Brake shoes and pads are constructed in a similar manner. The pad or shoe is composed of a metal backing plate and a friction lining. The lining is either bonded (glued) to the metal, or riveted. Generally, riveted linings provide superior performance, but good quality bonded linings are perfectly adequate.

Friction materials will vary between manufacturers and type of pad and the material compound may be referred to as: asbestos, organic, semi-metallic, metallic. The difference between these compounds lies in the types and percentages of friction materials used, material binders and performance modifiers.

Generally speaking, organic and non-metallic asbestos compound brakes are quiet, easy on rotors and provide good feel. But this comes at the expense of high temperature operation, so they may not be your best choice for heavy duty use or mountain driving. In most cases, these linings will wear somewhat faster than metallic compound pads, so you will usually replace them more often. However, when using these pads, rotors tend to last longer.

Semi-metallic or metallic compound brake linings will vary in performance based on the metallic contents of the compound. Again, generally speaking, the higher the metallic content, the better the friction material will resist heat. This makes them more appropriate for heavy duty applications, but at the expense of braking performance before the pad reaches operating temperature. The first few applications on a cold morning may not give strong braking. Also, metallics and semi-metallics are more likely to squeal. In most cases, metallic compounds last longer than non-metallic pads, but they tend to cause more wear on the rotors. If you use metallic pads, expect to replace the rotors more often.

When deciding what type of brake lining is right for you, keep in mind that today's modern cars have brake materials which are matched to the expected vehicle's performance capabilities. Changing the material from OEM specification could adversely affect brake feel or responsiveness. Before changing the brake materials, talk to your dealer or parts supplier to help decide what is most appropriate for your application. Remember that heavy use applications such as towing, stoping and going driving, driving down mountain roads, and racing may require a change to a higher performance material.

Some more exotic materials are also used in brake linings, among which are Kevlar and carbon compounds. These materials have the capability of extremely good performance for towing, mountain driving or racing. Wear characteristics can be similar to either the metallic or the non-metallic lining, depending on the product you buy. Most race applications tend to wear like metallic lining, while many of the street applications are more like the non-metallics.

Questions

1. What are the main components of the hydraulic system?

2. How does the hydraulic brake system work?

3. What kinds of material are used in brake linings?

Passage Two   Bleeding the Brakes

Bleeding the brakes is flushing the old brake fluid out of the master cylinder, brake lines, calipers and wheel cylinders and replacing it with fresh fluid.

Bleeding is necessary for the following reasons:

1. To remove air bubbles that may have entered the system while repairs were being made, because of a leak or because the fluid level got too low. The air must be removed because it is compressible and can prevent a full, firm pedal.

The individual brake lines must be bled in a specified sequence, which varies from vehicle to vehicle depending on the design of the brake system to remove all the air from the lines. On some ABS-equipped vehicles, special bleeding procedures may be required, which also requires special equipment in some cases such as a scan tool to cycle the ABS solenoids.

The brakes can be bled manually by attaching a piece of clear tubing to the bleeder screw on each caliper and wheel cylinder, opening the screw and manually stroking the brake pedal to force fluid through the lines, or with power bleeding equipment. Most professionals use power bleeding equipment because it's faster and easier.

2. To remove moisture contamination. Brake fluid needs to be replaced periodically because DOT 3 and 4 brake fluids are glycol-based and absorb moisture over time. This occurs whether a vehicle is driven 30,000 miles a year or just sits in a garage because fluid contamination is a function of time and humidity rather than mileage. Moisture enters the system past seals and through microscopic pores in hoses. It also enters every time the fluid reservoir is opened.

After only a year of service, DOT 3 fluid may contain as much as 2% water. After 18 months, the level of contamination can be as high as 3%. And after several years of service, it's usual to find brake fluid that has soaked up as much as 7%–8% water. Many vehicles that are six, seven or eight years old have never had the brake fluid changed!

As the fluid soaks up moisture, it thickens and becomes less able to withstand heat and corrosion. The result is a significant drop in the fluid's boiling temperature, which may under the right conditions allow the fluid to boil in the calipers. Once brake fluid turns to vapor, the bubbles

cause an increase in the distance the pedal must travel to apply the brakes. This condition should not be confused with "brake fade" that occurs when the brake linings get too hot as a result of prolonged braking. Brake fade requires greater and greater pedal effort to stop the vehicle while fluid boil increases pedal travel and makes the pedal feel soft or mushy.

The danger of fluid boil is the most important for front-wheel drive cars because of the higher operating temperatures that are generated in today's downsized front brakes, and because the hydraulic system is split diagonally. Semi-metallic linings compound the heat problem by conducting heat from the rotors to the calipers. If the fluid contains a lot of moisture and can't take the heat, it'll probably boil.

DOT 3 brake fluid, which has long been used in most domestic cars and light trucks, has a minimum dry boiling point of 401 degrees F. A 3% level of water contamination will lower this by 25% or 100 degrees! DOT 4 "extra heavy-duty" brake fluid, which is used in many European cars, has a higher dry boiling point of 446 degrees F. DOT 4 soaks up moisture at a slower rate than DOT 3 but suffers a greater drop in heat resistance as moisture builds up. Only 2% moisture in DOT 4 fluid will lower its boiling point by almost 50% or 200 degrees!

CAUTION: Use the type of brake fluid specified by the vehicle manufacturer. Never substitute DOT 3 for DOT 4. But you can safely substitute DOT 4 for DOT 3.

Though the owner's manuals for most domestic vehicles have no specific time or mileage recommendations for replacing brake fluid, recommending a change every two years for preventative maintenance is a good way to minimize the danger of fluid boil and internal corrosion in the brake system. At the very least, the fluid should always be replaced when the brakes are relined.

Some people say using DOT 5 silicone fluid eliminates moisture contamination problems. The premium-priced fluid, which is silicone based, does not absorb moisture and is theoretically a "lifetime" brake fluid. What's more, DOT 5 fluid has a higher dry boiling point of at least 500 degrees F. and a wet boiling point of 356 degrees F. But DOT 5 silicone brake fluid is very expensive (up to ten times as much as regular brake fluid). It does not mix with DOT 3 or 4 fluid, which means all the old fluid has to be removed if switching to DOT 5 to prevent "slugs" of moisture-contaminated DOT 3 and 4 fluid from forming in the system. And it is not recommended for any vehicle equipped with ABS because it contains a higher percentage of dissolved air that may cause foaming when the fluid is cycled rapidly. Other than that, it's great stuff.

Questions

1. What is "bleeding the brakes"?

2. Why is that sometimes necessary?

3. What kinds of brake fluid are used in brake system?

Unit 7　Antilock Brake System

The purpose of an electronic anti-lock, or anti-skid, braking system (ABS) is to prevent wheel lockup under heavy braking conditions on virtually any type of road surface. It has been used on aircraft for years, and some domestic cars were offered with an early form of antilock braking in the late 1960s and 1970s. Modern antilock systems may be the greatest advance in vehicle safety since the seatbelt. The most efficient braking takes place when the wheels are still revolving. If the driver slams on the brakes and the wheels lock, the following situations will occur:

1. Driving stability is lost, and the vehicle skids;
2. The vehicle cannot be steered;
3. The braking distance increases;
4. The risk of an accident increases.

Briefly Operational Principle

Anti-lock braking system is designed to provide the best deceleration and stability during hard braking by adjusting the hydraulic pressure at each wheel to prevent wheel lock.

There are many different variations and control algorithms for ABS systems. Regardless of the type, all work in a similar manner.

The system's main components are the wheel sensors, the electronic control unit and the hydraulic control unit. The wheel speed sensors continuously send wheel speed signals to the control unit. The control unit compares these signals to determine whether any of the wheels is about to lock. If any wheel is about to lock, the control unit signals the hydraulic unit to maintain or reduce hydraulic pressure at the appropriate wheel. Pressure is modulated by electrically operated solenoid valves in the hydraulic unit, as shown in Figure 3-9.

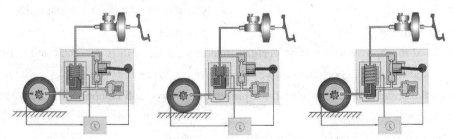

(a) maintaining braking pressure　(b) reducing braking pressure　(c) increasing braking pressure

Figure 3-9　ABS Operating Principle

Some Occasional Things about the ABS

When starting the vehicle, an anti-lock braking system light will illuminate on the instrument panel for a few seconds. This is normal. But if ABS light stays on, the ABS is not working; if the

ABS light and brake warning light both stay on, the brakes do not exist.

When the ABS is active, various ABS sound or feel different and this is normal. Some of the effects are as follows:

(1) A groaning noise;

(2) A rapid pulsing of the brake pedal;

(3) A periodic dropping of the brake pedal;

(4) A hard rake pedal;

(5) A light that turns on to say "low" traction.

Brake pedal will pulsate as the ABS engages; the driver may feel the brake pedal pulsating. This is caused by the system applying and releasing pressure to the brakes. If the brakes squeal under normal braking, this may mean that the brake pads are worn and need replacing. A pulsing brake pedal applied every time may mean warped brake rotors and or seized brake calipers that require servicing.

The ABS works by comparing the speed of the wheels. When replacing tires, use the same size originally supplied with the car. Tire size and construction can affect wheel speed and may cause the system to work inconsistently.

A car with an ABS may require a longer distance to stop on loose or uneven surfaces than an equivalent car without anti-lock.The ABS can not make up for road conditions or bad judgment. It is still your responsibility to drive at reasonable speeds for weather and traffic conditions, and to leave a margin of safety.

Self-checking

The ABS is self-checking. If anything goes wrong, the ABS indicator on the instrument panel comes on. This means the anti-lock function of the braking system has shut down. The braking still work like a conventional system, providing normal stopping ability. During this process, the control unit monitors the operation of the wheel sensors, solenoid, pump and faults; it shuts off power to the motor and solenoid. The ABS indicator light on the instrument panel comes on. The brakes then work like a conventional system without anti-lock capabilities.

The Advantages of ABS

Developed to improve the running performance of vehicle, ABS is designed on the principle that makes good use of the coefficient of wheel and ground. When the ABS senses a wheel lockup, it modulates the brake hydraulic pressure; the proper brake force will be applied to the wheel.

The advantages of ABS are as follows:

(1) It can decrease the distance of brake on even surfaces.

(2) It enhances the stability of moving vehicle. The accident proportion will decrease by about 8% for the vehicle equipped with ABS.

(3) It improves the wear properties of tires.

(4) It can be used easily and can work steadily.

Words and Expressions

1. stability　[stə'biliti]　*n.* 稳定性

2. diagnostic　[,daiəg'nɔstik]　*adj.* 诊断的，(有)特征的

3. illuminate　[i'lju:mineit]　*v.* 照亮，发光

4. activate　['æktiveit]　*v.* 使……活动，对……起作用；起动，开动

5. retrieve　[ri'tri:v]　*v.* 更正，纠正；弥补恢复；重获

6. anti-skid　['æntiskid]　*n.* 防滑装置

7. anti-lock　['ænti]　*n.* 防抱死

8. solenoid　['səulinɔid]　*n.* 电磁线圈

9. coefficient　[kəui'fiʃənt]　*n.* 系数

10. property　['prɔpəti]　*n.* 属性，特性

11. needle　['ni:dl]　*n.* 指针

12. nozzle　['nɔzl]　*n.* 喷嘴

13. regulator　['regjuleitə]　*n.* 调节器

14. exciter　[ik'saitə]　*n.* 振荡器，激发器，励磁机

15. instrument panel　仪表板

16. warning light　警告灯

17. magnetic induction　磁感应

Notes

1. Anti-lock braking system(ABS) is designed to provide best deceleration and stability during hard braking by adjusting the hydraulic pressure at each wheel to prevent wheel lock.

防抱死制动系统(ABS)是为汽车急刹车时提供最佳减速度和稳定性而设计的，它通过调节每个车轮的制动液压来防止车轮抱死。

2. If any wheel is about to lock, the control unit signals the hydraulic unit to maintain or reduce hydraulic pressure at the appropriate wheel.

若有车轮将抱死，控制器将向液压装置发出信号，维持或减少在相应车轮上的制动液压。

3. A pulsing brake pedal applied every time may mean warped brake rotors or seized brake calipers that require servicing.

若每次刹车时踏板跳动，则说明制动盘倾斜，或者钳体卡住，需要维修。

Exercises

A. Vocabulary

I. Translate the following expressions into Chinese.

1. anti-lock brake system

2. the wheel speed sensor

3. the electrical control unit

4. instrument panel

5. lock up

6. rear-wheel drive

7. hydraulic actuator

8. driving stability

9. warning light

10. magnetic induction

II. Identify the English names of the battery according to the picture.

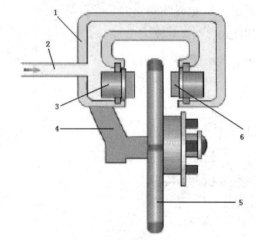

1. _____ 2. _____ 3. _____ 4. _____ 5. _____

B. Comprehension

I. Discuss the following questions in groups and write down your answers.

1. What is the true advantage of ABS ?

_____

2. What are the main components of a disc brake?

_____

3. How can the ABS solve the lockup problem?

_____

II. Read the following passage carefully and fill in the blanks with the proper forms of the given words.

| *instrument* | *go* | *stop* | *panel* |
| *conventional* | *shut* | *operation* | *solenoid* |

The ABS is self-checking. If anything _____ wrong, the ABS indicator on the instrument _____ comes on. This means the Anti-lock function of the braking system has _____ down. The braking still work like a _____ system, providing normal _____ ability. During this process, the control unit monitors the _____ of the wheel sensors, solenoid, pump, and faults; it shuts off power to the motor and _____. The ABS indicator light on the _____ panel comes on. The brakes then work like a conventional system without anti-lock capabilities.

C. Translation

I. Translate the following sentences into Chinese.

1. Anti-lock brake systems solve this lockup problem by rapidly pumping the brakes whenever the system detects a wheel that is locked up.

2. ABS wheel speed sensors are installed at each wheel, and they transmit wheel and tire speed information to the computer.

3. Rear-wheel ABS is designed to maintain directional stability and prevent the vehicle from skidding sideways in emergencies.

II. Translate the following sentences into English.

1. 相对于没有装备防抱死装置的同等车辆来说，装备了防抱死装置的同等车辆在不平整或松软的路面上行驶时就需要一个更长的制动距离。

2. 为提高汽车行驶性能而研发的防抱死装置，其工作原理是充分利用轮胎和地面之间的附着系数。

3. 车轮防抱死制动系统具有自诊断功能。

Reading Material

Read the following passages and answer the questions according to the information given in the passages.

Passage One　Typical Brake System

The typical brake system is composed of the following basic components: master cylinder, brake lines and brake hoses, and brake fluid.

Master Cylinder

As a modern system, the master cylinder is power-assisted by the engine. A typical master cylinder has actually two completely separate master cylinders in one housing, each handling two wheels. This way if one side fails, you will still be able to stop the car. A master cylinder is made up of a reservoir of fluid, two pistons, and two brake lines. When the brake pedal is depressed, the pistons move to create pressure in the cylinder. This pressure compresses the fluid evenly through each brake line and into the wheel cylinder that moves the brake calipers. In case of failure of a brake line, the master cylinder will redirect hydraulic pressure to the remaining lines, thereby avoiding catastrophic failure of the brakes.

Brake Lines and Brake Hoses

The brake fluid travels from the master cylinder to the wheels through the brake lines, that is, a series of steel tubes and reinforced rubber hoses. Rubber hoses are only used in places that require flexibility, such as at the front wheels, which move up and down as well as steer. The rest of the system uses non-corrosive seamless steel tubing with special fittings at attachment points. If

a steel line requires a repair, the best procedure is to replace the complete line. If this is not practical, a line can be repaired by using special splice fittings that are made for brake system repair. You must never use brass "compression" fittings or copper tubing to repair a brake system. They are dangerous and illegal.

Brake Fluid

Brake fluid is special oil that has specific properties. It is designed to withstand cold temperatures without thickening as well as very high temperatures without boiling. If the brake fluid should boil, it will cause you to have a spongy pedal and the car will be hard to stop.

The brake fluid reservoir is on top of the master cylinder. Most cars today have a transparent reservoir so that you can see the level without opening the cover. The brake fluid level will drop slightly as the brake pads wear. This is a normal condition and no cause for concern. If the level drops noticeably over a short period of time or goes down to about two thirds full, you're your brakes checked as soon as possible. Keep the reservoir covered expect for the amount of time you need to fill it and never leave a can of brake fluid uncovered. Brake fluid must maintain a very high boiling point. Exposure to air will cause the fluid to absorb moisture which will lower that boiling point.

Questions

1. What does the typical brake system consist of?

2. How does the disc brake work?

3. What is the function of the master cylinder?

Passage Two   Power Brakes

Most cars and trucks have vacuum-assist power brakes. If you've noticed that the brake pedal seems harder and requires more effort to apply the brakes, you may have a problem with the brake booster.

To check the booster, pump the brake pedal with the engine off until you've bled off all the vacuum from the unit (the pedal will feel firmer and you won't hear any sounds from the booster). Then hold the pedal down and start the engine. You should feel the pedal depress slightly as engine vacuum enters the booster and pulls on the diaphragm. If there's no change, the vacuum hose to the booster may be loose or blocked. If the vacuum hose is okay, the problem is in the booster and the booster needs to be replaced.

If your brake booster has failed, your brakes will still work but will require increased pedal effort. The pedal will feel much harder and will take a lot more pressure to stop the vehicle. Driving with a bad booster can be dangerous because the vehicle may not be able to stop as quickly as in a short distance. So don't delay. Have the problem diagnosed and repaired as soon as possible.

If your vehicle has an "integral" antilock brake system where the ABS system is combined with the master cylinder assembly, power brake assist is provided by pump pressure stored in the ABS accumulator.

NOTE: If your vehicle has a "nonintegral" ABS system, it has a conventional vacuum brake booster. If there's an ABS pump or accumulator failure, power assist will be lost and the ABS warning light should come on alerting you that a problem has occurred.

WARNING: If the ABS warning light is on, the ABS system is usually deactivated which means the ABS system can't prevent skidding when braking on wet or slick surfaces. You should have the system checked out and repaired as soon as possible.

Hydro-boost

Though not as common as vacuum booster power brake systems, some vehicles are equipped with Bendix "Hydro-Boost" power brakes. This system uses hydraulic pressure generated by the power steering pump rather than engine vacuum to provide power assist.

Pressure generated by the power steering pump is stored in an accumulator, which is then routed to the master cylinder by the Hydro-Boost unit when you step on the brakes. Problems can be caused by leaks inside the Hydro-Boost unit, by a worn power steering pump, slipping or broken pump drive belt, or hose connections.

A simple way to test the Hydro-Boost system is to pump the brakes five or six times with the engine off to discharge the accumulator. Then press down hard on the pedal (about 40 lbs. of force) and start the engine. Like a vacuum booster, you should feel the pedal fall slightly when the engine starts, then rise.

The leakdown of the accumulator can be checked by pumping the brakes several times while the engine is running, then shutting it off. Let the car sit for about an hour, then try the brakes without starting the engine. You should get 2 or 3 soft brake applications before it takes more effort to push the pedal.

Questions

1. How can I tell if my power brakes are working properly?

2. How does the vacuum-assist power brakes work?

3. What is the function of the hydro-boost?

Unit 8　GPS Navigation System

An GPS navigation system is a satellite navigation system designed for use in auto mobiles. Unlike other GPS systems, it uses position data to locate the user on a road in the unit's map database. Using the road database, the unit can give directions to other locations along roads also in its database. Dead reckoning using distance data from sensors attached to the drive train and a gyroscope can be used for greater reliability, as GPS signal loss and/or multi-path can occur due to urban canyons or tunnels.

History

Honda claims to have created the first navigation system starting in 1983, and culminating with general availability in the 1990 Acura Legend. This analog system used an accelerometer to

judge location, as the GPS system was not yet generally available.

Pioneer claims to be the first with a GPS-based auto navigation system, in 1990.

Magellan, a GPS navigation system manufacturer, claims to have created the first GPS-based vehicle navigation system in the US in 1995.

Introduction to In-car Navigation

Just a few years ago, adding a navigation system to your vehicle meant purchasing bulky components that required complex installation and the use of multiple CD-ROMs or DVD-ROMs to download the appropriate maps. Nowadays, many navigation systems come preloaded with maps and features designed to suit just about any budget and level of use.

Use this introduction to determine whether you want an in-dash setup that preserves your car's factory look, a plug-and-play GPS that is easy to use and install, or a handheld GPS that you can use in the mountains, on the water and in your car.

Types of in-car navigation systems are as follows:

1) In-dash Navigation

If you want to maintain the factory look of your dash and add the convenience of a large fold out monitor, look for an in-dash navigation system. A typical in-dash navigation system consists of a car stereo with a built-in monitor, a hideaway connection box that contains A/V inputs and outputs, and an external GPS antenna. The stereo mounts in the factory stereo slot in your dash. The hideaway box is usually mounted behind the dash or under a front seat. In addition to CD playback and AM/FM reception, most in-dash systems include DVD playback, so you can watch a movie on the built-in screen when parked. Installation of an in-dash system, can be complex, as they require connection to power, ground, the vehicle speed sensor and the parking brake.

- Warning

  Removing your seat could deactivate your vehicle's SRS system.

- Use

  In-dash Navigation Shopping Guide for more tips on how to choose an in-dash system.

2) Remote-mount navigation system

A remote-mount navigation system consists of a self-contained GPS receiver that must be connected to a compatible in-dash stereo. See the Navigation Installation Guide for more information on installation.

3) Plug-and-play navigation system

Compact and easy to use, plug-and-Play GPS receivers are ideal for anyone who wants the convenience of in-car navigation without the hassle of a permanent installation. These portable units attach quickly to the windshield or dash and use a simple cigarette lighter adapter to draw power, which makes it easy to transfer them from vehicle to vehicle. Featuring with bright color screens that range from 3.5 to 7, most plug-and-play GPS receivers also include touchscreen controls, voice prompts, a built-in speaker and an integrated GPS antenna. Best of all, touchscreen user interfaces have evolved to the point where many people find they can start using a plug-and-play GPS receiver without first reading the owner's manual although you'll always get

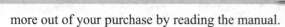

more out of your purchase by reading the manual.

4) Portable GPS

Portable GPS receivers include models designed for camping, boating, driving (plug-and-play), and even for use as a personal digital assistant(PDA). If you plan to use a GPS receiver primarily in your car, look for either an in-dash, remote-mount, or plug-and-play system, as these include special features designed specifically for use while operating a vehicle, such as voice prompts, large, bright screens, and built-in speakers. But if you're looking for a GPS device that you can use in the mountains, on the ocean, on the road, and while traveling, check out our portable GPS Shopping Guide for tips on choosing the right handheld model for your needs.

More Stories on this Topic

Nonetheless, auto manufacturers, suppliers and government agencies are working on various new technologies that can aid in an emergency. The developments include everything from advanced navigation systems to emergency brake sensors to car-to-car wireless communication systems, which rely on a sensor network to warn vehicles (and, in turn, drivers) of inclement weather, road closures or accidents up ahead.

According to experts, one of the most helpful technologies currently available is in-car navigation systems, which most automakers sell as an option for about $2,000. Nestled in the front dash, navigation screens display road maps of the majority of the country. The maps are culled from data stored on a DVD in the car. GPS locators then synchronize data on the car's whereabouts to cast the right map onto the screen. That information alone can lower a driver's likelihood of getting stuck somewhere, because the driver at least has a sense of direction and a path toward safety. Even in a remote location out of range of a cellular connection, navigation systems can still download predictive maps that give drivers an idea where they are.

Words and Expressions

1. navigation [ˌnævi'geiʃən] *n*. 航海，导航，航行

2. satellite ['sætəlait] *n*. 人造卫星

3. database ['deitobeis] *n* [计]数据库，资料库

4. gyroscope ['gaiərəskəup] *n*. 陀螺仪

5. accelerometer [ækˌselə'rɔmitə] *n*. 加速计

6. CD-ROM *n*. 光盘驱动器

7. compact [kəm'pækt] *adj*. 紧凑的，紧密的

8. hassle ['hæsl] *n*. 激战

9. evolve [i'vɔlv] *v*. (使)发展，(使)进化

10. drive train 动力传动系统

11. database 数据库

12. GPS-based 基于 GPS 的

13. parking brake 驻车制动

14. voice prompt   声音提示

15. built-in   内置

16. analog system   模拟系统

Notes

1. Dead reckoning using distance data from sensors attached to the drive train and a gyroscope can be used for greater reliability, as GPS signal loss and/or multi-path can occur due to urban canyons or tunnels.

由于城市地道的存在会出现 GPS 信号损失或多路径情况，为增强可靠性，可利用从连接到驱动列车和陀螺仪的传感器所获得的远程数据来作出判断。

2. Just a few years ago, adding a navigation system to your vehicle meant purchasing bulky components that required complex installation and the use of multiple CD-ROMs or DVD-ROMs to download the appropriate maps.

仅在几年前，车上加装巡航控制系统意味着要买大量的部件进行复杂的安装，且需要多种 CD 或 DVD 存储器来下载适当的地图。

Exercises

A. Vocabulary

I. Translate the following expressions into Chinese.

1. In-car Navigation

2. multi-path

3. bulky components

4. In-dash Navigation

5. stereo

6. anteo

7. SRS system

8. handsfree

9. core competency

10. walkie talkie

B. Comprehension

I. Discuss the following questions in groups and write down your answers.

1. What's the principle of a automobile navigation system?

2. What does a typical in-dash navigation system consist of?

3. How many types of in-car navigation systems are there?

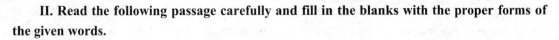
II. Read the following passage carefully and fill in the blanks with the proper forms of the given words.

factory	*monitor*	*parking*	*consist*	*connection*
usually	*playback*	*watch*	*complex*	*output*

If you want to maintain the _____ look of your dash and add the convenience of a large fold out _____, look for an in-dash navigation system. A typical in-dash navigation system _____ of a car stereo with a built-in monitor, a hideaway connection box that contains A/V inputs and _____, and an external GPS antenna. The stereo mounts in the factory stereo slot in your dash. The hideaway box is _____ mounted behind the dash or under a front seat. In addition to CD _____ and AM/FM reception, most in-dash systems include DVD playback, so you can _____ a movie on the built-in screen when parked. Installation of an in-dash system, can be _____, as they require _____ to power, ground, the vehicle speed sensor and the _____ brake.

C. Translation

I. Translate the following sentences into Chinese.

1. Removing your seat could deactivate your vehicle's SRS system.

2. In-dash Navigation Shopping Guide for more tips on how to choose an in-dash system.

3. Pioneer claims to be the first with a GPS-based auto navigation system in 1990.

II. Translate the following sentences into English.

1. 汽车通信系统就是驾驶员在驾车中能与其他人进行自由和安全交流的一种系统。

2. 当前的导航系统包括两部分：全球定位系统和车辆自动导航系统。

3. 汽车导航设备一般包含GPS天线、集成显示屏幕和功能按键的主机及语音输出设备。

Reading Material

Read the following passages and answer the questions according to the information given in the passages.

Passage One   Automobile Communication

Automobile communication systems are systems that allow motorists to communicate freely and safely with others while driving. Such systems typically use voice as the main method of communication, and can be built from simple devices such as walkie-talkies, cellular phones, or more sophisticated devices specifically made to address the needs of the system. The desirability of vehicular communication systems arises in scenarios where a motorist needs information (e.g. directions or notification of a flat-tire), and wants to send a message to a nearby motorist.

Overview

The underlying motivation for vehicular communication systems is convenience. Take the scenario of a motorist driving in a new, unfamiliar area. He is looking to get to his friend's house, but has taken a wrong turn and now he is lost. Does he stop and get out to ask for directions? This may seem like a logical solution, but it poses an inconvenience to the motorist. Moreover, chances are that there will be other nearby drivers who are local to the area and can easily direct him.

Although the driver could receive the directions to his destination, he does not have the means to communicate with another nearby motorist whom he does not know. This is the type of situation where a vehicular communication system is designed to address.

Other communication systems have been developed worldwide to support a vast assortment of needs. For instance, the cellular phone industry in recent history has experienced massive growth, from 7.6 million subscribers in 1991 (in the U.S. alone) to more than 120 million in 2001. Currently it is estimated that 2/3 of adult Americans own a cell phone. However, despite the popularity of cell phones and other technologies such as E-mail or Internet chat, none of these technologies can adequately be used to build an effective intra-vehicular voice communication system. These systems are meant for, person-to-person communication rather than vehicle- to-vehicle. Moreover, they require prior kowledge or some means of identifying the other person to contact. Thus, another key motivation for creating such vehicular communication systems is that they have not yet been developed.

State of the Art

Cellular phones are a popular wireless communication method for drivers today. Two friends who are traveling to the same destination can keep in contact with each other, relaying information regarding their location and estimated time of arrival. However, with regard to vehicular communication systems, cellular phone technology is inadequate. Cell phones have been shown to detract from the visual attention of the driver, possibly leading to more accidents. Additionally, in order for two people to communicate using cell phones, one person must know the other person's phone number. Thus, cell phones lack the ability to address a core competency of vehicular communication systems the ability for a driver to safely communicate with any other driver, regardless of their identity. The system like ESIT rack give the alternative with handsfree communication, so the vehicle can only call to one number, or received from any number.

Other devices such as walkie-talkies can address this problem by allowing messages to be broadcasted using radio waves, but have an inherent flaw. By design, walkie-talkies are half-duplex-in other words, a user cannot both forward and receive messages simultaneously. Moreover, walkie-talkies operate on low radio frequencies which can easily be intercepted, jeopardizing the confidentiality of the message.

Integrated automobile devices like OnStar have begun to make a presence on U.S. markets, with automobile manufacturers like GM offering them as options on their vehicles. The third party companies use these devices to offer services such as directions and emergency assistance to their customers. Although these devices may add an extra level of safety and peace of mind, they do not offer drivers the freedom to communicate with each other.

Questions

1. What is the automotive comunication network?
2. What's the function of the navigation system?
3. How does the cellular phone work?

Passage Two   A Trouble Shooting to the Front-Wheel Drive Car

My front-wheel drive car makes a clicking sound when turning. Is anything wrong? Yes. A clicking sound when turning is one of the classic symptoms of a worn or damaged "constant velocity" (CV) joint. Your car has four such joints on the two front axles: two inboard joints and two outboard joints. The outboard joints are the ones that make a clicking sound when they go bad.

Inside the joint are six steel balls, positioned in grooves between an inner race and an outer housing. The balls are held in position by a cage that looks something like a wide bracelet with windows or slots cut in it. When the joint is new, the balls fit tightly into the cage windows. But as the joint accumulates miles, the cage windows become worn and allow the balls to rattle around. The grooves in the inner race and outer housing also wear, which further contributes to noise.

When driving straight, a worn CV joint is usually quiet (constant noise would indicate a bad wheel bearing or other problem). But when the wheels are turned to either side, the joint bends cause the balls to click as they slide around in their cage windows and grooves. The noise is usually the loudest when backing up with the wheels turned. Repacking the joint with grease won't help because the joint is worn and needs to be replaced.

The "normal" life of a CV joint is usually 100,000 miles or more. But a joint can fail prematurely if the rubber boot that surrounds it is damaged or develops a leak.

CV Joint Boots

The boot, which is made of rubber or hard plastic, serves two purposes: it keeps the joint's vital supply of special grease inside, and it keeps dirt and water out. After five or six years of service, it's usual for the boot to develop age cracks or splits. Boots can also be damaged by road hazards or a careless tow truck operator who uses J-hooks to tow your vehicle.

Once the boot seal is broken, the inside grease quickly leaks out. Starved for lubrication, the CV joint soon fails. Dirt and water can also enter the boot and contaminate any grease that's left inside. Either way, a damaged boot is bad news for the joint.

CV joint boots should be inspected periodically (when the oil is changed is a good time) to make sure they are not cracked or torn, and that the clamps are tight. If you see grease on the outside of the boot, it is leaking and needs to be replaced (the sooner the better). If a clamp is loose and the boot is leaking grease at one end, the clamp needs to be replaced.

Original equipment boots are a one-piece design, which means the driveshaft and CV joint have to be removed from the vehicle and disassembled to replace a bad boot. However, there are aftermarket "split-boots" designed for easy do-it-yourself installation. The split-boots eliminate the need to remove and disassemble the joint and driveshaft. You simply cut off the old boot, clean out as much of the old grease as possible from the joint, pack the joint with fresh high temperature CV joint grease (never ordinary chassis grease), then install the new boot. Most split-boots have a seam that is glued together. The seam must not have any grease smeared on it and the glue must be applied carefully for a good seal. Also, the vehicle must not be driven until

the glue has cured (about an hour or so).

NOTE: Most professional mechanics do not use split-boots because they don't think a split-boot is as reliable or as long-lived as a one-piece original equipment style boot, and they don't like the idea of installing a new boot on a questionable joint.

By the time a damaged or leaky boot is noticed, the joint has usually lost most of its grease and/or been contaminated by dirt. Unless the joint is removed, disassembled, cleaned and inspected, there's no way to know if it is still in good enough condition to remain in service. If it's making noise, replacing the boot would be a waste of time because the joint is bad and needs to be replaced (most new joints come with a new boot, clamps and grease). But even if the joint isn't making any noise, it may still have wear or internal damage that will soon cause it to fail.

WARNING: A CV joint failure can cause loss of steering control under certain circumstances. If the joint locks up, it can prevent the wheels from being turned.

Questions

1. What's the "constant velocity" (CV) joint?
2. What's the function of the CV Joint Boots?
3. My front-wheel drive car makes a clicking sound when turning. Is anything wrong with it?

Unit 9　Frame and Suspension

The frame is a load-carrying beam structure consisting of tough steel sections welded, riveted, or bolted together. The frame looks like a steel ladder, though it sometimes has an X shape for extra strength. It forms a foundation for the car body and the parts of the several systems.

The frame of an automobile provides the support for the engine, body and transmission members. The frame transmits the load through suspension system and axles to the wheels. The frame's function is that of a beam, augmenting the body strength and stiffness, both in bending and in torsion. It withstands the static and dynamic loads within permissible deflection. It should be stiff and strong to resist the severe twisting and bending forces to which it is subjected to during motion of the vehicle on the road.

The frame is a fabrication of box, tubular, channel, angle, sections etc. The cross members reinforce the frame and also provide support for the engine and wheels. The frame is up swept at the front and rear and it may be having a lower height in the center for lowering the center of gravity of the vehicle. The frame is made narrow at the front end to have a better steering lock. The wider frame at the rear end provides more space for the body etc.

The engine is attached to the three or four place. To prevent the noise and vibrations of the engine through the frame rubber pads or washers are placed in between the engine and the frame.

Some of the modern cars use the body itself as a frame. No separate frame is provided on which the body is to be placed. The lower plate of the body is a steel pressing and reinforced with suitable member. To the lower body plate, suspension system is attached which transmits the weight of the body and other components to the axles and wheels.

The frame of the vehicle is attached to the rear and front wheel and axles with the help of spring and shock absorbers. In some cases, torsion bar is also used. Leaf springs and helical coil springs are generally used. Springs, torsion bar and other components necessary for jointing purposes are called the members of the suspension system.

The function of the suspension system is to absorb the road shocks and to prevent them from being transmitted to the other components of the vehicle, as shown in Figure 3-10. They protect the components from impact and dynamic working and their life is increased. The occupants of the vehicle are not subjected to the jerks due to the presence of the suspension system and their journey becomes much smoother and less tiring. The suspension system maintains the stability of the vehicle during pitching or rolling in motion.

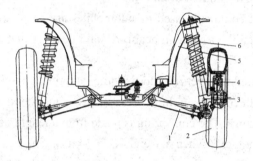

Figure 3-10　A Front-Suspension System Using Coil Springs

1—transverse arm　2—wheel　3—steering knuckle　4—shock absorber　5—frame　6—coil spring

The suspension system supports the weight of the engine, transmission, car body, and whatever the car body is carrying. This system has parts that link the wheels and tires to the frame or unit body. Springs are the key part of the suspension. They absorb the shocks of the road surface so that passengers can have a comfortable ride.

There are two basic suspension systems in use today. One is the solid leaf spring axle; the other is the independent suspension using long and short swinging arms. There are various adaptations of these systems, but the basic principles are the same.

The solid axle suspension uses a solid steel dead axle (does not turn with wheels) with a leaf spring at each side. The wheels swivel on each end via a pivot arrangement between the axle and the wheel spindle.

With independent suspension, each wheel is free to move up and down with minimum (the least attainable) effect on the other wheel. There is also far less twisting motion imposed on the frame.

The Front Suspension

The front suspension is more complicated than the rear suspension. This is because the front wheels must move in several different directions. The wheel must move up and down with the suspension and turn left to right with the steering. Since the car goes in the direction in which the

front wheels point, the alignment of the front wheels is important. The wheels must point in just the right direction for the car to move straight down the road and turn properly.

Practically modern cars use the independent front suspension in which each front is independently supported by a coil, torsion-bar, or leaf spring. In this system, each wheel mounts separately to the frame and has its own individual spring and shock absorber. Thus the wheels act independently of one another, when one wheel hits a bump or hole in the road, the other wheel does not deflect.

The Rear Suspension

The rear suspension may be of the solid axle or independent design. May cars have solid axle rear suspension. Either design may have different kinds of springs, including torsion bars. However, the coil spring and leaf spring types are most popular.

Leaf springs, Coil springs and Torsion bar

The leaf springs most commonly used in automobiles are made up of several long plates or leaves. The leaf spring acts like a flexible beam. A solid beam strong enough to support the car weight would not be very flexible.

The leaf spring mounted transversally does require additional bracing, control arms and strut rods are therefore used with coil spring. In the rear-suspension systems of many cars, coil springs are used instead of leaf springs. The coil spring is made from a length of steel rod. The coil spring is very elastic and will compress when a weight is put on it. The heavier the weight, the more spring will compress.

The coil springs are assembled between spring seats in the car frame and pads on the axle housing. Two control arms or links are used. They are attached upward or downward movement of the axle housing with respect to the car frame. They prevent side movement or forward and backward movement.

In the torsion-bar front-suspension system, two steel bars serve as the springs. The end of the bar is locked the across member or to the body. The other end of the bars is attached to the lower control arms. In operation, the lower control arms pivot up and down, twisting the torsion bars. The effect is very similar to the actions of the coil and leaf springs. Torsion bars that run across the car are called transverse torsion bars. When the torsion bars are installed, they run from front to rear on the car, they are called longitudinal torsion bars.

Shock Absorber

In the past, a wide variety of direct and indirect shock absorbing devices were used to control the spring action of passenger cars. Today, direct and double-acting hydraulic shock absorbers struts have almost universal application. Shock absorbers are filled with fluid. In operation, wheel movement causes the shock absorber to force this fluid through small openings. Since fluid can pass through restricted openings rather slowly, this puts a restraint on wheel and spring movement. The restraint imposed prevents excessive wheel movement. It also damps the spring oscillations quickly after the hole or bump is passed.

Words and Expressions

1. frame [freim] *n.* 车架；结构

2. assemble [ə'sembl] *v.* 装配

3. alignment [ə'lainmənt] *n.* 呈直线，准直

4. transverse [træns'və:s] *adj.* 横向的

5. longitudinal ['lɔndʒi'tju:dinəl] *adj.* 纵向的

6. beam [bi:m] *n.* 梁，横梁

7. elastic [i'læstik] *adj.* 弹性的，有弹力的

8. coil [kɔil] *n.* 线圈，螺旋弹簧

9. front suspension　前悬架

10. rear suspension　后悬架

11. torsion bar　扭杆弹簧

12. coil spring　螺旋弹簧

13. leaf spring　钢板弹簧

14. shock absorber　减震器

Notes

1. The frame's function is that of a beam, augmenting the body strength and stiffness, both in bending and in torsion.

车架的作用是增加车身的强度和刚度，以承受弯曲和扭曲载荷。

2. The wheels swivel on each end via a pivot arrangement between the axle and the wheel spindle.

通过装在车桥和轮轴之间的驱动轴，两端的车轮可以转动。

3. There is also far less twisting motion imposed on the frame.

车架的扭动也会大大减少。

Exercises

A. Vocabulary

I. Translate the following expressions into Chinese.

1. rated suspension spring capacity

2. front and rear springs

3. rear axle assembly

4. sprung weight and unsprung weight

5. riding comfort

6. solid axle beam

7. single-leaf spring

8. rear axle housing

9. compression type coil spring

10. MacPherson strut suspension system

II. Identify the English names of the battery according to the picture.

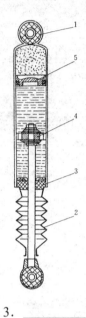

1. _____ 2. _____ 3. _____ 4. _____ 5. _____

B. Comprehension

I. Discuss the following questions in groups and write down your answers.

1. What types of springs are used in suspension?

_____

2. What are the advantages of the torsion bar?

_____

3. How does the shock absorber work?

_____

II. Read the following passage carefully and fill in the blanks with the proper forms of the given words.

fille	prevent	variety	restrict
absorber	damp	movement	bump

In the past, a wide _____ of direct and indirect shock absorbing devices were used to control the spring action of passenger cars. Today, direct, double-acting hydraulic shock _____ struts have almost universal application. Shock absorbers are _____ with fluid. In operation, wheel movement causes the shock absorber to force this _____ through small openings. Since fluid can pass through _____ openings rather slowly, this puts a restraint on wheel and spring _____. The restraint imposed _____ excessive wheel movement. It also _____ the spring oscillations quickly after the hole or _____ is passed.

C. Translation

I. Translate the following sentences into Chinese.

1. It also damps out the spring oscillations quickly after the hole or bump is passed.

2. The coil springs are assembled between spring seats in the car frame and pads on the axle housing.

3. The front suspension is more complicated than the rear suspension.

II. Translate the following sentences into English.

1. 实际上，现代轿车都使用独立前悬架。在这种结构中，每个前轮都由螺旋弹簧、扭杆弹簧或钢板弹簧独立支撑。

2. 钢板弹簧是横向悬架，需有额外的支撑，因此要使用控制臂和横摆臂。

3. 由于油液通过受封限制的孔隙时速度很慢，就对车轮和弹簧的运动产生了阻碍作用。

Reading Material

Read the following passages and answer the questions according to the information given in the passages.

Passage One   The MacPherson Strut Suspension

The MacPherson strut suspension has become very popular on both imported and American vehicles. The MacPherson strut suspension uses a single lower control arm connected to a long, tubular assembly called a strut. The shock absorber, strut and spindle are a combined unit that is supported by the coil spring at the upper end and by the lower control arm at the bottom. A ball joint is attached to the lower part of the spindle. The lower control arm is sometimes referred to as a track control arm or transverse link. The lower arm is held in position by a sway bar and frame-mounted rod called a strut rod, or by a stabilizer bar that functions as a combined strut rod and sway bar.

In the strut assembly, the shock absorber is called a cartridge and fits inside the strut housing. A metal dust cover is used on some units to protect the strut cartridge assembly. A coil spring is held in place by a lower spring seat welded to the strut housing and an upper spring seat bolted to the shock absorber piston rod. The upper mount is bolted to the vehicle body, through two or three studs that go through the vehicle shock tower or fender well. A rubber bumper fits on the piston rod and protects it in case the shock absorber is compressed to its limit.

Some vehicles use a suspension system described as a modified MacPherson strut. This suspension has a lower control arm and coil spring similar to that used on the shaft, long arm suspension. Instead of an upper control arm, a strut assembly connects the top of the steering knuckle to the body. In this case, the strut does not have a spring attached to it. The strut acts as the upper control arm and shock absorber.

Questions

1. What's the role of the sway bar?

2. Why is MacPherson is used widely?

3. Please describe the construction of MacPherson suspension.

Passage Two Shock Absorbers Replacement

You need new shocks (struts) if your original shocks (struts) are worn out, damaged or leaking. Leaking is easy enough to see (just look for oil or wetness on the outside of the shock or strut) as is damage (broken mount, badly dented housing, etc.). But wear is often more of a subjective thing to judge. There are also instances where the original equipment shocks may not be worn, damaged or leaking, but may not be adequate for the job they're being asked to do. In such cases, upgrading the suspension with stronger, stiffer or some type of special shock (or strut) may be recommended to improve handling, for towing trailer, hauling overloads or other special uses.

Shocks and struts do not require replacing at specific mileage intervals like filters or spark plugs, but they do wear out and eventually have to be replaced. How long a set of original equipment shocks will last is depending on anybody's guess. Some original equipment shocks may be getting weak after only 30,000 or 40,000 miles. Struts usually last upwards of 50,000 or 60,000 miles.

But when exactly a shock or strut needs to be replaced is hard to say. Because the damping characteristics of shocks and struts deteriorate gradually over time, the decline in ride control often passes unnoticed. So by the time to think you need new shocks or struts, it usually passed the point when they should have been replaced.

One way to evaluate your need for new shocks or struts is to consider how your vehicle has been handling and riding lately. Does it bounce excessively when driving on rough roads or after hitting a bump? Does the nose dip when braking? Does the body roll or sway excessively when cornering or driving in crosswinds? Does the suspension bottom out when backing out of the driveway or when hauling extra passengers or weight?

A "bounce test" is still a valid means of checking the dampening ability of shocks and struts. If the suspension continues to gyrate more than one or two times after rocking and releasing the bumper or body, your shocks or struts are showing their age and need to be replaced.

Why Replace Them?

Weak shocks and struts won't necessarily create a driving hazards if you continue to drive on them, but there are studies that show worn shocks increase the distance it takes to stop a vehicle on a rough surface. Increased body sway due to weak shocks or struts can also increase the risk of skidding on wet or slick surfaces.

Worn shocks and struts also increase suspension wear (though marginally) but can have an effect on tire wear.

The reason why most people decide to have worn shocks or struts replaced, however, is to improve overall ride quality. If you're sick of bouncing and rocking on rough roads, a new set of shocks or struts will firm up your suspension and restore proper ride control.

If you're interested in performance handling, you can upgrade to premium "gas" charged shocks or struts. These are charged with high pressure nitrogen gas to help minimize foaming in the hydraulic fluid inside the shock. This lessens "fade" on rough roads and helps the vehicle maintain better ride control when cornering.

There are also "heavy-duty" replacement shocks and struts that have larger diameter pistons than stock. These too, provide increases resistance for greater control—but may be a little too harsh for everyday driving. So some shocks have special valving or adjustable valving that allows the amount of resistance to vary.

Another option to consider if you tow a trailer or haul extra cargo is to overload or air-assist shocks. Overload shocks have a coil spring around them to increase the load carrying capacity of the suspension (these also tend to ride stiffer than standard replacement shocks). Air-assist shocks have an adjustable air bladder that acts like a spring to carry extra weight. With this type of shock, air can be added on an "as needed" basis when hauling extra weight.

Replacement

Shocks and struts are generally replaced in pairs—though this isn't absolutely necessary if only one shock or strut is leaking or has suffered damage at a low mileage.

Shocks are a popular do-it-yourself item on most vehicles because they're fairly easy to replace. But struts are not. Most struts require a fair amount of suspension disassembly. What's more, the wheels must usually be realigned after replacing a strut. For this reason, you're probably better off letting a professional replace your struts.

Questions

1. What's the role of the shock absorbers?

2. Why should we replace shock absorbers?

3. How do you know if your vehicle really needs new shock absorbers?

Unit 10   Electronic Stability Program

Electronic Stability Program (ESP) is a computerized technology that improves the safety of a vehicle's stability by detecting and minimizing skids. When ESP detects loss of steering control, ESC automatically applies the brakes to help "steer" the vehicle where the driver intends to go. Braking is automatically applied to individual wheels, such as the outer front wheel to counter oversteer, or the inner rear wheel to counter understeer.

During normal driving, ESP works in the background, continuously monitoring steering and vehicle direction. ESP compares the driver's intended direction (by measuring steering angle) to the vehicle's actual direction (by measuring lateral acceleration, vehicle rotation (yaw), and individual road wheel speeds).

ESC only intervenes when it detects loss of steering control, i.e. when the vehicle is not going where the driver is steering. This may happen, for example, when skidding during emergency evasive swerves, understeer or oversteer during poorly judged turns on slippery roads, or hydroplaning. ESP calculates (since all states are not readily available, this calculation is

actually an "estimation" according to the control terminology) the direction of the skid, and then applies the brakes to individual wheels asymmetrically in order to create torque about the vehicle's vertical axis, opposing the skid and bringing the vehicle back in line with the driver's commanded direction.

ESP can work on any surface, from dry pavement to frozen lakes. It reacts to and corrects skidding much faster and more effectively than the typical human driver, often before the driver is even aware of any imminent loss of control. In fact, this led to some concern that ESP could allow drivers to become overconfident in their vehicle's handling and their own driving skills. For this reason, ESP systems typically inform the driver when they intervene, so that the driver knows that the vehicle's handling limits have been approached. Most activate a dashboard indicator light and/or alert tone; some intentionally allow the vehicle's corrected course to deviate very slightly from the driver-commanded direction, even if it is possible to more precisely match it.

Indeed, all ESP manufacturers emphasize that the system is not a performance enhancement nor a replacement for safe driving practices, but rather a safety technology to assist the driver in recovering from dangerous situations.

ESP incorporates yaw rate control into the anti-lock braking system (ABS). Yaw is rotation around the vertical axis, i.e. spinning left or right. Anti-lock brakes enable ESP to brake individual wheels. Many ESP systems also incorporate a traction control system (TCS or ASR), which senses drive-wheel slip under acceleration and individually brakes the slipping wheel or wheels and/or reduces excess engine power until control is regained. However, ESP achieves a different purpose than ABS or Traction Control.

The ESP system uses several sensors to determine what the driver wants (input). Other sensors indicate the actual state of the vehicle (response). The control algorithm compares driver input to vehicle response and decides, when necessary, to apply brakes and/or reduce throttle by the amounts calculated through the state space (set of equations used to model the dynamics of the vehicle). The ESP controller can also receive data from and issue commands to other controllers on the vehicle such as an all wheel drive system or an active suspension system to improve vehicle stability and controllability.

The sensors used for ESP have to send data at all times in order to detect possible defects as soon as possible. They have to be resistant to possible forms of interference (rain, holes in the road, etc.). The most important sensors are as follows:

(1) Steering wheel angle sensor: determines the driver's intended rotation, i.e. where the driver wants to steer.

(2) Yaw rate sensor: measures the rotation rate of the car, i.e. how much the car is actually turning. The data from the yaw sensor is compared with the data from the steering wheel angle sensor to determine regulating action.

(3) Lateral acceleration sensor: is often based on the Hall effect and measures the lateral acceleration of the vehicle.

(4) Wheel speed sensor: measures the wheel speed.

Other sensors can include the following:

(1) Longitudinal acceleration sensor: similar to the lateral acceleration sensor in design but can offer additional information about road pitch and also provide another source of vehicle acceleration and speed.

(2) Roll rate sensor: similar to the yaw rate sensor in design but improves the fidelity of the controller's vehicle model and correct for errors when estimating vehicle behavior from the other sensors alone.

ESP uses a hydraulic modulator to assure that each wheel receives the correct brake force. A similar modulator is used in ABS. ABS needs to reduce pressure during braking, only. ESP additionally needs to increase pressure in certain situations and an active vacuum brake booster unit may be utilized in addition to the hydraulic pump to meet these demanding pressure gradients.

The heart of the ESP system is the Electronic Control Unit (ECU). The various control techniques are embedded in it. Often, the same ECU is used for diverse systems at the same time (ABS, traction control system, climate control, etc.). The input signals are sent through the input-circuit to the digital controller. The desired vehicle state is determined based upon the steering wheel angle, its gradient and the wheel speed. Simultaneously, the yaw sensor measures the actual state. The controller computes the needed brake or acceleration force for each wheel and directs via the driver circuits the valves of the hydraulic modulator. Via a CAN interface the ECU is connected with other systems such as ABS so as order to avoid giving contradictory commands.

Many ESP systems have an "off" override switch so the driver can disable ESP, which may be desirable when badly stuck in mud or snow, or driving on a beach, or if using a smaller-sized spare tire which would interfere with the sensors. However, ESP defaults to "On" when the ignition is re-started. Some ESP systems that lack an "off switch", such as on many recent Toyota and Lexus vehicles, can be temporarily disabled through an undocumented series of brake pedal and handbrake operations. Furthermore, unplugging a wheel speed sensor is another method of disabling most ESP systems.

Words and Expressions

1. stability [stə'biliti]　*n.* 稳定性

2. automatically　[,ɔ:tə'mætikəli]　*adv.* 自动地

3. understeer ['ʌndəstiə]　*n.* 驾驶盘失灵

4. monitor ['mɔnitə]　*n.* 监控器

5. actual　['æktjuəl]　*adj.* 实在的

6. yaw [jɔ:]　*n.* 偏航；偏离角

7. emergency [i'mə:dʒənsi]　*n.* 紧急情况

8. evasive [i'veisiv] *adj.* 逃避的

9. hydroplaning   湿路打滑

10. deviate ['di:vieit] *vi.* 脱离；越轨

11. road wheel   车轮

12. lateral acceleration   横向加速度

13. override switch   超越控制开关

Notes

1. Braking is automatically applied to individual wheels, such as the outer front wheel to counter oversteer, or the inner rear wheel to counter understeer.

制动力自动作用在某个车轮上，比如作用在外侧前轮防止转向过多，或作用在内后轮上防止转向不足。

2. It reacts to and corrects skidding much faster and more effectively than the typical human driver, often before the driver is even aware of any imminent loss of control.

这一系统常常在驾驶员意识到汽车即将失去控制之前比典型的人类驾驶员更能及时有效地纠正侧滑。

3. Lateral acceleration sensor is often based on the Hall effect and measures the lateral acceleration of the vehicle.

横向加速度传感器通常基于霍尔效应，测量汽车的横向加速度。

Exercises

A. Vocabulary

Translate the following expressions into Chinese.

1. electronic stability program

2. steering control

3. background

4. slippery road

5. frozen lake

B. Comprehension

I. Discuss the following questions in groups and write down your answers.

1. Describe driver assistant system briefly.

_____

_____

2. What does driver assistant systems include?

_____

_____

3. What advantages does a parking assistant system have?

_____

_____

II. Read the following passage carefully and fill in the blanks with the proper forms of the given words.

> *effectively*   *react*   *control*   *handle*   *approach*
> *surface*   *intervene*   *tone*   *correct*   *precisely*

ESP can work on any ____ from dry pavement to frozen lakes. It ____ to and corrects skidding much faster and more ____ than the typical human driver, often before the driver is even aware of any imminent loss of ____. In fact, this led to some concern that ESP could allow drivers to become overconfident in their vehicle's ____ and their own driving skills. For this reason, ESP systems typically inform the driver when they ____, so that the driver knows that the vehicle's handling limits have been ____. Most activate a dashboard indicator light and/or alert ____; some intentionally allow the vehicle's ____ course to deviate very slightly from the driver-commanded direction, even if it is possible to more ____ match it.

C. Translation

I. Translate the following sentences into Chinese.

1. ESP uses a hydraulic modulator to assure that each wheel receives the correct brake force.

2. ESC automatically applies the brakes to help "steer" the vehicle where the driver intends to go.

3. During normal driving, ESP works in the background, continuously monitoring steering and vehicle direction.

II. Translate the following sentences into English.

1. 驾驶员辅助系统的目的是使车辆具有感知其周围环境的能力。
2. 紧急制动的车辆具有探测系统，它会发现障碍物的位置和车辆的运动方向。
3. 传感器会为车辆提供这些技术参数。

Reading Material

Read the following passages and answer the questions according to the information given in the passages.

Passage One   ESC

In 1987, the earliest innovators of ESC, Mercedes-Benz, BMW and Toyota introduced their first traction control systems. Traction control works by applying individual wheel braking and throttle to keep traction while accelerating but unlike ESC, it is not designed to aid in steering.

In 1990, Mitsubishi released the Diamante (Sigma) in Japan. It featured a new electronically controlled active trace & traction control system (the first integration of these two systems in the world) that Mitsubishi developed. Simply named TCL in 1990, the system has since evolved into Mitsubishi's modern Active Skid and Traction Control (ASTC) system or ESC. Developed to help the driver maintain the intended line through a corner, an onboard computer monitored several vehicle operating parameters through various sensors. When too much throttle has been used when taking a curve, engine output and braking are automatically regulated to ensure the proper line through a curve and to provide the proper amount of traction under various road

surface conditions. While conventional traction control systems at the time featured only a slip control function, Mitsubishi's newly developed TCL system had a preventive (active) safety function which improved the course tracing performance by automatically adjusting the traction force (called "trace control") thereby restraining the development of excessive lateral acceleration while turning. Although not a "true" modern stability control system, trace control monitors steering angle, throttle position and individual wheel speeds although there is no yaw input. The TCL system's standard wheel slip control function enables better traction on slippery surfaces during cornering. In addition to the TCL system's individual effect, it also works together with Diamante's electronic controlled suspension and four-wheel steering that Mitsubishi had equipped to improve total handling and performance.

BMW, working with Robert Bosch GmbH and Continental Automotive Systems, developed a system to reduce engine torque to prevent loss of control and applied it to the entire BMW model line for 1992. From 1987 to 1992, Mercedes-Benz and Robert Bosch GmbH co-developed a system called Elektronisches Stabilitätsprogramm (Germany "Electronic Stability Programme" trademarked as ESP) a lateral slippage control system, the electronic stability control (ESC).

Questions

1. What's the function of adaptive light control?

2. How many kinds of driver assistant system are there? What are they?

3. When did BMW develop a system to reduce engine torque?

Passage Two   The Bosch Mot Series Motortesters

This article introduces the Bosch MOT 240, 250 and 251 Motortesters with digital ignition stacked and multi-oscilloscope.

MOT 240 — with liquid-crystal display, portable and independent of mains (powered by vehicle battery). The ideal engine tester featuring a digital memory oscilloscope for mobile service.

MOT 240 — with mains adapter, equipment trolley, DIN A4 printer and exhaust gas analyzer — the Motortester is also designed for the exhaust gas analysis (AU) station.

MOT 250 — the convenient, mobile Motortester with cable boom, lockable tool cabinet and spacious cabinets.

MOT 251 — The compact Motortester complete with space-saving equipment trolley and swiveling monitor.

MOT 240, MOT 250 and MOT 251 clearly informed about brands, types and systems.

All MOTs are compatible with exhaust gas analysis due to RS 232 interface.

The Motortesters 240, 250 and 251 with digital oscilloscope plus measuring unit with connecting cables and sensors. The oscilloscope has a picture memory with a capacity to recall 32 display pictures. The Motortesters are therefore the universal measuring devices for all necessary measurements during tests of engine and electronic system. This enables selective trouble — shooting, e.g. on various ignition and fuel management systems.

These Motortesters can be upgraded and networked with other Bosch testers (PDR record printer, ETT 008.21/…8.42 exhaust gas tester, input keyboard for exhaust gas analysis).

Via 3 serial (RS 232) interfaces using an additional interface switch, it is also possible to connect the RTT 100/110 exhaust gas smoke meter.

When combined with an appropriate exhaust gas analyzer or smoke meter, these MOTs can also be used for the exhaust gas analysis on spark-ignition and diesel engines.

All measurement functions are grouped in special test programs appropriately for use in the following practice:

- Engine test;
- Ignition;
- Multi-test;
- Stacked oscilloscope;
- Exhaust gas (including exhaust gas analysis);
- Multi-oscilloscope;
- Injection test.

The measured values and the oscilloscope pattern are shown on the digital screen. As many as three measured values are shown with a small oscilloscope pattern or the large representation of the oscillogram is shown with the engine speed.

All measured values and the oscilloscope pattern can be printed out in clear, customer-friendly form in DIN A4 size with the PDR 200 record printer.

The sensors and connecting cables are clearly arranged in the frame of the measuring unit in brackets and plug-in sockets.

Power is from the mains and is automatically adapted to all voltages from 100v to 240v at 50/60 Hz. The MOT 240 can also be powered from the vehicle battery. The engine tests are operated with seven hardkeys (keys with a fixed function) and six softkeys (keys with a variable function).

The hardkeys have the following functions: permanent short-circuiting (suppression of ignition), storage and read-out of measured values, operation of the report printer, information key and RETURN key for branching back from the current program, and changeover between operation for oscilloscope and measuring functions. Depending on the program selected, each of the six functions keys has a different function which is indicated by symbols on the screen.

An information key "i " can be used by the operator to access information and instructions for the respective measurement or operation, e.g. regarding the connection to the vehicle or the scope of the measuring functions.

All operating and system software is stored on the program module which is accessible from the outside. This means high flexibility in case changes are required to test new vehicle and ignition systems.

Testing includes the following:

- Engines with up to 12 cylinders with automatic recognition of cylinder number and ignition system;

- Ignition systems ranging from the contact-controlled ignition with one or two distributors to fully electronic ignition system with single-spark ignition coil (EFS) or dual-spark ignition coil control;
- Simultaneous display of up to three measured values together with a small oscillogram;
- Large representation of oscillogram together with engine speed.

Measuring functions are as follows:

- Engine speed via TDC sensors, No. 1 cylinder or signal from terminal 1;
- Ignition point with TDC sensor (with automatic recognition) or stroboscope;
- Dwell angle in % or degrees of distributor shaft and closing time in ms;
- Injection time or other times, measured at the valve or suitable measuring points;
- Automatic cylinder comparison, absolute or relative drop in engine speed;
- Dynamic compression measurement based on starter current;
- Voltages related to ground or floating, voltage of lambda sensor and at terminal 1, dynamic or static;
- Current of up to 1,000A or 20A with current-measuring pickup, up to 500mA with current-measuring shunt (both = special accessories);
- Resistances from milliohm to megaohm level;
- Temperature by means of oil temperature sensor;
- Primary and secondary ignition, shown as parade, raster or individual displays, in ignition systems with or without distributors;
- Signals from vehicle electrical and electronic systems as curves of voltage and current. This turns your MOTs into full-feature laboratory oscilloscopes;
- Memory mode with picture memory (32 displays) for examining irregularities in detail (sporadic defects).

The following are some tests actually displayed on a 12 screen (MOT 240: 10 screen) and represent just a small selection of the extensive capabilities of the MOTs: test programs supported by oscilloscope display of measured values.

Engine test includes the following:

- Measurement of battery voltage or the supply voltage of the ignition coil;
- Measurement of electric current, e.g. starter power, or temperature;
- Engine speed;
- Ripple content of alternator on oscilloscope or oscilloscope: primary side.

Measurement of ignition-primary side includes the following:

- Measurement of contact voltage or at terminal 1 (-) of ignition coil;
- Measurement of dwell angle in degrees of distributor shaft (_DS)or in %;
- Closing time in ms;
- Engine speed;
- Oscilloscope: primary side.

Measurements are performed per ignition circuit in ignition systems with two distributors or direct firing.

Measurement of ignition point includes the following:

- Absolute ignition advance;
- Relative/delta ignition advance;
- Engine speed;
- Oscilloscope: secondary side.

Cylinder comparison are as follows:

- Measurement of temperature and engine speed;
- Start button;
- Oscilloscope: secondary side measurement;
- Speed in RPM and % with and without delta HC;
- Dynamic compression measurement on basis of starter current.

Measurements are performed per ignition circuit in ignition systems with two distributors or direct firing.

Multitest are as follows:

- Voltage-related measurement (relative to engine earth);
- Measurement of electric current;
- Potential-free voltage measuring cable and measurement of current;
- Measurement of electrical resistance;
- Measurement of temperature;
- Zero calibration;
- Measurement of voltage or current using oscilloscope.

Injection test are as follows:

- Measurement of temperature;
- Lambda sensor voltage;
- Duration of injection;
- Pulse duty factor;
- Measurement of voltage using oscilloscope.

Exhaust gas test/process of exhaust gas analysis are as follows:

- Display of exhaust gas constituents in accordance with analyzer used;
- Measurement of oil temperature and engine speed;
- Adjustment of engine-specific data;
- Type of engine/number of cylinders;
- Various ignition systems;
- Various TDC sensor systems with position of marks;
- Automatic recognition of engine type;
- Memory fields for standard engine types.

Basic adjustments are as follows:

- Input of workshop address;
- Changeover of units of measurement;

- Selection printer driver for report driver and language;
- Input of report head for workshop address;
- Input of exhaust gas analysis testing agency;
- Selection of printout (test record or screen contents);
- Input of workshop address for PDR 200 report printer.

Information includes the information for each measurement.

Digital ignition oscilloscope with parade, stacked and individual display and multi-oscilloscope, each with picture memory (32 display) and curve measurement for precise signal analysis.

Ignition oscilloscope includes primary and secondary ignition voltage, shown as parade, stacked or individual displays in ignition systems with or without distributors.

Multi-oscilloscope includes the following:

- Recording of signals from electric and electronic vehicle systems to be displayed as curves of voltage or current;
- Injection signal measured with red multi-clip;
- Primary current of a TZ-I ignition system measured with a clamp-on pickup;
- Alternator ripple measured via the positive (red) battery terminal (B+).

Memory mode and measurement of signal curves includes the following:

- The memory mode, the measurement of signal curves and the adjustment menus are available in both ignition oscilloscope and multi-oscilloscope;
- Memory mode with forward and return picture memory (32 displays) for examining scope displays in detail, e.g. for evaluating defects;
- Measurement of signal curves during memory mode, e.g. measurement of combustion duration and combustion voltage in the secondary oscillogram.

Adjustment menus

- Change of X-and Y-deviation and displacement of the zero line for more accurate study of signals;
- Shift of start of display to align the signal curve, e.g. in the center of the screen;
- Selection of various trigger facilities to determine when the measurement is to begin (signal size, rising or falling slope, etc.).

Questions

1. What's a Bosch Motortesters?

2. How many types of Bosch Motortesters are there? What are they?

3. How do the Bosch Motortesters work?

Chapter 4　Electrical Equipment

Unit 1　Charging System

The charging system, as shown in Figure 4-1, provides electrical energy for all of the electrical components on the vehicle.

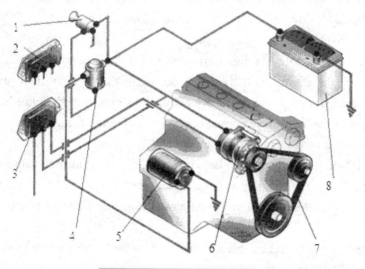

Figure 4-1　Charging System

1—ignition switch　2—power module　3—external voltage regulator
4—starter relay　5—starter　6—drive belt　7—alternator　8—battery

The main parts of the charging system include the battery; the alternator; the voltage regulator, which is usually integral to the alternator; a charge warning, or indicator light; and wiring that completes the circuits.

The battery provides the electrical energy for starting. It is an electrochemical device. The purpose of the battery is to store electrical energy. It does this by converting the electrical energy supplied to it into chemical energy so that when an electrical current is required the energy change is reversed.

Once the engine is running, the alternator supplies all electrical components of the vehicle. The alternator is an alternating current (AC) generator driven by engine power to produce electricity. A set of diodes in the rectifier allows the generated alternating current to pass in only one direction, thus converting the AC current into DC.

The voltage regulator prevents over-charging. It is necessary to control the maximum voltage

and current output developed by the alternator. This is done by using the regulator. The voltage regulator keeps the alternator voltage constant over the entire engine speed and under varying load conditions.

The most commonly used charging indicator device is a simple on/off warning lamp. It is normally off and can be designed to come on when the alternator is not satisfying electrical load required, not charging at all, or if voltage is either too high or too low. It also lights when the ignition switch is turned on, before the engine starts for a check of the lamp circuit. An ammeter is used on some vehicles instead of the warning light to inform the driver of the state of the charging system output.

If your battery is dead, keeping running down or cranking your engine slowly, you may have a charging problem. Likewise, if the alternator or battery warning light is on, or the amp or voltage gauge is reading low, this probably indicates a charging problem.

A quick way to check the charging system is to start the car and turn on the headlights. If the headlights are dim, it indicates the lights are running off the battery and that little or no juice is being produced by the alternator. If the lights get brighter as you rev the engine, it means the alternator is producing some current but may not be producing enough at idle to keep the battery properly charged. If the lights have normal brightness and don't change intensity as the engine is revved, your charging system is functioning normally.

You can also check the charging system by connecting the leads of a voltmeter to the battery. When the engine starts, the charging voltage should jump to about 14.5 or higher. If the reading doesn't change or rises less than a volt, you have a charging problem that will require further diagnosis.

Alternators are pretty rugged, but can succumb to excessive heat and overwork. They can also be damaged by sudden voltage overloads (as when someone attempts to jump to start a dead battery and crosses up the jumper connections or if someone disconnects a battery cable from the battery while the engine is running).

Sometimes alternators can partially fail. In the back of every alternator is a "diode trio" that converts the alternators AC (alternating current) output to DC (direct current). If one or more of these diodes fail, the alternator's amperage output will be reduced. It may continue to produce some current, but not enough to keep the battery fully charged — especially at idle or low speed.

Most service facilities have test equipment that can identify these kind of problems. So if you suspect a weak alternator, you should have it tested to see if it needs to be replaced.

Most service facilities do not repair or rebuild alternators because it's a waste of time and requires special parts. Most will replace your old unit with a new or remanufactured unit. Your old alternator is usually traded in or exchanged for a credit (so it can be remanufactured and sold to someone else).

CAUTION: If you're replacing an alternator yourself, always disconnect the battery before unhooking the wiring on the alternator. This step will eliminate the possibility of accidentally shorting out a hot ware and damaging something or starting a fire.

The alternator drive belt should be inspected at this time, and replaced if it is cracked, oil soaked, glazed, badly worn or otherwise damaged. The belt should be adjusted for proper tension by following the vehicle manufacturer's guidelines. Too much tension can overload the alternator's bearings and shorten the unit's life (as well as belt life), while too little tension may allow the belt to slip.

Words and Expressions

1. alternator ['ɔ:ltə(:)neitə] *n.* 交流发动机

2. electrochemical [i'lektrəu'kemikəl] *adj.* 电化学的，电化的

3. ammeter ['æmitə] *n.* 安培计，电流表

4. voltmeter ['vəult'mi:tə] *n.* 电压表，伏特计

5. intensity [in'tensiti] *n.* 激烈、强烈

6. diode ['daiəud] *n.* 二极管

7. headlight ['hedlait] *n.* 前大灯

8. rug [rʌg] *n.* 小地毯

9. eliminate [i'liminеit] *vt.* 消除

10. remanufacture [ri: 'mænju'fæktʃə] *n.* 再制造、改制

11. charging system   充电系统

12. chemical energy   化学能

13. alternating current   交流电

14. voltage gauge   电压表

15. over-charging   过充电

16. alternator drive belt   发电机皮带

17. start a fire   着火

18. vehicle manufacturer's guideline   车辆制造者指导规范

Notes

1. The battery does this by converting the electrical energy supplied to it into chemical energy so that when an electrical current is required the energy change is reversed.
蓄电池通过将供给的电能转变成化学能完成此项功能，而当需要电能时此转换反过来进行。

2. The most commonly used charging indicator device is a simple on/off warning lamp.
最常用的充电指示器是简单的开关警告灯。

3. It is necessary to control the maximum voltage and current output developed by the alternator.
限制最高电压和发电机的最大输出电流是必需的。

4. If you're replacing an alternator yourself, always disconnect the battery before unhooking

the wiring on the alternator.

如果你自己动手更换发电机，记住在解下发电机电缆之前要先和蓄电池断开。

5. Too much tension can overload the alternator's bearings and shorten the unit's life, while too little tension may allow the belt to slip.

发电机的皮带太紧会使得发电机轴承过载并缩短其寿命，而太松又会导致打滑。

Exercises

A. Vocabulary

I. Translate the following expressions into Chinese.

1. charging system

2. chemical energy

3. alternating current

4. voltage gauge

5. over-charging

6. alternator drive belt

7. starting a fire

8. warning lamp

9. direct current

10. charging indicator

II. Identify the English names of the battery according to the picture.

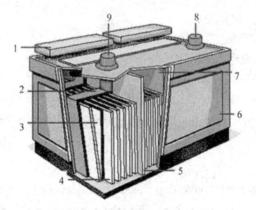

1. _____ 2. _____ 3. _____ 4. _____

5. _____ 6. _____ 7. _____ 8. _____

9. _____

B. Comprehension

I. Discuss the following questions in groups and write down your answers.

1. What is the charging system composed of ?

_____

_____

2. What's the function of the battery?

_____

_____

3. How do I know whether my alternator is charging properly?

_____

_____

II. Read the following passage carefully and fill in the blanks with the proper forms of the given words.

dim	normally	properly	headlight	current
alternator	intensity	idle	normal	engine

A quick way to check the charging system is to start the car and turn on the ____. If the headlights are ____, it indicates the lights are running off the battery and that little or no juice is being produced by the ____. If the lights get brighter as you rev the ____, it means the alternator is producing some ____ but may not be producing enough at ____ to keep the battery ____ charged. If the lights have ____ brightness and don't change ____ as the engine is revved, your charging system is functioning ____.

C. Translation

I. Translate the following sentences into Chinese.

1. Sometimes alternators can partially fail. In the back of every alternator is a "diode trio" that converts the alternators AC (alternating current) output to DC (direct current).

2. It is necessary to control the maximum voltage and current output developed by the alternator.

3. Most service facilities do not repair or rebuild alternators because it's too time consuming and requires special parts.

II. Translate the following sentences into English.

1. 最常用的充电指示器是简单的开关警告灯。充电系统包括蓄电池、发电机、电压调节器和充电报警或指示灯等。

2. 蓄电池的功能是为汽车中的许多系统和部件提供电能。

3. 电压调节器可以防止过充电。

Reading Material

Read the following passages and answer the questions according to the information given in the passages.

Passage One   The Fuse

A fuse is a protection device that is designed to blow if the ampere load in a circuit exceeds the "safe" limit for that circuit. Fuses are built with a specific ampere rating which is marked on the fuse. The wiring and design load of the circuit dictates the size of fuse that's required to protect the circuit. Circuits that draw a lot of power need fuses with high amp ratings (20 or 30

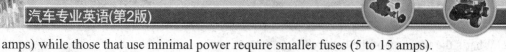

amps) while those that use minimal power require smaller fuses (5 to 15 amps).

When the current in a circuit exceeds the normal limit for whatever reason, the metal element in the fuse melts and opens the circuit stopping the flow of current. A short, for example, causes a runaway electrical current. If not stopped, wires can start to melt and things can catch on fire. So respect the amp ratings specified for fuses (which can usually be found in your vehicle owner's manual, on the fuse block or a fuse block reference decal).

What will happen if you install a fuse with the wrong amp rating? If you install a 20 amperes fuse in a circuit designed for 10 amps, you're asking for trouble. A difference of 10 amps might not sound like much, but it may be enough to fry a sensitive electronic component or to overheat wires to the point where the insulation may start to melt.

WARNING: Under no circumstances should you ever bypass or eliminate a fuse. No electrical circuit should ever be operated without fuse protection. This is extremely dangerous, especially if you've had problems with a fuse blowing before.

If a fuse keeps blowing, it usually means something is amiss in the circuit. The wiring should be checked along with the components in the circuit to determine if there's a short or other problem.

The fuse for the windshield wiper circuit, for example, may blow if ice or debris builds up in the cool areas and interferes with the movement of the wiper arms. If a fuse blows in a motor circuit (heater blower motor, cooling fan motor, power seat or window, electric fuel pump, etc.), it often indicates a shorted motor. If a fuse in a light circuit blows, look for wiring or connector shorts. Adding driving lights may also overtax the headlight circuit unless a separate circuit is provided for the driving lights. An A/C fuse will blow if the system is low on refrigerant and is working unusually hard, or if the compressor is hanging up. Stereo systems with high amp boosters should also have their own electrical circuit with fuse protection to avoid overloading the normal radio circuit.

Questions

1. Your car keeps blowing fuses. Should you install a larger fuse?

2. If a fuse keeps blowing, what does it usually mean?

3. Under what situation may the fuse for the windshield wiper circuit blow?

Passage Two   Battery Check

How can I tell if my battery is low and needs to be recharged?

The first and most likely indication of a low battery would be a hard starting problem caused by slow cranking. If the battery seems weak or fails to crank your engine normally, it may be low. To figure it out, you need to check the battery's "state of charge".

A battery is nothing more than a chemical storage device for holding electrons until they're needed to crank the engine or run the lights or other electrical accessories on your vehicle. Checking the battery's state of charge will tell you how much juice the battery has available for such purposes.

If your battery is low, it needs to be recharged, not only to restore full power, but also to prevent possible damage to the battery. Ordinary automotive lead-acid storage batteries must be kept at or near full charge to keep the cell plates from becoming "sulfated" (a condition that occurs if the battery is run down and left in a discharged condition for more than a few days). As sulfate builds up, it reduces the battery's ability to hold a charge and supply voltage. Eventually the battery becomes useless and must be replaced.

Checking the State of Charge

The charge level depends on the concentration of acid inside the battery. The stronger the concentration of acid in the water, the higher the specific gravity of the solution, and the higher the state of charge.

On batteries with removable caps, state of charge can be checked with a "hydrometer". Some hydrometers have a calibrated float to measure the specific gravity of the acid solution while others simply have a number of colored balls. On the kind with a calibrated float, a hydrometer reading of 1.265 (corrected for temperature) indicates a fully charged battery, 1.230 indicates a 75% charge, 1.200 indicates a 50% charge, 1.170 indicates a 25% charge, and 1.140 or less indicates a discharged battery. On the kind using floating balls, the number of balls that float tells you the approximate level of charge. All balls floating would indicate a fully charged battery, no balls floating would indicate a dead or fully discharged battery.

Some sealed-top batteries have a built-in hydrometer to indicate charge. The charge indicator only reads one cell, but usually shows the average charge for all battery cells. A green dot means the battery is 75% or more charged and is okay for use or further testing. No dot (a dark indicator) means the battery is low and should be recharged before it is returned to service or tested further. A clear or yellow indicator means the level of electrolyte inside has dropped too low, and the battery should be replaced.

On sealed-top batteries that do not have a built-in charge indicator, the state of charge can be determined by checking the battery's base or open circuit voltage with a digital voltmeter or multimeter. This is done by touching the meter leads to the positive and negative battery terminals while the ignition key is off.

A reading of 12.66 volts indicates a fully charged battery; 12.45 volts is 75% charged, 12.24 volts is 50% charged, and 12.06 volts is 25% charged.

Recharging the Battery

CAUTION: Do not attempt to recharge a battery with low (or frozen) electrolyte! Doing so risks blowing up the battery if the hydrogen gas inside is ignited by a spark.

Your charging system should be capable of recharging the battery if it is not fully discharged. Thirty minutes or so of normal driving should be enough.

If your battery is completely dead or extremely low, it should be recharged with a fast or slow charger. This will reduce the risk of overtaxing and damaging your vehicle's charging system. One or both battery cables should be disconnected from the battery prior to charging it with a charger. This will eliminate any risk of damage to your vehicle's electrical system or its onboard electronics.

Questions

1. How do you know if your battery is low and needs to be recharged?

2. How to check the state of charge?

3. How to recharge a battery?

Unit 2   Starting System

The starting system is a necessity for internal-combustion engines, because the Otto cycle requires the pistons already to be in motion before the ignition phase of the cycle. This means that the engine must be started in motion by an outside force before it can power itself.

Originally, a hand crank was used to start the engine, but it was inconvenient and rather hard work to crank the engine up to speed. It was also highly dangerous; when the engine did finally start up, the crank would begin to spin on its own at high speed. The operator had to pull away immediately or else risk a broken wrist.

The starting system provides the power to turn the internal combustion engine over until it can operate under its own power. To perform this task, the starting motor receives electrical power from the battery, and it converts this energy into mechanical energy, which transmits through the drive mechanism to the engine's flywheel.

The starting system is a type of electrical circuit that converts electrical energy into mechanical energy. The electrical energy contained in the battery is used to crank a starter motor. As the motor turns, the engine is turned for starting. The system includes the starter motor, a drive and clutch mechanism, and a solenoid that is used to switch on the heavy current in the circuit.

A considerable amount of mechanical power is necessary to crank and start a car engine. About 250–500 amps of electricity is normally needed. The amperage is higher on a diesel engine. Because of the high amounts of current, heavy cable must be used to energize the heavy-current circuits. The typical starting system has five components, as shown in Figure 4-2.

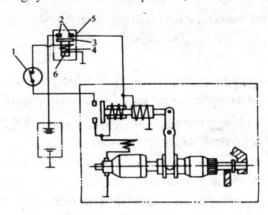

Figure 4-2   Engine Starting System

1—starting switch   2—contact point   3—contact plate

4—magnetic coil   5—starting breaker   6—magnetic core

Safety switches or interlock devices are used with all automatic transmissions and on many late-model cars with manual transmissions. The starting safety switch is also called a neutral start switch. It is a normally open switch that prevents the starting system from operating when the automobile's transmission is in gear. If the car has no starting safety switch, it is possible to spin the engine with the transmission in gear. This will make the car lurch forward, or backward which could be dangerous. The safety switch can be an electrical switch that opens the control circuit if the car is in gear. It can also be a mechanical interlock device that will not let the ignition switch turn to start if the car is in gear.

The starter motor converts electrical energy from the battery into mechanical energy to turn the engine. It does this through the interaction of magnetic fields. When current flows through a conductor, a magnetic field is formed around the conductor. If the conductor is placed in another magnetic field, the two fields will be weakened at one side and strengthened at the other side. An automotive starter motor has many conductors and uses a lot of current to create enough rotational force to crank the engine.

Figure 4-3 shows a cutaway view of a starter motor. The armature is the collection of conductors that will spin to crank the engine. The starter drive gear is mounted on the armature shaft. The pole pieces are the stationary magnetic fields. The motor housing encloses the armature and pole pieces, holds the bearings that support the armature shaft, and provides the terminals for connecting the motor to the rest of the starting system.

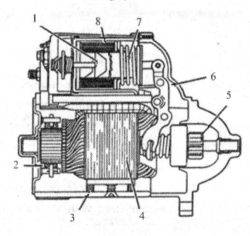

Figure 4-3   Starter Motor

1—plunger   2—bruch   3—field coils   4—armature

5—starter drive gear   6—shift fork   7—return spring   8—solenoid

Words and Expressions

1. inconvenient [ˌinkən'viːnjənt]   *adj.* 不便的，有困难的

2. wrist [rist]   *n.* 手腕，腕关节

3. typical ['tipikəl]   *adj.* 典型的；象征性的

4. cable ['keibl]　*n.* 电缆, 海底电报, 缆, 索

5. resistance [ri'zistəns]　*n.* 反抗, 抵抗, 抵抗力; 阻力, 电阻, 阻抗

6. circuit ['sə:kit]　*n.* 电路; 一圈; 周游, 巡回

7. actual ['æktʃuəl]　*adj.* 实际的, 真实的; 现行的, 目前的

8. solenoid ['səulinɔid]　*n.* [电]螺线管

9. relay ['ri:lei]　*n.* 继电器　*vt.* (消息, 货物等)分程传递; 使接替; 转播

10. electromagnetic [i,lektrəumæg'netik]　*adj.* 电磁的

11. coil [kɔil]　*v.* 盘绕, 卷

12. armature ['ɑ:mətʃə]　*n.* 盔甲, 电枢(电机的部件)

13. plunger ['plʌndʒə]　*n.* 跳进(水中)的人; 潜水者; 活塞

14. overload [,əuvə'ləud]　*vt.* 使超载, 超过负荷　*n.* 超载, 负荷过多

15. horsepower ['hɔ:s,pauə]　*n.* 马力

16. electromagnetic field　电磁场

17. starting system　起动系统

18. starter motor　起动机

19. magnetic switch　磁力开关

20. contact point　触点

21. solenoid-actuated　电磁阀控制的

Notes

1. The starting system is a necessity for internal-combustion engines, because the Otto cycle requires the pistons already to be in motion before the ignition phase of the cycle.

起动系统是内燃机必需的, 因为奥托循环在点火阶段前需要活塞已经处于运动状态。

2. Because of the high amounts of current, heavy cable must be used to energize the heavy-current circuits.

由于起动时需要大电流, 因此必须用很粗的电缆为起动电路供电。

3. Safety switches or interlock devices are used with all automatic transmissions and on many late-model cars with manual transmissions.

所有自动变速器和很多新款的手动变速器汽车上安装了安全开关或闭锁装置。

4. An automotive starter motor has many conductors and uses a lot of current to create enough rotational force to crank the engine.

汽车起动机上有很多导线并依靠大电流产生足够的旋转力来起动发动机。

5. The motor housing encloses the armature and pole pieces, holds the bearings that support the armature shaft, and provides the terminals for connecting the motor to the rest of the starting system.

起动机壳体封装着电枢和磁极, 壳体两端的轴承支撑着电枢转轴, 并将起动机和起动系统的其他部分相连。

Exercises

A. Vocabulary

I. Translate the following expressions into Chinese.

1. starting system

2. in motion

3. starting motor

4. electrical circuit

5. starting safety switch

6. starting solenoid

7. in gear

8. interaction of magnetic field

9. contact point

10. solenoid-actuated

II. Identify the English names of the starting system according to the picture.

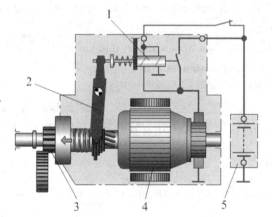

1. _____ 2. _____ 3. _____ 4. _____ 5. _____

B. Comprehension

I. Discuss the following questions in groups and write down your answers.

1. Why is the starting system a necessity for internal-combustion engines?

_____

_____

2. What is a typical starting system composed of?

_____

_____

3. What's the function of the starter motor?

_____

_____

II. Read the following passage carefully and fill in the blanks with the proper forms of the given words.

> *battery*   *alternator*   *electrochemical*   *current*
> *service*   *ignition*   *electrical*   *storage*   *recharge*

The automotive _____, also known as a lead-acid _____ battery, is an _____ device that produces voltage and delivers current. In an automotive battery we can reverse the electrochemical action, thereby _____ the battery, which will then give us many years of _____. The purpose of the battery is to supply _____ to the starter motor, provide current to the _____ system while cranking, to supply additional current when the demand is higher than the _____ can supply and to act as an _____ reservoir.

C. Translation

I. Translate the following sentences into Chinese.

1. It is a normally open switch that prevents the starting system from operating when the automobile's transmission is in gear.

2. If the car has no starting safety switch, it is possible to spin the engine with the transmission in gear. This will make the car lurch forward, or backward which could be dangerous.

3. The armature is the collection of conductors that will spin to crank the engine.

II. Translate the following sentences into English.

1. 起动系统是将电能转换成机械能的一种电路。

2. 起动机包括定子、转子或电枢及辅助设备，如直流电机的电刷等。

3. 要使发动机自行运转，必须先用外力转动发动机的曲轴，使活塞做往复运动。

Reading Material

Read the following passages and answer the questions according to the information given in the passages.

Passage One   Battery Testing

Life of average battery is only about four to five years under the best circumstances and sometimes as short as two to three years in extremely hot climates such as Arizona and New Mexico. But the battery may become "sulfated" prematurely if it is chronically undercharged (charging problems or frequent short-trip driving), or if the water level inside the battery drops below the top of the cell plates as a result of hot weather or overcharging and allows the cell plates to dry out.

Battery testing is something that you can't really do yourself, so you need to take your vehicle to a service facility that has the proper test equipment. The battery's condition can be determined one of two ways: with a carbon pile "load test" (that applies a calibrated load to the battery) or electronically with a special tester that measures the battery's internal resistance.

Equipment that uses a carbon pile for load testing requires the battery to be at least 75% charged. If the battery is less than 75% charged, a good battery may fail the test. So the state of charge must be checked to see if the battery needs to be recharged prior to testing. If it is low the battery should be recharged.

NOTE: The battery does NOT have to be fully charged prior to testing if an electronic tester that measures internal resistance is being used.

If load testing with a carbon pile, apply a load that is equal to half of the battery's cold cranking amps (CCA) rating. A good battery should be able to supply half of its CCA rating for fifteen seconds without dropping below 9.5 volts.

Questions

1. How long is the life of average battery?
2. What is the battery testing?
3. How can you tell whether your battery is good or bad?

Passage Two　Battery Replacement

Does a replacement battery have to be the same size as my old one? No. If your old battery has reached the end of the road and needs to be replaced, or if you think you need a battery with a bigger amp capacity for easier cold weather starting or to handle added electrical accessories (such as a killer stereo system, driving lights, etc.), then there's no reason why you have to install a battery that's the same size as your old one.

The word "size" may be a bit confusing here because what we're really talking about is the battery's ampere or power rating, not the physical dimensions of its case.

A battery with a bigger case is not necessarily a more powerful battery. Battery manufacturers can cram a lot of amps into a relatively small box by varying the design of the cell plates and grids, so two batteries with identical exterior dimensions may have significantly different power ratings.

Batteries come in many different sizes and configurations (which are referred to as "group" sizes) because the vehicle manufacturers can't get together and standardize anything. Therefore, when you're choosing a battery, you have to consider three things: ①the group size (height, width, length and post configuration); ②whether your battery has top or side posts; ③how many amps will be needed for reliable cold starting and vehicle operation.

Group Sizes

Because there are 57 different group sizes, many aftermarket replacement battery suppliers consolidate group sizes to simplify inventory requirements, so some replacement batteries may not fit exactly the same as the original. The battery may be slightly shorter, taller, narrower or wider than the original. But as long as it fits the battery tray and there are no interference problems (a too tall battery may cause the cables to make contact with the hood causing a dangerous and damaging electrical short!), it should work fine.

Some replacement batteries come with both side and top posts to further consolidate applications. Some also have folding handles to make handling and installation easier.

Battery Ratings

Though many replacement batteries are marketed by the number of "months" of warranty coverage provided (36, 48, 60, etc.), what's more important in terms of performance is the

battery's power rating which is usually specified in "Cold Cranking Amps" (CCA) rating. The CCA rating tells you how many amps the battery can deliver at 0 degree F. for 30 seconds and still maintain a minimum voltage of 1.2V per cell.

In the past, the rule of thumb was to always buy a battery with a rating of at least one CCA per cubic inch of engine displacement. But twice that is probably a better recommendation for reliable cold weather starting.

At the very least, you should buy a replacement battery with the same or better CCA rating as your old battery or one that meets the vehicle manufacturer's requirements. For most small four-cylinder engines, this would be a 450 CCA or larger battery, for a six cylinder application, a 550 CCA or larger battery, and for a V8 a 650 CCA or larger battery. Bigger is usually better. Extra battery capacity is recommended if your vehicle has a lot of electrical accessories such as air conditioning, power windows, seats, electric rear defogger, etc.

Battery Installation

Most batteries are "dry charged" at the factory, which means they're activated as soon as acid is poured into the cells. Even so, the battery may require some charging to bring it all the way up to full charge.

Most experts recommend charging the battery before it is installed regardless of whether it is dry charged or not. This will ensure the battery is at full charge and lessen the strain on your charging system.

When the battery is installed, it must be locked down and held securely by a clamp, strap or bracket. This will not only keep the battery from sliding around on its tray (which might allow the positive cable to touch against something and short out the battery or start a fire!), but will also help to minimize vibration that can damage the battery.

The battery cables should also be inspected to make sure they're in good condition, too. If the cables are badly corroded, don't fit the battery posts or terminals tightly, or have been "fixed" by installing temporary clamps on the ends, the cables should be replaced. At the very least, you should clean the cable clamps and battery posts with a post cleaner, sandpaper or a wire brush to ensure good electrical contact. A light coating of grease, petroleum jelly and/or installing chemically treated felt washers under the cable clamps will help prevent corrosion.

Questions

1. Does a replacement battery have to be the same size as the old one?

2. Why do we say that what's more important in terms of performance is the battery's power rating?

3. How should you do a battery installation?

Unit 3　Ignition System Basic

The ignition system of an internal-combustion engine is an important part of the overall engine system. It provides for the timely burning of the fuel mixture within the engine. Not all engine types need an ignition system, for example, a diesel engine relies on compression-ignition, that is, the rise in temperature that accompanies the rise in pressure within the cylinder is sufficient to ignite the fuel spontaneously. All conventional petrol (gasoline) engines, by contrast, require an ignition system. The ignition system is usually switched on/off through a lock switch, operated with a key or code patch.

The ignition system is divided into two circuits: the primary and the secondary. The primary circuit is the low-voltage side of the system and controls the secondary circuit, which is the high-voltage side of the system, as shown in Figure 4-4.

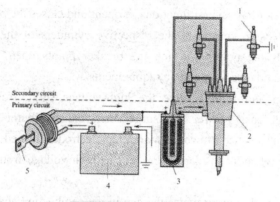

Figure 4-4　Ignition System

1—spark plug　2—distributor　3—ignition coil　4—battery　5—ignition switch

The following are the basic parts of the primary ignition circuit:

1. Battery and/or alternator. The battery is the heart of the total electrical system. In regard to the primary circuit, its function is to supply voltage and current flow to the primary windings of the ignition coil in order to produce an electromagnet.

2. Ignition switch. The purpose of the ignition switch is to connect and disconnect the ignition system from the battery, so the engine can be started and stopped as desired.

3. Primary wires. Low-voltage wires are used to connect the electrical components of the primary circuit.

4. Ignition coil primary winding. When current passes through the coil, the function of it is to create a very strong electromagnetic field. In other words, the coil becomes an electromagnet with N and S poles. The magnetic field from this coil, in turn, induces a voltage in the secondary windings that is necessary to cause an arc at the spark plug gap.

5. Electronic control unit. It contains a switching transistor controlled by a speed sensor and is used to open and close the primary circuit.

6. Speed sensor, or pickup. It produces a pulsating voltage that signals the generation of an ignition spark.

The following are the basic parts of a secondary ignition circuit:

1. Ignition coil secondary winding, which has a high voltage (40,000 V or more) induced in it each time the primary magnetic field collapses.

2. Coil wire, which is heavily insulated wire that feeds high voltage from the ignition coil to distributor cap.

3. Distributor rotor. It operates in conjunction with the distributor cap to distribute the high voltage from the ignition coil to the individual spark plug wires in the firing order. The rotor itself mounts on the upper distributor shaft and rotates with it. As a result, the rotor electrode moves from one cap spark plug electrode to another, following the specific firing order of the engine.

4. Distributor cap, which is insulated cap that transfers high voltage from the distributor rotor to spark plug wires.

The ignition distributor has several functions. It opens and closes the primary ignition circuit. It distributes the high tension current to the respective cylinders of the engine. It also has a mechanism that controls the point at which the breaker points open, thereby advancing or retarding the spark in accordance with engine requirements.

The distributor cap and rotor receive the high-voltage surge from the secondary coil windings through a high-tension wire. This surge enters the distributor cap through its center terminal, which is known as the coil tower to spark plug electrodes formed into the rim of the cap.

5. Spark plug wire. Heavily insulated wire carries high voltage from the distributor to the spark plugs.

6. Spark plug. The spark plug provides the gap in the combustion chamber across which the high-tension electrical spark jumps to ignite the combustion charge.

A spark plug consists of a pair of electrodes, as shown in Figure 4-5, called the center and ground electrodes, separated by a gap. A spark is produced by applying a high voltage (from approximately 6 kV to 40 kV) between the center electrode and ground. Once the arc is started, a much lower voltage is required to sustain the arc to ignite the air/fuel mixture.

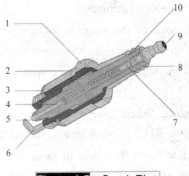

Figure 4-5 Spark Plug

1—hex nut 2—spark plug body 3—gasket 4—center electrode 5—gap
6—ground electrode 7—resistance 8—spline 9—terminal 10—ceramic insulator

Words and Expressions

1. electrode [ɪˈlektrəʊd] *n.* 电极

2. gap [gæp] *n.* 缺口，间隙，缝隙；差距

3. primary ['praiməri] *adj.* 第一位的，主要的；初步的，原来的

4. wire ['waiə] *n.* 金属丝，电线

5. spark [spɑːk] *n.* 火花；瞬间放电

6. sensor ['sensə] *n.* 传感器

7. terminal ['təːminl] *n.* 端子，终端，接线端

8. pulse [pʌls] *n.* 脉搏，脉冲

9. distribute [dis'tribju(ː)t] *vt.* 分发，分配；散布；分区 *v.* 分发

10. collapse [kə'læps] *n.* 倒塌，崩溃，*vi.* 倒塌，崩溃，瓦解

11. electromagnet [i'lektrəu'mægnit] *n.* 电磁铁，电磁

12. winding ['waindiŋ] *n.* 绕，缠；绕组，线圈

13. ignition system　点火系统

14. electric arc　电弧

15. spark plug　火花塞

16. center electrode　中央电极

17. primary winding　初级绕组

18. ignition coil　点火线圈

19. distributor cap　分电器盖

Notes

1. Not all engine types need an ignition system, for example, a diesel engine relies on compression-ignition, that is, the rise in temperature that accompanies the rise in pressure within the cylinder is sufficient to ignite the fuel spontaneously.

并非所有发动机都需要点火系统，例如，柴油机依靠压燃，即随着缸内压力增高，温度增高到足以使得柴油自燃。

2. The primary circuit is the low-voltage side of the system and controls the secondary circuit, which is the high-voltage side of the system.

初级回路是系统的低压回路，它控制着次级回路也就是系统的高压回路。

3. The battery is the heart of the total electrical system.

蓄电池是整个电气系统的心脏。

4. Heavily insulated wire feeds high voltage from the ignition coil to distributor cap.

高绝缘的高压线将高压电从点火线圈送到分电器盖。

5. The distributor cap and rotor receive the high-voltage surge from the secondary coil windings through a high-tension wire.

分电器盖和分火头通过高压线从次级绕组接收到高压电。

Exercises

A. Vocabulary

I. Translate the following expressions into Chinese.

1. ignition system

2. electric arc

3. spark plug

4. primary winding center electrode

5. ignition coil

6. distributor cap

7. the secondary circuit

8. ignition switch

9. high-tension wire

10. center and ground electrodes

II. Identify the English names of the spark plug according to the picture.

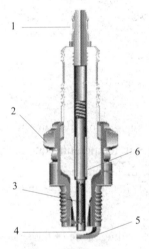

1. _____ 2. _____ 3. _____
4. _____ 5. _____ 6. _____

B. Comprehension

I. Discuss the following questions in groups and write down your answers.

1. The ignition system is the necessity of an internal-combustion engine. Is it true? Why?

_____

_____

2. What is the primary ignition circuit composed of?

_____

_____

3. What are the basic parts of a secondary ignition circuit?

_____

_____

II. Read the following passage carefully and fill in the blanks with the proper forms of the given words.

primary	*point*	*retarding*	*cylinder*	*rotor*
camshaft	*body*	*arm*	*ignition*	*fire*

A distributor is a device in the ____ system of an internal combustion engine that routes high voltage from the ignition coil to the spark plugs in the correct firing order. It consists of a rotating ____ or ____ inside the distributor cap, on top of the distributor shaft, but insulated from it and the ____ of the vehicle (ground). The distributor shaft is driven by a gear on the ____.

The ignition distributor has several functions. It opens and closes the ____ ignition circuit. It distributes the high tension current to the respective ____ of the engine. It also has a mechanism that controls the ____ at which the breaker points open, thereby advancing or ____ the spark in accordance with engine requirements.

C. Translation

I. Translate the following sentences into Chinese.

1. In regard to the primary circuit, its function is to supply voltage and current flow to the primary windings of the ignition coil.

2. As a result, the rotor electrode moves from one cap spark plug electrode to another, following the specific firing order of the engine.

3. It opens and closes the primary ignition circuit. It distributes the high tension current to the respective cylinders of the engine.

II. Translate the following sentences into English.

1. 汽车点火系统分为初级和次级两个电路。

2. 点火系统的作用是在正确的时刻把电火花提供给汽缸，点燃混合气。

3. 火花塞提供空气间隙，保证高电压的电弧通过，以点燃混合气。

Reading Material

Read the following passages and answer the questions according to the information given in the passages.

Passage One　The Exhaust Gas Recirculation(EGR) Valve

When combustion temperatures exceed 2,500 degree F., atmospheric nitrogen begins to react with oxygen during combustion. The result is various compounds called nitrogen oxides (NO_X), which play a major role in urban air pollution. To reduce the formation of NO_X, combustion temperatures must be kept below the NO_X threshold. This is done by recirculating a small amount of exhaust through the "exhaust gas recirculation", or EGR valve.

The EGR valve controls a small passageway between the intake and exhaust manifolds. When the valve opens, intake vacuum draws exhaust through the valve. This dilutes the incoming air/fuel mixture and has a quenching effect on combustion temperatures which keeps NO_X within acceptable limits. As an added benefit, it also reduces the engine's octane requirements which lessens the danger of detonation (spark knock).

The EGR valve consists of a poppet valve and a vacuum diaphragm. When vacuum is applied to the EGR valve diaphragm, it pulls the valve open allowing exhaust to pass from the exhaust manifold into the intake manifold. Some engines have "positive backpressure" EGR valves, while others have "negative backpressure" EGR valves. Both types contain a second diaphragm that modulates the action of the valve. This prevents the valve from opening unless there is a certain level of exhaust backpressure in the system. EGR valves are calibrated for specific engine applications. The wrong valve may flow too much or not enough exhaust and cause emission, driveability and detonation problems.

EGR valves do not normally require maintenance or replacement for preventative maintenance. But the valve can become clogged with carbon deposits that cause it to stick or prevent it from closing properly. Dirty EGR valves can sometimes be cleaned, but replacement is necessary if the valve is defective.

Some newer engines are so clean from a NO_X emissions standpoint that no EGR valve is required.

Questions

1. What's the meaning of "EGR"?

2. What does the EGR valve consist of ?

3. What is the EGR valve and what does it do?

Passage Two   Voltage Regulator Service

My mechanic says I have a bad voltage regulator, and he has to replace my alternator. How come? The voltage regulator controls or regulates the alternator's output. Think of it as the brains of the charging system. It senses how much voltage is needed by your vehicle, then modifies the field current within the alternator so it puts out just the right amount of current. Too little current can allow the battery to run down while too much can damage it and other electrical and electronic components. When the regulator fails, the charging system usually ceases to function — except in cases where the nature of the failure causes the alternator to run wild and overcharge the battery. In any event, the only cure for a dead or defective regulator is replacement.

In older vehicles, the regulator was a separate component usually mounted somewhere in the engine compartment. If this type of regulator failed, it could be easily replaced in a matter of minutes with a new one. But for the last decade or more, most regulators have been mounted in or on the alternator itself. This was done by the vehicle manufacturers to simplify wiring and assembly. It was also made possible by advances in electronics that allowed the regulator to be reduced in size to a small chip.

Charging systems that have a separate regulator mounted away from the alternator are referred to as "externally regulated" charging systems, while those have the regulator in or on the alternator are called "internally regulated" charging systems. On some vehicles there is no regulator at all! Voltage regulation is controlled by the engine computer.

Unfortunately, internally regulated alternators are packaged as a unit, which means that if either component fails (alternator or regulator), both must be replaced. This is because internal regulators are not available separately (at least not to the general public or the typical service facility). Electrical shops and remanufacturers who rebuild alternators can get them and can replace the regulator separately if that's all wrong with the unit—but they'll usually charge you the same as if you bought a rebuilt alternator.

The truth is, the high cost of labor today has made it impractical for most service facilities to fool around trying to rebuild or repair components like alternators, starters, carburetors, front-wheel driveshafts, transmissions and even engines. It's faster, easier and usually cheaper to simply replace the old unit with a new or remanufactured one than to try to overhaul or fix it. Besides, most new and remanufactured parts come with a guarantee.

Questions

1. My mechanic says I have a bad voltage regulator, and he has to replace my alternator. Why?

2. What is the function of a voltage regulator?

3. Internally regulated alternators are packaged as a unit. What is the result?

Unit 4　Electronic Ignition System

In the early 1970s many American vehicles began to install electronic ignition systems which now operate as part of an electronic engine-control system. This action was necessary not only to meet stricter emission control standards but to increase the fuel economy of the vehicle. All the function that used to be done mechanically can now be done through electronics. Centrifugal and vacuum-advance mechanisms in the distributor have been eliminated, and ignition timing is controlled by the engine computer.

Although the electronic system costs more to install than the standard system, the advantages that it offers more than outweigh the drawbacks of increased cost. These advantages include the following:

(1) greater available secondary voltage, especially at high engine rpm;

(2) reliable and consistent system performance at any and all engine speeds;

(3) a potential for more responsive and variable ignition advance curves;

(4) decreased maintenance cost of the system.

Figure 4-6 shows the modern electronic ignition system of Toyota：

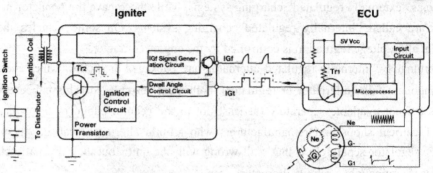

Figure 4-6　Electronic Ignition System of Toyota

Igniter Operation

When the IGt signal goes high, the primary circuit power transistor TR2 turns on, allowing current to flow in the coil primary winding. When the IGt signal goes low, the igniter interrupts primary circuit current flow, causing voltage induction into the coil secondary winding.

Spark Confirmation IGf

Once a spark event takes place, an ignition confirmation signal called IGf is generated by the igniter and sent to the ECU. The IGf signal tells the ECU that a spark event has actually occurred. In the event of an ignition fault, after approximately eight to eleven IGt signals are sent to the igniter without receiving an IGf confirmation, the ECU will enter a fail-safe mode, shutting down the injectors to prevent potential catalyst overheating.

Ignition Timing Strategy

The ECU determines ignition timing by comparing engine operating parameters with spark advance values stored in its memory. The general formula for ignition timing are follows:

Initial timing + Basic advance angle + Corrective advance angle = Total spark advance

Basic advance angle is computed using signals from crankshaft angle (G1), crankshaft speed (Ne) and engine load (Vs or PIM) sensors. Corrective timing factors include adjustments for coolant temperature (THW) and presence of detonation (KNK).

Distributor-Less Ignition Igniter System (DLI)

DLI, as the name implies, as shown in Figure 4-7, is an electronic spark distribution system which supplies secondary current directly from the ignition coils to the spark plugs without the use of a conventional distributor. The DLI system contains the following major components: Cam Position Sensor, Igniter and Ignition Coils.

The following checks assume that the engine runs but timing will not advance.

The design of the Variable Advance Spark Timing (VAST) system will allow the ignition system to function at initial timing in the event that the IGt signal does not reach the igniter. If this condition occurs, the ignition system will be locked at initial timing regardless of engine speed or load. The ECU has no way to monitor for this fault, so there will be no indication of this condition other than a loss of engine performance.

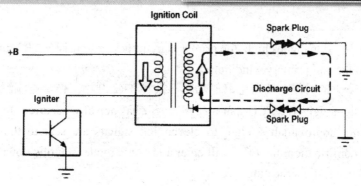

Figure 4-7　Distributor-Less Ignition Igniter System

You can follow the following steps to check for this condition:

(1) Monitor the IGt wire at the igniter using an oscilloscope or logic probe.

(2) If a good signal is being sent out on IGt, check the connection at the igniter.

(3) Once connections are confirmed, the igniter is the last item left which can cause the problem.

Words and Expressions

1. emission　[i'miʃən]　*n.* 排放，发射

2. outweigh　[aut'wei]　*v.* 胜过，优于

3. consistent　[kən'sistənt]　*adj.* 始终如一的，一贯的

4. maintenance　['meintinəns]　*n.* 维护，保养

5. interrupt　['intə'rʌpt]　*v.* 中断，打断

6. confirmation　[,kɔnfə'meiʃnel]　*n.* 确认

7. catalyst　['kætəlist]　*n.* 催化剂，触媒

8. parameter　[pə'ræmitə]　*n.* 参数

9. detonation　['detə'neiʃən]　*n.* 爆震，爆燃

10. oscilloscope　[ɔ'siləskəup]　*n.* 示波器

11. monitor　['mɔnitə]　*n.* 监督员　*v.* 监控

12. vacuum-advance mechanism　真空提前装置

13. IGt signal　点火信号

14. IGf signal　点火反馈确认信号

15. basic spark advance angle　基础点火提前角

16. Variable Advance Spark Timing (VAST)　可变点火正时

17. logic probe　逻辑探测仪

18. fail-safe mode　故障安全模式

19. engine performance　发动机性能

20. Cam Position Sensor　凸轮轴位置传感器

Notes

1. When the IGt signal goes high, the primary circuit power transistor TR2 turns on, allowing current to flow in the coil primary winding.

当 IGt 信号变大的时候，初级电路的功率三极管 TR2 开始工作，电流流过初级线圈。

2. The IGf signal tells the ECU that a spark event has actually occurred. In the event of an ignition fault, after approximately eight to eleven IGt signals are sent to the igniter without receiving an IGf confirmation, the ECU will enter a fail-safe mode, shutting down the injectors to prevent potential catalyst overheating.

IGf 告诉电脑点火信号已有效发生。若在这个过程中点火失效，大约 8 到 11 个 IGt(点火时刻控制)信号发送到点火器后而没有接收到 IGf 信号时，电脑将会进入故障防护模式，关闭喷油器以防止催化剂可能会过热。

3. Basic advance angle is computed using signals from crankshaft angle (G1), crankshaft speed (Ne), and engine load (Vs or PIM) sensors. Corrective timing factors include adjustments for coolant temperature (THW) and presence of detonation (KNK).

基本提前角是电脑利用曲轴转角 G1 的信号、曲轴转速 Ne 的信号和发动机负荷传感器的信号来计算的。修正正时的因素包括冷却剂温度和爆燃。

4. DLI, as the name implies, is an electronic spark distribution system which supplies secondary current directly from the ignition coils to the spark plugs without the use of a conventional distributor.

顾名思义，DLI 是直接从点火线圈到火花塞提供次级电流而无须传统分电器的无分电器点火系统。

5. If this condition occurs, the ignition system will be locked at initial timing regardless of engine speed or load. The ECU has no way to monitor for this fault, so there will be no indication of this condition other than a loss of engine performance.

如果发生这种情况，不论发动机速度或者负荷如何变化，点火系统将锁定在初始正时提前角。电脑无法监测这种故障，因此除了发动机的性能将会降低外，没有产生这种状况的迹象。

Exercises

A. Vocabulary

I. Translate the following expressions into Chinese.

1. vacuum-advance mechanism
2. IGt signal
3. IGf signal
4. basic advance angle
5. Variable Advance Spark Timing (VAST)
6. logic probe
7. fail-safe mode

8. engine performance

9. Cam Position Sensor

10. presence of detonation

II. Identify the English names of the electronic ignition system according to the picture.

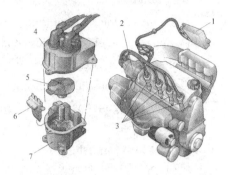

1. _____ 2. _____ 3. _____ 4. _____

5. _____ 6. _____ 7. _____

B. Comprehension

I. Discuss the following questions in groups and write down your answers.

1. What are the advantages of electronic ignition systems?

_____

_____

2. How does an igniter operate?

_____

_____

3. What's the meaning of the DLI system? What are the major components of DLI?

_____

_____

II. Read the following passage carefully and fill in the blanks with the proper forms of the given words.

ECU	*technology*	*efficiency*	*precise*	*distributorless*
coil	*unit*	*wire*	*distributor*	*spark*

In recent years, you may have heard of cars that need their first tune-up at 100,000 miles. One of the _____ that enable this long maintenance interval is the _____ ignition.

The _____ in this type of system works the same way as the larger, centrally-located coils. The engine control _____ controls the transistors that break the ground side of the circuit, which generates the _____. This gives the _____ total control over spark timing.

Systems like these have some substantial advantages. First, there is no _____, which is an item that eventually wears out. Also, there are no high-voltage spark-plug _____, which also wear out. And finally, they allow for more _____ control of the spark timing, which can improve _____, emissions and increase the overall power of a car.

C. Translation

I. Translate the following sentences into Chinese.

1. When the IGt signal goes low, the igniter interrupts primary circuit current flow, causing voltage induction into the coil secondary winding.

2. The following checks assume that the engine runs but timing will not advance.

3. You can according to the following steps to check for this condition:

(1) Monitor the IGt wire at the igniter using an oscilloscope or logic probe.

(2) If a good signal is being sent out on IGt, check the connection at the igniter.

(3) Once connections are confirmed, the igniter is the last item left which can cause the problem.

II. Translate the following sentences into English.

1. 电脑通过对发动机运行参数和存储器存储的点火提前量进行比较来确定点火时刻。

2. 初始正时＋基本的提前角＋修正的提前角＝全部的点火提前角。

3. VAST 系统设计时有这样的功能：点火系统如果没有 IGt 信号送达点火器则点火按照初始提前角工作。

Reading Material

Read the following passages and answer the questions according to the information given in the passages.

Passage One   Primary Circuit Checks

The following procedures assume that a spark tester reveals no spark at two different cylinders while the engine is cranked.

Preliminary checks

(1) Ensure battery condition prior to ignition system analysis.

(2) Check and confirm good connections at distributor, igniter and coil.

(3) Basic secondary leakage checks at coil and coil wire.

Primary circuit checks

(1) Confirm power supply to igniter and coil positive (+) terminal. Confirm connections at coil positive and negative (−) terminals.

(2) Using a test light or logic probe, check for primary switching at the coil (−) terminal. Blinking light confirms primary switching is taking place; check coil wire, coil secondary winding resistance, or secondary leakage in distributor cap.

(3) The power transistor(s) in the igniter get their ground through the igniter case to the vehicle chassis. Always confirm good ground continuity prior to trouble shooting.

(4) Confirm coil primary and secondary windings resistance. Confirm primary windings are not grounded.

(5) Confirm signal status from Ne and G pickups to ECU (ESA system) or to igniter (VAST

system) using an oscilloscope or logic probe.

If a fault is detected, check pickup(s) for proper resistance and shorts to ground. Check electrical connections.

If signal amplitude is low, check signal generator gap(s).

(6) Confirm signal status from ECU IGt circuit to igniter using an oscilloscope or logic probe.

(7) On 7M-GTE, check power transistor in igniter. Bias transistor base using a remote 3 volts battery as power source. Use ohmmeter to check for continuity from primary circuit to ground.

(8) Check pickup gaps and coil resistances against specifications. If gap and/or resistance is not within specification, replace faulty component.

Questions

How to check when a spark tester reveals no spark at two different cylinders while the engine is cranked?

Passage Two   Electronic Control System

To meet stringent emission control requirements in the early 1970s, automotive engineers began to apply electronic control to basic automotive systems. The use of electronics was first applied to ignition timing and later to fuel metering. Electronic control introduced a degree of precision that electromechanical and vacuum-operated systems could not achieve in matching fuel delivery and ignition timing with engine load and speed requirements. With electronic control came a significant decrease in emission levels, major improvements in drive-ability, and increased reliability of the systems.

Electronic ignitions appeared first, followed a few years later by electronic fuel metering systems which were quickly integrated with the electronic ignitions to form the early engine management systems. By the early 1980s, many automotive systems were controlled by an onboard computer. In addition, the control system includes a series of sensors and various actuators.

We have dealt with the functions, logic and software used by a computer. The software consists of the programs and logic functions stored in the computer's circuitry. The hardware is the mechanical and electronic parts of the computer.

The electronic control system can be organized into three basic elements: input, processor and output. The input signal is usually the cause of a change in the system, and the output action which occurs as a result of the input is called the effect, while the response of the system to an input signal is called the process, where the input is processed to effect the desired output. A system can be purely analogue in nature, purely digital, or a mixture both.

Initially, a system senses external information, converting it to a form that can be handled internally. Then decisions are made, based on the input information, by process or manipulation. In making a decision a system may store the information for a time, or process it as the result of other information stored permanently in memory. Finally, as the result of the decision, an action outside the system takes place.

This three-element system configuration is very simple. Typically, each element consists of more than one process.

Sensors convert physical quantities into electronic signals and apply them to the input circuits. Usually the sensors feed data to the computer in the form of voltage signals. The computer then processes the sensor data according to its internal program and then signals the actuators to exercise the desired control over the subsystems that require adjustment.

Actuators are devices such as solenoid valves, relays and motors that deliver motion in response to an electrical signal. Actuators respond to output commands issued by the microcomputer. Today's automotive computers are capable of issuing up to 600,000 commands per second.

The most common actuator is a valve powered by a solenoid. By energizing and de-energizing the solenoid coil, the movable core of the solenoid can be made to open or close valves. The valve, in turn, controls vacuum, fuel vapor, air, oil, or water flow. Both normally open and normally closed solenoid valves are used. A normally open solenoid valve remains open when no voltage is applied. A normally closed solenoid valve remains closed when no voltage is applied.

Any control system can be classified as open-loop or closed-loop.

In an open-loop system, the control circuits do not monitor the system's output to determine if the desired control action was achieved.

In a closed-loop system, on the other hand, a feedback sensor and circuit continually monitor the system's output by developing a correction signal applied to the control circuit, which adjusts the output towards the desired value. generally, control systems comprise only closed-loop systems are not accurate due to their very nature.

The microprocessor is a very large scale integration circuit whose final function is determined by the sequence of instructions, known as the program, given to it. Individual instructions enable the microprocessor to carry out each step towards completion of a complex circuit function. The basic microprocessor is therefore not a dedicated device confined to one particular application, although the majority of microprocessors used for control purposes do have built-in mask-programmable storage circuits which allow them to be dedicated to specific control functions.

The microprocessor can do nothing on its own, requiring a certain amount of supporting hardware, memory and input/output circuits. The microprocessor is the central control function for the system, sometimes called the central processing unit (CPU). It performs this processing control function under the direction of instructions stored in the system memory. These instructions make up the system program.

The computer memory function is provided by other integrated circuit (IC) devices. These simply store the computer operating program, system sensor input data and system actuator output data for use by the CPU. The memory also provides storage of data, function tables and decision tables. When used for engine management systems, it would be programmed with all the information necessary to control functions such as fuel injection quantities and ignition advance characteristics. For example, the memory might contain 16 load and 16 speed parameters which would permit the use of 256 ignition advance positions based on a combination of these stored values. But the microprocessor has also to consider other parameters when deciding the actual ignition timing point-starting period, coolant temperatures, dwell time, combustion knock, etc.

Input ports allow inputs of system data from sensors and manual controls into the system. The microprocessor interprets the data and implements output control decisions under the guidance of the program stored in memory. Output ports provide the means for the microprocessor to send the output control signal to the device that carries out the desired action.

The microprocessor communicates with the other elements of the internal system by sending digital binary codes along conductors called buses. Initially, the microprocessor may send a binary address code which determines which input/output port or memory location is to be brought into action. Control signals are then sent, which determine the direction of data flow and when the transfer of data is to take place. Finally data codes are sent to or from the microprocessor along the data bus.

Each action the microprocessor takes is under the direction of an instruction from memory. Thus, the microprocessor must know where the instruction is located in memory and it must fetch the instruction code from memory before the instruction can be carried out. Once inside the microprocessor an instruction decoder circuit interprets the instruction, then a controller generates the required control signals to carry out the instruction. This sequence of addressing memory and fetching instructions, decoding and executing instructions, is repeated for all instructions in the program.

Questions

1. Why do we need an electronic control system?

2. How does an electronic control system work?

3. What is the difference between open-loop or closed-loop?

Unit 5　Air Bag System

Air bags supplement the protection provided by safety belts by protecting the head and chest in moderate to severe front-end collisions. If a vehicle collides with a solid object, the occupants are thrown forward against the dashboard, windshield and protruding objects, particularly the steering wheel. In the event of a moderate to severe front-end collision, tough nylon bags, similar to large balloons, inflate in a fraction of a second so that the driver and passenger are cushioned as

they are thrown forward. As a result, the air bag absorbs the energy of the forward motion of the occupants with little or no injury to them.

Driver deaths in frontal crashes are about 20 percent lower with air bags than in similar cars without them. At the time of publication, it has been estimated that more than 2,500 lives have been saved. But in some circumstances, air bags can cause injuries, mostly minor, but occasionally serious or, in rare cases, fatal. The most serious injuries occur when people are very close to air bags when they first begin to inflate. Some of the deaths have been infants in rear-facing restraints and unrestrained or improperly restrained children. This risk can be eliminated by making sure all youngsters travel in the back seat.

Although different manufacturers' systems vary slightly, the air bag system is composed of a few basic parts. Each air bag module contains an inflator, an igniter, and the folded air bag. When electrical current flows through the igniter, it produces heat, which ignites the generant material within the inflator. This solid generant burns in an enclosed chamber to produce harmless nitrogen gas. This gas is cooled and filtered prior to inflating the air bag, as shown in Figure 4-8.

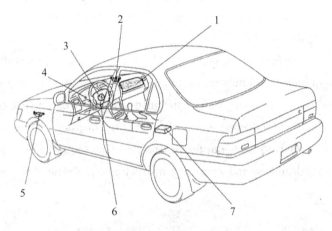

Figure 4-8　Air Bag System

1—front passenger airbag assembly　2—front airbag sensor RH　3—spiral cable　4—SRS warning light
5—front airbag sensor LH　6—steering wheel pad (with airbag)　7—center airbag sensor assembly

The system performs three main functions, which are listed as following:

(1) Detects an impact;

(2) Provides a ground to the air bags for deployment;

(3) Monitors system readiness.

If an air bag should inflate by error under normal driving conditions, it could cause an accident. Similarly, should it fail to inflate as expected in a collision, occupants could be injured. To prevent either from happening, the system utilizes five electromechanical crash sensors (three front crash sensors and two safety sensors) to monitor and respond to appropriate impact forces. The three front crash sensors are mounted across the front of the vehicle to differentiate between moderate crashes that do not warrant air bag deployment and severe crashes that do. The system will not deploy the air bags unless it gets confirmation from one of the two safety crash sensors that there is sufficient vehicle deceleration to warrant deployment. The purpose of these safety crash sensors is to make sure that the air bags will not deploy inadvertently in the event of an electrical short in one of the crash sensors or wiring.

The system has an indicator lamp activated by the ignition key to let you know the system is working. If the car is involved in a frontal crash equivalent to running into a stationary barrier at least 10-12 mph, the sudden deceleration (impact) causes the sensor to activate a gas cartridge that instantly inflates the air bag preventing the occupants from contacting the inside of the car. The air cushions absorb the impact.

The air bags themselves are porous and the air is actually beginning to escape as they are being inflated. The entire process (sensing, inflation and partial deflation) is completed in about 125th of a second, or about the time it takes to blink your eye.

Words and Expressions

1. frontal ['frʌntl] *n*. 前沿

2. cushion ['kuʃən] *n*. 垫子，软垫，衬垫

3. inflate [in'fleit] *vt*. 使膨胀；使得意；使(通货)膨胀；使充气 *vi*. 充气，膨胀

4. supplement ['sʌpliment] *v*.；*n*. 增补，补充；增补

5. moderate ['mɔdərit] *n*.；*v*. 缓和，缓冲；减轻，节制

6. occupant ['ɔkjupənt] *n*. 占有人，占有者

7. protrude [prə'truːd] *vt*. 使伸出，突出

8. fraction ['frækʃən] *n*. 片断，片刻，小部分

9. fold [fəuld] *v*. 折叠，笼罩；对折起来

10. differentiate [,difə'renʃieit] *v*. 区分，分别；使变异

11. deploy [di'plɔi] *v*. 展开，调度

12. warrant ['wɔrənt] *v*. 认为正当，担保；授权；批准 *n*. 正当理由，根据；授权证，许可证

13. inadvertently ['inəd'vəːtəntli] *adj*. 不经心的，疏忽的

14. buffer ['bʌfə] *n*. 缓冲器

15. restraint [ris'treint] *n*. 抑制，制止，克制

16. deceleration [diː,selə'reiʃən] *n*. 减速

17. cartridge ['kɑːtridʒ] *n*. 弹药筒

18. lap [læp] *n*. (坐时的)大腿前部，膝盖，下摆

19. supplemental restraint system　辅助约束系统

20. front-end collision　前端碰撞

21. crash sensor   碰撞传感器

22. safety sensor   安全传感器

23. indicator lamp   指示灯

24. under normal driving conditions   正常行驶状态

25. air bag   气囊

26. ignition key   点火开关

27. spiral cable   螺旋电缆

28. in the event of   如果……发生

29. as a result   结果，因此

30. fail to do   不能做……

31. as expect   如所期望的

Notes

1. Air bags supplement the protection provided by safety belts by protecting the head and chest in moderate to severe front-end collisions.

在汽车发生中度至重度的正面碰撞时，安全气囊作为安全带的辅助保护装置可使司机的头部和胸部免受伤害。

2. Driver deaths in frontal crashes are about 20 percent lower with air bags than in similar cars without them.

装配有安全气囊的汽车发生正面碰撞造成的驾驶员死亡率比没有装配安全气囊的汽车低 20%。

3. When electrical current flows through the igniter, it produces heat, which ignites the generant material within the inflator.

当电流流过点火器时，产生的热量会点燃气体发生器内的某种物质。

4. If the car is involved in a frontal crash equivalent to running into a stationary barrier at least 10-12 mph, the sudden deceleration (impact) causes the sensor to activate a gas cartridge that instantly inflates the air bag preventing the occupants from contacting the inside of the car.

如果汽车以至少每小时 10～12 英里的车速与静止障碍物发生正面碰撞，突然的降速会导致传感器激发气体发生器工作，从而瞬间为气囊充气以防止乘员和汽车内的物体相撞。

5. If an air bag should inflate by error under normal driving conditions, it could cause an accident.

正常行驶状态下如果错误地激发了气囊，就会导致事故。

Exercises

A. Vocabulary

I. Translate the following expressions into Chinese.

1. supplemental restraint system

2. front-end collision

3. crash sensor

4. safety sensor

5. cause an accident

6. under normal driving conditions

7. air bag

8. ignition key

9. spiral cable

10. stationary barrier

II. Identify the English names of the airbag system according to the picture.

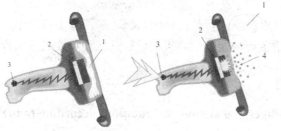

1. _____ 2. _____ 3. _____ 4. _____

B. Comprehension

I. Discuss the following questions in groups and write down your answers.

1. Why are more and more cars equipped with air bags?

_____

_____

2. What is the air bag system composed of?

_____

_____

3. How does the air bag system work?

_____

_____

II. Read the following passage carefully and fill in the blanks with the proper forms of the given words.

firmly   belt   component   excessive   injury

supplemental   airbag   inertia   accident

Vehicle ____ restraint systems are designed to protect occupants during ____. Namely, in case of a head-on collision, they pull the seat ____ tighter around the upper part of the body and press it ____ against the seat's backrest. These prevent ____ forward displacement of the body caused by mass ____ and protect the occupants against ____. The ____ are necessary for system operation. They are ____, Crash Sensors, Spring Cable and ECU, etc.

C. Translation

I. Translate the following sentences into Chinese.

1. Although different manufacturers' systems vary slightly, the air bag system is composed of a few basic parts.

2. The purpose of these safety crash sensors is to make sure that the air bags will not deploy inadvertently in the event of an electrical short in one of the crash sensors or wiring.

3. The air bags themselves are porous and the air is actually beginning to escape as they are being inflated.

II. Translate the following sentences into English.

1. 车辆辅助约束系统用于在发生事故时保护乘员。

2. 侧安全气囊通常设在座位背部的外侧边缘、车门或车门顶部。

3. 安全气囊系统的主要功能是检测碰撞、打开气囊和读取系统数据。

Reading Material

Read the following passages and answer the questions according to the information given in the passages.

Passage One   Clear Coated Wheel

Most original equipment aluminum wheels are clear coated for corrosion resistance. You can generally use any type of wax or sealer specially formulated for alloy wheels, or any product that is designed for a base coat, clear coat finish.

CAUTION: Do not use any wax or polish that contains abrasives on a clear coated wheel (chrome polish, rubbing compound, ordinary wax designed for ordinary painted finishes or that "restores faded paint"). The abrasives in such products will scratch and dull the clear coat on the wheels.

If your wheels are not clear coated, or the original coating is worn away or damaged, you can clean the wheels with "mag wheel polish" or fine steel wool to remove surface oxide and dirt (and what's left of the old finish)—then repaint the wheels with a durable clear coat epoxy or paint designed for this purpose.

Unprotected aluminum wheels quickly corrode and pit when exposed to road salt and excessive moisture. If the corrosion continues unchecked for too long, the cosmetic damage may be too great to reverse. So if you don't want to drive around with ugly, pitted alloy wheels, use some type of coating (wax, sealer and/or paint) to protect them from the elements.

When an aluminum wheel is mounted against a steel brake drum or rotor, the different compositions of the two metals often lead to electrolytic corrosion. Aluminum is the more reactive of the two, so the wheel can corrode and "weld" itself to the rotor or drum making removal very difficult. To prevent this from happening, the face of the rotor or drum (or the back face the alloy wheel) should be painted. Another alternative is to apply a light coat of lithium, silicone or synthetic brake grease to the back of the wheel where it butts up against the rotor or drum.

Another problem that sometimes plagues alloy wheels is porosity leaks. When an alloy wheel is cast, microscopic pores and voids may be left in the metal that allows air to slowly leak out of the tire. High pressure casting techniques have reduced, but not entirely eliminated this problem. So some alloy wheels are painted or coated on the inside to help seal the metal. If you've experienced this kind of problem, and your wheels are not coated or painted inside, they might need it.

Questions

1. What should you pay more attention to when work on a clear coated wheel?

2. What problems do the alloy wheel have?

3. What do you recommend for protecting aluminum wheels?

Passage Two　Brief Introduction of Some Equipments

Right tool for the right job. Without servicing equipments, a car can't be maintained or repaired well. Some key automobile servicing equipments are introduced as follows:

1　Vulker Water Cleaner

The water cleaners from the Lavorwash range have been designed and constructed to meet the most different use requirements and to guarantee the longest life and max reliability. The Vulker water cleaner is an extremely versatile machine, it can be used both as a professional machine and as a hobby appliance. The Vulker is necessary to perfectly wash cars, machinery, agricultural and garden tools, floors or outer coverings. In particular, it is recommended for the disinfestation of rooms and for sandblasting walls and railings. It is a powerful machine produced in strictest compliance with the CE norms in order to guarantee the max safety conditions for the operator. High-pressure pump having a brass head with 3 high-reliable ceramic pistons. Boiler made in quality steel with cathode painting treatment, forced ventilation to obtain a higher thermal efficiency. Double winding tube-shaped coil in drawn steel for a high heat-exchange. Electric motor-fan assembly of new construction, directly coupled with pressure pump and with gas oil pump. Automatic sensor zeroing and self-test sequence upon start-up.

2　Multigas

Gas and smoke analysis

Coordinated use of gas and smoke analyzers

Multigas 488 and Multigas 488 Plus are exhaust analyzers for gasoline engines. They can be used autonomously of managed by Visa family or Flex centers. Multigas 473 Box is an exhaust gas analyzers for gasoline engines. It has to be used with Visa family or Flex centers.

Smokemeter 495/01 is a smoke analysis cell for diesel engines managed by Visa family or Flex centers.

Multigas Plus

CO, CO_2, HC, O_2, NO_X

$LAMBDA(\lambda)$, $TEMP(℃)$, rpm

Mod 488

Infrared exhaust gas analyzer

Multigas 488 Plus is an infrared exhaust gas analyzer for gasoline engines.

Tests conducted with 488 allow operators to measure the carbon monoxide (CO), carbon dioxide (CO_2), unburnt hydrocarbons (HC) and oxygen (O_2) values according to which the LAMBDA coefficient is automatically calculated. This is essential as a reference in order to correctly tune the engine. Moreover, for the countries which apply to obtain it, the calculation of the correct CO is also available. The operator's work is facilitated since the rpm and oil temperature values can be kept under control at the same time. Kit is also available as an optional in order to measure nitrogen oxides (NO_X).

Multigas 488 Plus is used by Car Manufacturers and has been approved according to the standards in force in numerous European countries:

Italy (DM 628 del 23/10/96-Classe 1), Germany (AU), United Kingdom (OIML1 and OIML 1996), France (Class 1 DRIRE), Austria (KDV 32), Belgium, Slovakia, Czech Republic, Portugal and in various Asian nations.

Measuring range	
Induction rpm counter	0–9990 rpm
Thermometer	5℃–200℃
Operating temperature	5℃–40℃
Measuring gas flow	8L/min.(about)
Flow control inside and automatic	
Tightness test automatic	
Condensate discharge continuous and automatic	
Response time	<10 sec.
Heating time	max 15 min
Mains power supply	110/220/240 V(±15%)
Mains frequency	50/60 Hz(±3%)
Zero setting electronic and automatic	
Calibration electronic and automatic	
Serial output	RS232
Clock printed date and time	
Printer	24 column
LCD	2×16 column
Storage temperature	min −20℃; max +60℃
Dimension	400 mm×180 mm×420 mm
Weight	13.5kg

3　Tech 2 Flash Scan by OTC

Supports on-board diagnostics for all GM systems

1992　through　1998

Authentic GM software means you are on equal footing with GM dealers

Removable hardware modules provide insurance against scan tool obsolescence

PC memory cards are available separately to expand and enhance the investment

Scanner is reprogrammable to keep pace with vehicle and tool evolution

Basic set includes OTC Tec 2 flash, vehicle power cables, necessary vehicle adapters and 10 MB '92-'98 GM PC diagnostic card in heavy duty storage case.

4　She-ff300 Fault Finder by Sheffield Pro

Electrical Wiring

Quickly track down short circuits, open connections, broken wires, current leaks

Operates on DC voltages from 6 to 36 volts

Positive detection of fault

Transmitter/receiver LED for open/short circuit

Adjustable speaker level on receiver

10″ flexible probe for hard to reach places

No wire piercing required

Wire tracing in bundles, conduits, behind panels, under carpets, upholstery, etc.

Variable flashing and beeping provides feedback on the proximity of the wire

5　Analyzer by OTC

Vision Premier

High Speed Ignition Scope, Lab Scope, and Engine Analyzer

Expandable and Updateable Via CD ROM

Fast, High Resolution Color Scope

Displays "live" digital ignition and Lab Scope Patterns

Largest and most detailed scope display

Intuitive, easy-to-use Software

Built-In, Robust, On-Line Help and Operator Guide

Personal Computer Based Tool

The Engine Analyzer Module is compatible with modern Personal Computers (You stay current with PC Technology).

Additional benefits:

Expandability protects your investment.

Modern technology keeps you current with new vehicle testing needs.

Long-term value for a moderate investment.

Catches and displays intermittent and high speed events that slower, hand-held and old technology analyzers miss — saving you diagnostic time.

Because the tool is easy to use, you will spend your time productively — not learning the tool. Quickly gets new technicians up-to-speed so they are productive.

Modern technology allows you to pick your PC platform and keep pace with the ever changing PC World.

You control the costs.

6　CO-210 Carbon Monoxide Probe

Accurately measure CO levels with easy-to-use probe

Features at a Glance

The Fluke CO-210 Carbon Monoxide Probe is an accessory for use with a digital multimeter with DC millivolt inputs. The CO-210 utilizes the newest generation of electro-chemical sensors (fast responding) and an intelligent microprocessor to provide higher accuracy and reliability. Use the CO-210 as an accessory to your digital multimeter for a display of carbon monoxide levels, or as a stand-alone indicator by relying upon the "sun-bright" LED and beeper which trigger with increasing frequency as the levels of CO rise.

Rugged case and electronics

Displays CO levels on multimeter from 0 to 1000 ppm

Acts as a stand-alone device with LED and beeper CO indicators

CO indicator beeper can be silenced

Automatic sensor zeroing and self-test sequence upon start-up

Easy to replace battery

Simple on/off switch operation

Replaceable sensor extends tool life

Includes C50 Soft Carrying Case, battery (installed) and instruction sheet

Detachable RJ-45 connection to probe and standard banana jack to multimeter

Automatic power-off after 20 minutes extends battery life.

Battery life 500 hours with alkaline battery

Stabilized electrochemical CO specific sensor with 2 seconds warm-up

Typical 3 years sensor life; one year calibration cycle

Specifications Range: 0 to 1000 ppm

Resolution: 1 ppm

Accuracy: 3%

Questions

1. What is the function of a Multigas?

2. What problems can the Analyzer solve?

3. What does a CO-210 Carbon Monoxide Probe do?

Unit 6　Air Conditioning

Air conditioning makes driving much more comfortable in hot weather. Your car's air conditioner cleans and dehumidifies (removes excess moisture) the outside air entering your car. It also has the task of keeping the air at the temperature you select. These are all big jobs. How do our cars keep our "riding environment" the way we like?

The air conditioner works much like the refrigerator used in your home. It has five basic parts: receiver, expansion valve, evaporator, compressor and condenser, as shown in Figure 4-9.

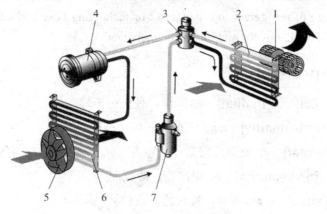

Figure 4-9　Air Conditioner

1—blower　2—evaporator　3—expansion valve　4—compressor　5—condenser　6—fan　7—drier

As the compressor raises the pressure of the refrigerant, it also heats it. The hot refrigerant is then pumped into the condenser, where it is cooled off by giving off heat to air passing over the condenser fins. As the refrigerant cools, it condenses into liquid. Still under high pressure, the refrigerant passes into the receiver.

The receiver acts as a storage tank to send refrigerant to the expansion valve at all times. From the receiver, the high-pressure liquid refrigerant passed to the expansion valve.

The expansion valve controls the flow of refrigerant into the evaporator, where a low pressure is maintained by the suction side of the compressor. As it enters the evaporator, the refrigerant begins to boil by absorbing the heat from the air passing over the evaporator core. Having given up its heat to boil the refrigerant, the air is cooled and passes into the passenger compartment. The refrigerant continues to boil in the evaporator until all the liquid has been vaporized. From the evaporator, the refrigerant flows back to the compressor to repeat the cycle.

Recharging the AC system

CAUTION: The high side of the AC system is under considerable pressure. If a can of refrigerant is connected to the high side service fitting, it may explode! The system must therefore

be recharged by using the low side service fitting only. If you are not sure which fittings should be used, do not attempt to recharge your air conditioner yourself. Wear eye protection and avoid direct contact with the refrigerant as it can cause frostbite on bare skin.

The basic recharging procedure goes as follows:

1. Identify the low side service fitting.

2. Determine the type of refrigerant required by the system. On most 1993 and older vehicles, this would be R12. On most 1994 and newer vehicles, it would be R134a.

CAUTION: R12 and R134a refrigerants are incompatible and must not be intermixed. Use the type of refrigerant required for your AC system only. On most 1993 and newer vehicles, there's an identification decal or sticker that tells what kind of refrigerant is required. Also, the size and design of R134a and R12 service fittings are different to avoid cross-contamination.

3. Connect a can of refrigerant to a gauge set or recharging hose and valve set. Follow the equipment supplier's directions for making the connections.

Words and Expressions

1. dehumidify [ˌdiːhjuːˈmidifai] v. 除湿，使……干燥

2. automotive [ɔːtəˈməutiv] adj. 汽车的，自动推进的

3. comfort [ˈkʌmfət] n. 安慰，舒适，安慰者 vt. 安慰，使(痛苦等)缓和

4. refrigerator [riˈfridʒəreitə] n. 电冰箱，冷藏库

5. receiver [riˈsiːvə] n. 接收者，接收器，收信机

6. evaporator [iˈvæpəreitə] n. 蒸发器，脱水器

7. compressor [kəmˈpresə] n. 压缩物，压缩机

8. condenser [kənˈdensə] n. 冷凝器；电容器

9. refrigerant [riˈfridʒərənt] adj. 制冷的 n. 制冷剂

10. storage [ˈstɔridʒ] n. 贮藏(量)，贮藏库，存储

11. boil [bɔil] n. 沸点，沸腾；疖子 v. 煮沸；激动

12. considerable [kənˈsidərəbl] adj. 相当地，可观地，重要地

13. frostbite [ˈfrɔstbait] n. 冻伤，冻疮 v. 使……冻伤

14. riding environment 驾乘环境

15. air conditioner 空调

16. expansion valve 膨胀阀

17. condenser fin 冷凝器肋片

18. high-pressure liquid refrigerant 高压液态制冷剂

19. evaporator core 蒸发器芯

20. passenger compartment 驾驶室

21. repeat the cycle 重复循环

22. recharge the AC system   重新加注制冷剂

23. bare skin   裸露皮肤

24. flow back   回流

Notes

1. Your car's air conditioner cleans and dehumidifies (removes excess moisture) the outside air entering your car.

汽车空调系统对进入汽车内的外部空气进行清洁和除湿。

2. The hot refrigerant is then pumped into the condenser, where it is cooled off by giving off heat to air passing over the condenser fins.

热的制冷剂此时被泵送进入冷凝器，在此其热量由流经冷凝器肋片的空气带走而被冷却。

3. The expansion valve controls the flow of refrigerant into the evaporator, where a low pressure is maintained by the suction side of the compressor.

膨胀阀控制着进入蒸发器的制冷剂流量，蒸发器中通过压缩机的进气侧保持一个低压状态。

4. Wear eye protection and avoid direct contact with the refrigerant as it can cause frostbite on bare skin.

戴好眼罩并且避免和制冷剂直接接触，因为它会在裸露的皮肤上造成冻伤。

5. On most 1993 and newer vehicles, there's an identification decal or sticker that tells what kind of refrigerant is required.

1993 年及以后的车上有识别标记或贴标说明所需制冷剂的类型。

Exercises

A. Vocabulary

I. Translate the following expressions into Chinese.

1. riding environment

2. expansion valve

3. condenser fin

4. high-pressure liquid refrigerant

5. bare skin

6. recharging procedure

7. evaporator core

8. passenger compartment

9. repeat the cycle

10. recharging the AC system

II. Identify the English names of the piston assemblies according to the picture.

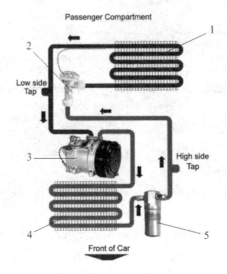

1. _____ 2. _____ 3. _____ 4. _____ 5. _____

B. Comprehension

I. Discuss the following questions in groups and write down your answers.

1. What's the function of the AC system?

_____

_____

2. What is the AC system composed of?

_____

_____

3. How to recharge the AC system?

_____

_____

II. Read the following passage carefully and fill in the blanks with the proper forms of the given words.

maintain	*boil*	*refrigerant*	*flow back*	*liquid*
vaporize	*suction*	*evaporator*	*give up*	*compartment*

The expansion valve controls the flow of _____ into the evaporator, where a low pressure is _____ by the _____ side of the compressor. As it enters the _____, the refrigerant begins to _____ by absorbing the heat from the air passing over the evaporator core. Having _____ its heat to boil the refrigerant, the air is cooled and passes into the passenger _____. The refrigerant continues to boil in the evaporator until all the _____ has been _____. From the evaporator, the refrigerant _____ to the compressor to repeat the cycle.

C. Translation

I. Translate the following sentences into Chinese.

1. As the refrigerant cools, it condenses into liquid. Still under high pressure, the refrigerant passes into the receiver.

2. Determine the type of refrigerant required by the system. On most 1993 and older vehicles, this would be R12. On most 1994 and newer vehicles, it would be R134a.

3. Connect a can of refrigerant to a gauge set or recharging hose and valve set. Follow the equipment supplier's directions for making the connections.

II. Translate the following sentences into English.

1. 空调系统由压缩机、冷凝器、蒸发器、储液器和膨胀阀五个基本配件组成。

2. 空调的任务包括冷却、干燥和循环。

3. 制冷剂沸腾或变成蒸气时，它从流过冷凝器肋片的空气吸收热量。

Reading Material

Read the following passages and answer the questions according to the information given in the passages.

Passage One   Coolant Leak

My cooling system keeps losing coolant, but I don't see any leaks. Where is it going?

You probably have an "internal" coolant leak inside your engine. The coolant is escaping into the combustion chamber or crankcase through cracks in the cylinder head or block, or through a leaky head gasket.

In rare instances, coolant may also leak into the automatic transmission fluid cooler if one is located inside the radiator. But usually when automatic transmission fluid leaks into the coolant it means the line is leaking.

Pressure testing the cooling system is necessary to diagnose an internal leak. A "cylinder leak-down test" can tell a mechanic if the coolant leak is in the combustion chamber. But to pinpoint an internal leak, it is usually necessary to remove the head(s) from the engine. The head may then be pressure tested and/or checked for cracks using special equipment.

Minor internal leaks can sometimes be temporarily sealed by adding a sealer to the cooling system. But large leaks or ones that do not respond to a sealer will have to be fixed.

If the problem is a cracked head or block, repairs may or may not be possible depending on the nature of the crack. Cracks in aluminum can often be repaired by welding while those in cast iron can be fixed by pinning the damaged area. But some cracks may be so bad that they are beyond repair or in a location that makes repair impossible. In such cases, the head or block must be replaced.

If a leaky head gasket is the culprit, replacing the gasket may only temporarily cure the problem if the head or block is warped. The mating surfaces on both the head and block should be

checked for flatness and resurfaced if necessary to restore flatness for a proper seal.

Questions

1. What does "internal leak" mean?

2. If the problem is a cracked head or block, what to do the next?

3. How to do a pressure testing for the cooling system?

Passage Two   Refrigerant Leak

The two most common ways for a do-it-yourselfer to find a leak is to visually inspect the system for telltale oil stains, or add a can of "leak detector" to the system and then look for the presence of the colored dye around hose connections and fittings.

When refrigerant leaks from the system, it immediately evaporates into thin air leaving no trace except possibly the compressor oil residue that leaks out with it. Wet oily areas around hose connections and fittings and/or greasy streaks radiating outward around the compressor clutch or on the underside of the hood just above the compressor are good visual clues to where the leak is.

Leak detecting dyes will often reveal tiny leaks that might escape visual detection. Some are fluorescent and require illumination with a special light before you can see them. Even so, even dyes can fail to show you where a leak is if the leak is in the evaporator (located inside the heater/defroster plenum under the dash) or in a hard-to-observe or hidden location.

Most professionals use an "electronic" leak detector that reacts to the presence of refrigerant in air. Such detectors are extremely sensitive and can detect leaks as small as 1/4 oz. of refrigerant per year!

Fixing Leaks

Once a leak has been identified and pinpointed, it should be fixed. Don't waste your time on "stop leak" products because they seldom work.

Leaks should be fixed for three reasons. First, leaks allow air and moisture to enter your A/C system. Moisture can react with refrigerant to form corrosive acids and sludge that can damage the compressor, plug up orifice tubes and/or eat pinholes in evaporators and condensers. Second, refrigerant is expensive. It may seem cheaper to keep recharging your system with additional refrigerant instead of having the leak fixed, but in the long run it won't be as the cost of R12 refrigerant continues to rise. Third, R12 refrigerant is an ozone-depleting CFC. When it leaks into the atmosphere, it drifts up into the stratosphere and destroys ozone that protects us from the sun's harmful ultraviolet radiation.

Before any attempt is made to repair a leak, any refrigerant that's still in your system should be recovered and recycled. All service facilities that do A/C work are required by law to have such equipment.

Once the old refrigerant has been pumped out of your system, it can be opened for repairs. The desiccant (crystals that absorb moisture and help protect the system against moisture contamination) in the accumulator or receiver/drier should also be replaced if the system has lost all its refrigerant or must be left open for more than a few hours for repairs.

After the leak has been repaired, the system must be connected to a vacuum pump to purge it of all air and moisture before it is recharged with refrigerant. Leaving air and moisture in the system will greatly reduce the cooling efficiency of the system and will lead to the formation of damaging acids and sludge.

It's also important to replace any compressor oil that was lost due to leakage or parts replacement. Use the type and quantity specified by the vehicle manufacturer.

CAUTION: Using the wrong type of compressor oil or too much or too little oil may result in compressor failure.

Questions

1. What does "leak detector" mean?

2. Your A/C system is leaking refrigerant. How can you find the leak?

3. How should you do when fixing leaks?

Chapter 5　Car Selling

Unit 1　Some Basic Marketing Theory

Marketing is more than sales. Marketing is the set of activities used to deal with the following matters:

(1) get your potential customers' attention;

(2) motivate them to buy;

(3) get them to buy actually;

(4) get them to buy again and again…

Marketing is a process regarding how to define your product, promote your product, distribute your product, and maintain a relationship with your customers.

Target Market

Target market is the group of potential customers selected for marketing. If you are looking to segment the market, you need to determine the different target markets for each segment.

Marketing theory is made up of the 5Ps, i.e. product, positioning, place, price and promotion. Each "P" contributes to your marketing mix.

Product

Product is, of course, the thing (or service) that you have to offer to the customers. There are a number of things you should evaluate regarding product.

It is important to understand your product from the customers' point of view.

1) Product Description

It is critical to be able to say in one clear sentence why your product is perfect for a specific buyer and what it does best.

2) Product Name

It is more important to be descriptive than creative for a product's name.

3) Functionality, Features & Benefits

In order to understand the product from a customer's point of view, list the functionality, the features and the benefits that the product has.

Positioning

Simply, positioning is how your target market defines you in relation to your competitors.

A good position is what makes you unique. This is considered a benefit by your target market.

This is necessary for a good positioning. So what if you are the only red-haired singer who only knows how to play a G minor chord? Does your target market consider this a good thing?

Positioning is important because you are competing with all the noise out there competing for your potential fans'attention. If you can stand out with a unique benefit, you have a chance at getting their attention.

It is important to understand your product from the customers'point of view relative to the competition.

There are three types of segmentation as follows:

- Mass Marketing or Undifferentiated Marketing: Go after the whole market with one offer and focus on common needs rather than differences.
- Product-variety Marketing or Differentiated Marketing: Target several market segments and design separate offers for each.
- Target Marketing or Concentrated Marketing: Large share of one or a few sub-markets. Good when company's resources are limited.

Place

Place, or distribution channel, is the method for making your product available to the consumers.

There are eight main functions for distribution channels in the following:

- Information: Gathering and distributing marketing research;
- Promotion: Developing and communicating offers;
- Contact: Communicating with prospective buyers;
- Matching: Fitting the offer to the buyer's needs;
- Negotiation: Reaching agreement on price and terms;
- Physical distribution: Transporting and storing the goods;
- Financing: Getting and using funds to cover the costs of channel work;
- Risk Taking: Assuming the risks of carrying out the channel work.

Price

Price is the amount of money charged for a product or service or the value exchanged for the benefits of the product or service.

For a new product, you must understand your positioning before you set a price. Make sure it is not too low, or the product will not be taken seriously. If it is too high, the potential customer will not take the risk.

There are five general pricing strategies as follows:

- Product Line: Setting price steps between product line items;
- Optional Product: Pricing optional or accessory products;
- Captive Product: Pricing products that must be used with the main product;
- By-Product: Pricing low value by-product to get rid of them;
- Product Bundle: Pricing bundles of products sold together.

There are two new product pricing strategies in the following:

(1) Market-Skimming: Initially set high prices to "skim" revenue layer by layer from the market in the following situations:

- Quality and image support the higher price;

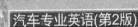 

- Enough buyers want the product at that price;
- Cost of producing a small volume cannot be high;
- Competitors should not be able to enter the market easily.

(2) Market Penetration: Set a low initial price in order to penetrate the market quickly and deeply to win a large market share in the following situations:

- Market is highly price sensitive;
- Production and distribution costs fall as sales volume increases;
- Low price must help keep out the competition.

Promotion

Promotion is the specific mix of advertising, personal selling, sales promotion and public relations a company uses to pursue its advertising and marketing objectives.

If you are an entrepreneur, you most likely have limited resources and you are still learning about the market. Information gather is extremely important at this stage of the game. The trick is to start the revenue stream without spending too much money.

Words and Expressions

1. descriptive [dis'kriptiv] *adj.* 叙述的

2. potential [pə'tenʃ(ə)l] *adj.* 潜在的

3. prospective [prəs'pektiv] *adj.* 预期的

4. distribution [ˌdistri'bjuːʃən] *n.* 分配，分销

5. entrepreneur [ˌɔntrəprə'nəː] *n.* 企业家

6. sensitive ['sensitiv] *adj.* 敏感的

7. penetration [peni'treiʃən] *n.* 渗透，穿透；侵入

8. marketing ['mɑːkitiŋ] *n.* 市场营销

9. promotion [prə'məuʃən] *n.* 促销

10. segmentation [ˌsegmən'teiʃən] *n.* 市场细分

11. competitor [kəm'petitə] *n.* 竞争者

12. advertising ['ædvətaiziŋ] *n.* 广告

13. marketing mix   营销组合

14. mass marketing   完全市场覆盖

15. product-variety marketing   专门化市场

16. target marketing   密集单一市场

17. market penetration   市场渗透

18. market-skimming   撇脂定价

19. sales volume   销量

20. personal selling   人员推销

21. sales promotion   促销
22. public relation   公共关系

Notes

1. It is critical to be able to say in one clear sentence why your product is perfect for a specific buyer and what it does best.

用言简意赅的一句话说明你的产品适宜特定的客户以及它在什么方面最好是很关键的。

2. In order to understand the product from a customer's point of view, list the functionality, the features, and the benefits that the product has.

为了从客户的角度理解产品，列出产品所具备的功能、特性和好处。

3. Target Marketing or Concentrated Marketing: Large share of one or a few sub-markets. Good when company's resources are limited.

密集单一市场：选择一个或几个细分化的专门市场作为营销目标，当企业资源有限的时候适合细分市场。

Exercises

A. Vocabulary

I. Draw lines to match the English and Chinese words.

a) marketing

b) product

c) positioning

d) place

e) promotion

f) price

g) pricing strategy

h) target market

i) marketing mix

j) mass marketing

k) product-variety marketing

l) target marketing

m) market penetration

n) market-skimming

o) sales volume

p) personal selling

q) sales promotion

r) public relation

s) segmentation

t) competitor

1. 产品
2. 分销
3. 促销
4. 目标市场
5. 促销
6. 人员推销
7. 定价策略
8. 公共关系
9. 市场营销
10. 营销组合
11. 密集单一市场
12. 价格
13. 完全市场覆盖
14. 销量
15. 专门化市场
16. 市场细分
17. 竞争者
18. 撇脂定价
19. 市场定位
20. 市场渗透

B. Description

I. Discuss the following questions in groups and write down your answers.

1. What is the definition of marketing ?

_____

_____

2. What is marketing theory made up of?

_____

_____

3. Is it important to understand your product from the customers point of view? Why?

_____

_____

4. What types of segmentation do you know?

_____

_____

II. Fill the missing words in the blanks of the following dialogue and role-play in pairs adapted from the dialogue.

Lisa: Hi, John. I heard that you have taken part in a training class of auto marketing recently, haven't you?

John: Yes, I have. I learned a lot.

Lisa: May I ask you some questions about auto marketing?

John: Certainly.

Lisa: Could you please tell me what the definition of target market is?

John: It is _____.

Lisa: What is 5P's made up of?

John: It's made up of _____.

Lisa: How to achieve a good position?

John: There are 2 points _____.

Lisa: Thank you for telling me so much knowledge regarding marketing.

C. Translation

I. Translate the following sentences into Chinese.

1. Promotion is the specific mix of advertising, personal selling, sales promotion and public relations a company uses to pursue its advertising and marketing objectives.

2. Market Penetration: Set a low initial price in order to penetrate the market quickly and deeply to win a large market share.

3. It is important to understand your product from the customers point of view relative to the competition.

4. It is critical to be able to say in one clear sentence why your product is perfect for a specific buyer and what it does best.

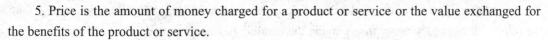

5. Price is the amount of money charged for a product or service or the value exchanged for the benefits of the product or service.

II. Translate the following sentences into English.

1. 要细分市场，就要为每个细分市场确定不同的目标客户。

2. 完全市场覆盖：针对消费者的共同需要，把整个市场作为一个大目标，不考虑细分市场间的区别。

3. 营销并非销售。营销是一整套活动，用来：①引起潜在客户的注意；②激发他们的购买欲望；③促使客户实施购买行为；④促使客户持续购买。

4. 产品就是你要提供给客户的实物或者服务。你需要对产品的以下几项特别注意。

5. 价格是为产品或者服务付出的金钱总额。

Reading Material

Read the following passages and answer the questions according to the information given in the passages.

Passage One   Four-square Basics — How the Dealer Works the Numbers

To help you get the best deal when you buy your next car, you should understand how the salespeople will "work the numbers" on a four-square worksheet as they negotiate. The worksheet, which covers everything from auto loan payments to trade-in price, helps the salespeople view the total profit to the dealership while reviewing the separate elements of the deal.

As the name suggests, the sheet is divided into the following four large squares:

1. Trade-in: How much the dealership will credit you for your trade-in. This figure is credited toward your purchase of a new vehicle. Dealers would like you to put 1/3 down. However, this figure is negotiable and can certainly be less than 1/3 the price of the car.

2. Purchase price of the dealer's car: This is the price of the car. Often a dealer will write the price of the car, then write "plus fees", indicating that, on top of the cost of the car, you will pay sales tax, title and licensing fees.

3. Down payment: How much cash are you willing to pay up front? Down payments made using a credit card are also considered "cash up front".

4. Monthly payments: How high a monthly auto loan payment are you willing to make? Car salespeople try to get the customer to focus on this figure since it most directly affects a person's budget.

As you can see, these four separate pieces are interconnected. If, for example, a customer is concerned about receiving the full value of her trade-in, the dealer will inflate the amount of the trade-in and then raise the monthly payment on the auto loan regarding the new car. Now the customer is satisfied, but the dealer is still making the same total amount of profit.

Avoid Being Trapped by the Four-square

First of all, try to keep the deal as simple as possible. Consider selling your old car rather than trading it in. With a little effort, you could save a lot of money, or secure outside auto

financing before you go to the dealership. Taking these advance steps will allow you to negotiate the price of the car only rather than playing the monthly payment game.

If you want to trade in your current vehicle and become a monthly payment buyer (sometimes dealers can offer attractively low interest rates), work the numbers yourself before you go to the dealership. Decide what your maximum down payment and monthly auto loan payment should be. Then, decide on your lowest figure for the trade-in. Now, write all these figures down so that you can control the whole deal to limit your expenses in the same way the dealer tries to maximize his profit.

Questions

1. What is a four-square worksheet?

2. What is the function of a four-square dealing?

3. How to avoid being trapped by the four-square?

Passage Two   Fluke

The new Fluke Automotive ScopeMeter test tool is a powerful instrument with a wild variety of capabilities.

Its menu-driven Interface has automatic configurations for most of your tests, so you will find that the test tool is easy to use.

Continuous AUTO RANGE, an exclusive Fluke feature，constantly acquires and displays the best possible signal.

The secondary ignition pickup and automated ignition functions make it easy for you to analyze an ignition system malfunction

The relative compression mode helps you quickly find a low compression cylinder.

The Secondary Ignition Single function displays the waveform along with the spark voltage，RPM，burn time and burn voltage.

Many problems you will encounter are under a load on a road test.

The Intermittent Record function can find and display such a problem. This record function can record up to 1,280 divisions of continuous information.

The Flight Record function records screen snapshots from 200ms per division up to full time base speed.

The Plot Readings function allows you to plot up to four different readings of a signal over time with a single connection.

Min/Max TrendPlot continuously monitors the minimum, maximum and average value of a signal's readings with time stamp.

The Automotive ScopeMeter test tool has a wide variety of accessories，designed to enhance the test tool's measurement power.

The optional diesel accessories allow you to set injection pump timing and rpm with confidence.

The optional 90i-610s Current Probe will let you measure and analyze electrical system problems quickly and easily.

The optional TR90 Temperature Probe will let you measure and analyze temperature measurements safe and easy.

Test lead extensions are included for most of your long distance measurements.

A wide variety of probes and clips are included to make connection to the vehicle quick and easy.

Additional probes are available as accessories easily connecting to the test leads.

Even though your instrument has been designed to configure itself to almost any test, review the following examples.

Automotive   Applications

Air Flow Sensors

Analog, Digital, and Potentiometer Sensors

ANALOG MASS AIR FLOW (MAF)SENSOR

This mass air flow sensor uses a heated-metal-foil sensing element to measure air flow entering the intake manifold. The sensing element is heated to a temperature of about 170°F (77°C), above the temperature of incoming air. As air flows over the sensing element, it cools the element, causing resistance to drop. This causes a corresponding increase in current flow, which causes supply voltage to decrease. This signal is seen by the ECU as a change in voltage drop(an increase in air flow causes an increase in voltage drop), and is used as an indication of air flow.

DIGITAL MASS AIR FLOW SENSOR (MAF)

This type of air flow sensor receives a 5 volt reference signal from the electronic control unit and sends back a variable frequency signal that is equivalent to the mass of air entering the engine . The output signal is a square wave, with amplitude fixed at 0 and 5 volts. Frequency of the signal varies from about 30 Hz to 150 Hz. Low frequency equals low air flow; high frequency equals high air flow.

AIR-FLOW METER (Potentiometer)

Air-flow meters have a spring-loaded vane that pivots on a shaft as it opens and closes in response to a volume of incoming air. A variable resistor "potentiometer" is connected to the vane at its pivot point, causing the output voltage signal to change as the air vane angle changes. When the vane is wild open, the ECU knows that a maximum amount of air is being drawn into the engine, and when it is closed, a minimum amount of air is entering the engine. The ECU responds by increasing or decreasing fuel injector pulse width accordingly.

The electronic control units use these signals to calculate fuel injector pulse width or ON time and ignition timing. Engine coolant temperature engine speed, manifold air temperature, and the air flow sensor signals enable the computer to make the necessary calculations and adjustments.

Vehicle Speed Sensor (VSS) — Magnetic, Hall-Effect and Optical

The VSS output signal is directly proportional to vehicle speed. The ECU controls torque-converter clutch lockup, electronic transmission shift levels, and other functions from this signal. There are three main sensor types used for the Vehicle Speed Sensor: magnetic, Hall-effect and optical.

Variable Reluctance Sensors (magnetic) do not require a separates power connection and have two connecting wires for the stationary magnet's coil. Small signal voltages are induced at the teeth of a trigger wheel，made of a low magnetic reluctance steel, pass through the magnetic field of a stationary magnet and coil.

Optical sensors use a rotor disk that separates LEDs from optical pickups. Small openings, or slits, in the rotor disk, allow light from the LEDs to energize the optical pickups. Each time a slit aligns with the LEDs and optical pickups，the pickup sends out a pulse.

Measurement Conditions

Raise the drive wheels off the ground and place the transmission in drive.

Connect the test tool to the sensor according to the instruments Connection Help and start the engine.

Monitor the VSS output signal at low speed while gradually increasing the speed of the drive wheels.

Questions

1. What are the functions of a Fluke Automotive ScopeMeter test tool?

2. How should one check air-flow meters with the Fluke?

3. Please introduce the Fluke to your classmates.

Unit 2　How to Be a Good Car Salesman

How to be a good car salesman, here are a few points:

1. One mistake that seems to be prominent in our business is for guys to continually move store to store. If you do that you can't build a clientele, repeat and referral business. Plus your integrity is shot to hell. How can a guy spend three months telling folks that fords are the greatest thing, then switch to a Chevy store and trash Ford?

2. Always ask questions. Listen to what your customers are telling you. Take a real interest in finding the vehicle that meets all of their needs within their budget. Usually a salesperson decides that Mr. Jones really needs a Miata, and decides what he will get. When Mr. Jones has already said he has three kids and likes to go camping, listen to what they want and need. Only after you have asked all the questions and gathered information should you present a car.

3. Know your product. I have been embarrassed to see people who work for me and did not know how to fold down the seats in a Tahoe. Take time each day to learn about a vehicle in your inventory. Learn the pros and cons, strengths and weaknesses, and how it compares to your competition.

4. Follow up religiously. Call the people who bought cars from you and make sure they are happy. Make sure you answer any questions they have. Do not leave them high and dry after you have made a sale. Remember that buying a car is a huge decision for people. They need to feel

comfortable with their choices. Part of that is your follow through.

5. Do not be afraid to ask for referrals. Your customers who bought from you have friends and family who need a car too. Talk to the clerk at the supermarket and the receptionist at the doctor's office.

6. Lastly — and the most importantly — always be honest with your customers. If you don't know an answer, say so, and find out for them. Don't promise anything you cannot deliver. Don't tell them a car has something when it doesn't. Don't mislead or lie to any of your customers. Sure, you can promise the sun and moon in order to make a big deal once. But it will come back to bite you a thousand times over. And, that customer will never send you a referral, and never come back to you again. Remember：Customer satisfaction is always No. 1. It's not selling cars, it's selling yourself, and make sure you learn the four most important steps.

1. Meet and greet-hand shake. Don't let there hand go till you get their whole name first and last.

2. Fact find. Find out what kind of car fits their needs, not what they want. How many kids, what they do for living, what purpose the vehicle will be used for. car, truck, SUV or van.

3. Check the Inventory — Show them what you have on your lot-do not let them walk around free, and keep in control of them let them follow you. In that way when it get close to the closing, YOU are in control.

4. Demonstration get them in the car and have them drive you around. This is where you find out about them while you make them love the vehicle.

Words and Expressions

1. prominent ['prɔminənt] *adj.* 显著的，突出的，杰出的

2. clientele [ˌkliːɑːn'teil] *n.* 老主顾

3. budget ['bʌdʒit] *n.* 预算

4. embarrassed [im'bærəs] *adj.* 尴尬的,局促的

5. demo ['deməu] *n.* 演示

6. van [væn] *n.* 货车

7. SUV *n.* 运动多用途车

8. referral [ri'fəːrəl] *n.* 推荐人

9. inventory ['invəntri] *n.* 库存

10. lot [lɔt] *n.* 车场，车店

11. pros and cons 正反两方面

12. customer satisfaction 客户满意

13. meet and greet 欢迎与问候

14. promise the sun and moon 对天发誓

15. close to the closing 临近尾声

Notes

1. One mistake that seems to be prominent in our business is for guys to continually move store to store.

干我们这一行的年轻人的一个突出错误就是频繁跳槽。

2. How can a guy spend three months telling folks that Fords are the greatest thing, then switch to a Chevy store and trash Ford?

如果一个年轻人在福特干了三个月，一直在夸福特是最棒的，转而又跳槽到雪佛兰贬低福特，那情况会怎样？

3. I have been embarrassed to see people who work for me and did not know how to fold down the seats in a Tahoe.

我曾很尴尬地看到为我工作的销售员不知如何放倒塔霍车的座椅。

4. You can promise the sun and moon in order to make a big deal once. But it will come back to bite you a thousand times over.

你可以为了一个大生意对天信誓旦旦。但结果是它会报复你很多次。

5. Do not leave them high and dry after you have made a sale.

千万不能做完买卖后就把他们晾起来。

Exercises

A. Vehicle Introduction

Introduce Some Cars According to the Following Summaries.

2009 Ford Mustang Summary

The 2009 Mustang is a 2-door, 4-passenger family coupe, sports coupe, convertible, or convertible sports car, available in 8 trims, ranging from the V6 Coupe to the GT Premium Convertible.

Upon introduction, the V6 Coupe is equipped with a standard 4.0-liter, V6, 210-horsepower engine that achieves 17-mpg in the city and 26-mpg on the highway. The GT Premium convertible is equipped with a standard 4.6-liter, V8, 300-horsepower engine that achieves 15-mpg in the city and 23-mpg on the highway. A5-speed manual transmission with overdrive is standard on both trims, and a 5-speed automatic transmission with overdrive is optional.

The 2009 Mustang is a carryover from 2008.

2009 Ford Escape Hybrid Summary

The 2009 Escape Hybrid is a 4-door, 5-passenger sport-utility, available in 4 trims, ranging from the FWD to the Limited 4WD.

Upon introduction, the FWD is equipped with a standard 2.5-liter, I4 , 153-horsepower, hybrid engine that achieves 34-mpg in the city and 31-mpg on the highway. The Limited 4WD is equipped with a standard 2.5-liter, I4 , 153-horsepower, hybrid engine that achieves 29-mpg in the city and 27-mpg on the highway. A variable speed automatic transmission with overdrive is standard on both trims.

The 2009 Escape Hybrid is a carryover from 2008.

2008 Rolls-Royce Drophead Summary

The 2008 Drophead is a 2-door, 4-passenger luxury sedan, available in one trim only, the Coupe.

Upon introduction, the Drophead is equipped with a standard 6.75-liter, V12, 453-horsepower engine that achieves 11-mpg in the city and 18-mpg on the highway. A6-speed automatic transmission with overdrive is standard.

2009 Chrysler Aspen Summary

The 2009 Aspen is a 4-door, up to 8-passenger sport-utility, available in two trims, the Limited 4X2 and the Limited 4X4.

Upon introduction, both trims are equipped with a standard 4.7-liter, V8, 303-horsepower engine. A 5-speed automatic transmission with overdrive is standard.

The 2009 Aspen is a carryover from 2008.

B. Practical Writing

Sales Contract
销售合同

在国际贸易中，只要一方发盘，另一方表示接受，就已达成交易。但作为一份受法律保护的合同，除了当事人双方的承诺之外，还需要具备其他条件，例如，当事人的合法资格、合同的标的(即交易的商品)和内容的合法性、合同订立的基础和互为有偿的条件等。对进出口贸易合同的形式和内容，各国都有不同的规定。按照我国《合同法》的规定，销售合同必须以书面形式订立，且一般应包括以下内容：

1. 当事人的名称或姓名、国籍和地址；

2. 合同的类型和标的种类、范围、质量、标准、规格、数量等；

3. 履行的期限、地点和方式；

4. 价格条件、支付金额、支付方式和附带费用；

5. 合同的转让和转让条件；

6. 违约的赔偿和其他责任及争议解决办法；

7. 合同使用的文字及其效力。

SAMPLE

SALES CONTRACT

Seller: Jinling Foodstuff Import & Export Corporation

Address: 57 Renmin Road, Nanjing, China

Buyer: Smith & Dowson Co. Ltd.

Address:228 Queens Avenue, Kuala Lumpur, Malaysia

Under this Sales Contract, the Seller agrees to sell and the Buyer agrees to buy the under-mentioned goods according to the terms and conditions stipulated below:

Commodity: Jinling Canned Ham

Quantity: 5,000 cases with 20 tins each

Unit Price: $20 per case CIF Kuala Lumpur

Total Value: $100,000

Insurance: To be covered by the Seller for 110% of invoice value against All Risks as per the relevant Ocean Marine Cargo Clauses of the People's Insurance Company of China.

Port of Shipment: Shanghai

Port of Destination: Kuala Lumpur

Time of Shipment: During December 2015.

Terms of Payment: The Buyer shall open a 100% irrevocable L/C at sight to reach the Seller 30 days before the month of shipment.

Commodity Inspection: It is mutually agreed that the Certificate of Quality and Quantity issued by the China Import & Export Commodity Inspection Bureau at the port of shipment shall be taken as the basis of delivery.

Discrepancy and Claim: Any claim by the Buyer on the goods shipped shall be filed within 30 days after the arrival of the goods at the port of destination and supported by a survey report issued by a surveyor approved by the Seller .

Arbitration: All disputes arising out of the performance of, or relating to this Contract, shall be settled by arbitration by the China Council for the Promotion International Trade, Nanjing Branch.

Signed on the date of July 5, 2015, by

The Seller   The Buyer

Liu Chunsheng   Nahong Thanakalan

Manager   Sales   Manager

Jinling Foodstuff Import & Export Corporation   Smith & Dowson Co.Ltd.

Notes

1. Insurance: To be covered by the Seller for 110% of invoice value against All Risks as per the relevant Ocean Marine Cargo Clauses of the People's Insurance Company of China.

保险：卖方按照发票总值的 110%，按照中国人民保险公司海洋货运有关条例投保综合险。

2. Commodity Inspection: It is mutually agreed that the Certificate of Quality and Quantity issued by the China Import & Export Commodity Inspection Bureau at the port of shipment shall be taken as the basis of delivery.

商检：双方同意以中国出口商品检验局在装船港签发的质量数量证明作为交货的依据。

I. Translate the following contract.

销售合同

卖方：金陵食品进出口公司

地址：中国，南京，人民路 57 号

买方：史密斯和道森有限公司

地址：马来西亚，科伦坡，皇后大街 228 号

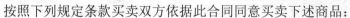

按照下列规定条款买卖双方依据此合同同意买卖下述商品：

商品：金陵火腿罐头

数量：500 件，每件 20 罐

单价：科伦坡到岸价 每件 20 美元

总价值：10 万美元

保险：由卖方按照发票总值的 110%，按照中国人民保险公司海洋货运有关条例投保综合险。

装运港：上海

目的港：科伦坡

装船时间：2015 年 12 月

支付条款：买方须在装船月前 30 天将开具的 100%不可撤销即期信用证送达卖方。

商品检查：双方同意以中国出口商品检验局在装船港签发的质量数量证明作为交货的依据。

异议与索赔：买方的任何关于运输商品的异议与索赔应于商品到港的 30 天内提出并同时提交卖方认可的检查员开具的检验报告。

仲裁：任何相关于合同或来自合同执行过程中产生的纠纷应由中国贸易促进会南京分会仲裁解决。

签订时间：2015 年 7 月 5 日

卖方：	买方：
刘春生	那红·他那客兰
经理	经理
金陵食品进出口公司	史密斯和道森有限公司

II. Write an English sales contract based on the following points.

提示：

销售合同

卖方：上海奇瑞汽车贸易进出口公司

地址：中国，芜湖，长春路 8 号

买方：玛利亚有限公司

地址：越南，胡志明市，沙土地大街 2 号

按照下列规定条款买卖双方依据此合同同意买卖下述商品：

商品：奇瑞轿车

数量：100 辆

单价：上海离岸价每辆 12 800 美元

总价值：1 280 000 美元

保险：由卖方按照发票总值的 110%，按照中国人民保险公司海洋货运有关条例投保综合险。

装运港：上海

目的港：胡志明市

装船时间：2015 年 12 月

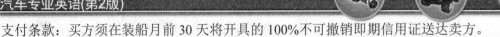

支付条款：买方须在装船月前 30 天将开具的 100%不可撤销即期信用证送达卖方。

商品检查：双方同意以中国出口商品检验局在装船港签发的质量数量证明作为交货的依据。

异议与索赔：买方的任何关于运输商品的异议与索赔应于商品到港的 30 天内提出并同时提交卖方认可的检查员开具的检验报告。

仲裁：任何相关于合同或来自合同执行过程中产生的纠纷应由中国贸易促进会上海分会仲裁解决。

签订时间：2015 年 10 月 5 日

卖方：　　　　　　　　　　　　　　　　买方：

尹同耀　　　　　　　　　　　　　　　　玛利亚

经理　　　　　　　　　　　　　　　　　经理

上海奇瑞汽车进出口公司　　　　　　　　玛利亚有限公司

Reading Material

Read the following passage and answer the questions according to the information given in the passages.

10 Steps to Selling Your Car

Selling is an art, selling your car is both an art and a skill. How to sell your car as quickly as possible? The 10 steps will do you a favor.

Step 1: Know the Market

Is your car going to be easy to sell? Is it a hot commodity? Or will you have to drop your price and search out additional avenues to sell it? Here are a few general rules to answer these questions:

- Family sedans, while unexciting to many, are in constant demand by people needing basic, inexpensive transportation.
- SUVs are very popular right now and often move quickly, even older models.
- The sale of convertibles and sports cars is seasonal. Sunny weather brings out the buyers. Fall and winter months will be slow.
- Trucks and vans, used for work, are steady sellers and command competitive prices. Don't underestimate their value.
- Collector cars will take longer to sell and are often difficult to price. However, these cars can have unexpected value if you find the right buyer.

Your first step is to check on-line classified ads to see how much others are asking for your type of car. For example, select the year and trim level of your car and see how many similar cars are currently on the market. Take note of their condition, mileage, geographic location and selling price so you can list your car at a price that will sell it quickly.

Step 2: Price Your Car Competitively

Once you have followed the prompts and gotten a specific price, you can also generate a "For Sale" sign. An Edmunds.com "For Sale" sign will give your price an air of authority.

There are always some exceptions to the rules of pricing, so you should follow your intuition. And be sure to leave a little wiggle room in your asking price. Ask for slightly more money than you are actually willing to accept. If you want to get $12,000 for the car, you should list the car at $12,500. That way, if you get $12,500 — great! But if you have to go lower, it won't be a terrible loss.

You may have noticed how creative used car dealers get in pricing cars. Their prices usually end in "995", as in $12,995. Are we not supposed to notice that the car basically costs $13,000? There is a lot of psychology in setting prices. A product that doesn't sell well at $20 might jump off the shelf at $19.95.

On the other hand, as a private party seller, you don't want to look like a car dealer. Therefore, you might want to take a simple approach and set your price at a round figure such as $12,750 or $12,500.

Step 3: Give Your Car "Curb Appeal"

When people come to look at your car, they will probably make up their minds to buy it or not within the first few seconds. This is based on their first look at the car. So you want this first look to be positive. You want your car to have "curb appeal".

Before you advertise your car for sale, make sure it looks as clean and attractive as realistically possible. This goes beyond just taking it to the car wash. Here is a to-do list that could help turn your heap into a cream puff:

- Make sure it is washed, waxed and detailed.
- Make sure your car is both mechanically sound and free from dents, dings and scrapes.
- Consider making low-cost repairs yourself rather than selling it "as is".
- Shovel out all the junk from the inside of the car. When prospective buyers go for a test-drive, you don't want them to feel like they've walked into your messy bedroom. Let them visualize the car as theirs.
- Wipe the brake dust off the wheel covers and clean the tires with a tire gloss product.
- Thoroughly clean the windows (inside and outside) and all the mirrored surfaces.
- Wipe down the dashboard and empty the ashtrays.
- Have all your maintenance records ready to show prospective buyers.
- If the car needs servicing or even a routine oil change, take care of that before putting it up for sale.
- Have your mechanic check out your car and issue a report about its condition. You can use this to motivate a buyer who is on the fence.
- Order a Carfax report and show it to the buyer to prove the car's title is clean and the odometer reading is accurate.

Step 4: Where to Advertise Your Car

Now that your car is looking great and running well, it's time to advertise it for sale. Traditionally, people advertise in newspaper classified ads. These ads can be expensive, but they get results. Online classified ads are becoming increasingly popular. Online ads are particularly

effective with hard-to-find or collector cars. In most cases, on-line classifieds reach a geographically wider area of buyers.

Here are the main markets for advertising used cars in the following:

- Online classified ads such as those on Edmunds.com
- Daily newspaper classified ads
- Weekly "shoppers" and giveaway newspapers
- Bulletin boards at your office, a local supermarket or a college campus
- Word of mouth — tell your friends and family you have a car for sale
- Put a "For Sale" sign in the car window

Creativity is required when it comes to advertising. Think of unusual places to put ads (skywriting is probably too expensive), and you will get results.

One last word of advice about advertising: if you run an expensive classified ad, be sure you are available to take phone calls from possible buyers. Many people won't leave a message for a return call. So answer the phone — and be polite. Creating a good first impression is the first step to getting buyers to come and see the car in person.

Step 5: Create Ads That Sell

When creating "For Sale" signs or putting a classified ad in the paper, you have an opportunity to show how eager you are to sell the car. This can be done by inserting the following abbreviations and phrases:

Must Sell: This often means the seller is leaving town and needs to dump the car at a fire sale price.

OBO: This stands for "or best offer" and it indicates that you are willing to entertain offers below the stated price. This usually means you are eager to sell the car.

Asking price: This also communicates the feeling that you will negotiate, but it is one notch below OBO on the eagerness scale.

Firm: This word is used to rebuff attempts to negotiate. It indicates that you aren't in a hurry to sell the car — you are most interested in getting your price.

Think about what you are telling people when you phrase your ad. Little words convey a lot. Besides the price, your ad should also include the year, make, model and trim level of the car you are selling along with the mileage, color, condition and popular options.

Step 6: Showing Your Car

Keep in mind that when you sell your car, people will also be evaluating you. They will be thinking something like, "Here's the person who's owned this car for the past few years. Do I trust him/her?" Make the buyers feel comfortable. They will probably be uneasy about making a big decision and spending money. Put them at ease and answer their questions openly.

Potential buyers will want to test-drive the car. If in doubt, check to make sure they have a driver license. Ride along with them so you can answer any questions about the car's history and performance. Also, they may not know the area, so you might have to guide them.

There are many unexpected bumps in the road that can arise while selling a used car. These will be handled easily if you are dealing with a reasonable person. So, as you are contacted by prospective buyers, use your intuition to evaluate them. If they seem difficult, pushy or even shady, wait for another buyer. With the right person, selling a used car should be simple.

Some sellers feel uncomfortable about having buyers come to their house to see the car. However, you can generally screen buyers on the phone. If they sound suspicious, don't do business with them. If you don't want people knowing where you live, arrange to show the car at a park or shopping center near your home. However, keep in mind that people will eventually see your address when you sign the title over to them.

Some buyers will want to take the car to a mechanic to have it inspected. If you have an inspection report from your mechanic, this might put their doubts to rest. However, if they still want to take the car to their mechanic, this is a reasonable request. By now, you should have a feeling for the person's trustworthiness. If you feel uncomfortable or have reason to think they will steal the car, decline the offer or go along with them.

Be ready for trick questions such as, "So, what's really wrong with the car?" If you get this, refer them to the mechanic's report or invite them to look over the car more carefully.

Step 7: Negotiate for Your Best Price

If a person comes to look at the car and it passes their approval after a test-drive, you can expect them to make an offer. Most people are uncomfortable negotiating, so their opening offer might take several forms.

"I like the car, but…" This is the softest way to negotiate on the price. They may not even state that the price seems too high. If they say, "I like the car, but…" and then lapse into uncomfortable silence, you might consider an appropriate response. If you really want to move the car, you could say, "How much would you be willing to pay?"

"What's your best price?" This is a more direct way to probe the seller to find out how much he or she will come down. If you get this from a prospective buyer, don't seem too eager to reduce your price.

"Would you accept…?" Now we're getting somewhere. This buyer has thought it over and is making an offer. But the offer is being presented in a polite manner designed to allow for a counter offer.

"Take it or leave it." This buyer is making an offer that supposedly leaves no room for a counter offer. In reality, this buyer might be bluffing. Still, they are sending a message that they are close to their final price. The only way to know for sure whether it really is a "take it or leave it" offer is to leave it — and let them leave. They may return tomorrow ready to pay your price.

The above are just a few of the openers you might encounter. Think of your responses ahead of time so you won't be caught unprepared. In general, it's a good idea to hold to your price when your car first goes up for sale. If you don't get any buyers right away, you'll know you have to be flexible about the price.

Step 8: Handling Complications

In some cases, you might reach an agreement with a buyer that is contingent on performing

repair work on the car. This can lead to misunderstandings down the line, so avoid this if you can. The best thing to do is have your car in good running order while being fully aware of any necessary repairs. If you state clearly in your ads that the car is being sold "as is", you can refer to this statement when it's time to close the deal.

Still, a trip to the prospective buyer's mechanic might turn up a new question about the car's condition. What to do?

This must be handled on a case-by-case basis. If the repair is needed, and you trust the mechanic's assessment, you could propose reducing the agreed-upon price by all, or part, of the amount for the repair. If the repair is questionable, but the buyer is insistent, split the difference, or have the car taken to your mechanic for further evaluation.

Remember, the older the car, the more a mechanic is likely to find. At some point, you have to draw the line. You may have to say to the buyer, "True, this work could be done. But the car drives well as it is. And the proposed repair isn't addressing a safety concern". After all, a used car — particularly an elderly one — isn't expected to be perfect.

Step 9: Finalize the Sale

Rules governing the sale of motor vehicles vary somewhat from state to state. Make sure you check with the department of motor vehicles (DMV) in your state, and keep in mind that much of the information is now available on DMV Web sites.

When selling your car, it's important to limit your liability. If someone drives away in the car you just sold, and they get into an accident, can you be held responsible? There are two ways to deal with this concern.

Once you have the money from the sale (it's customary to request either cash or a cashier's check), record the odometer reading and sign the car's title over to the buyer. In some states, the license plates go along with the car. A new title will be issued and mailed to the new owner. Additionally, in most states, a release of liability form can be downloaded from the DMV web site. Fill this out, along with the car's mileage, and mail it in as soon as the car is sold. This establishes the time at which the car left your possession.

But what if you still owe money on the car, and the bank is holding the title? One way to deal with this is to conclude the sale at the bank where the title is held. Call ahead and have the title ready. Then, once money has changed hands and the bank has been paid the balance of the loan, sign the title over to the buyer.

In some cases, however, an out-of-state bank might hold the title. In this instance, it is recommended that you go with the buyer to the DMV and get a temporary operating permit based on a bill of sale. Then, after you pay off the balance of the loan with the proceeds from the car sale, have the title mailed to the new owner. Sign it over to the new owner and the transaction is complete.

Finally, remember to contact your insurance agent to cancel your policy on the vehicle you have sold (or transfer the coverage to your new car).

Before your car drives away for the final time, take a last look through the glove compartment, the trunk and under the seats. You might find some long forgotten treasures you misplaced years ago.

Step 10: After the Sale

In most states, the condition of a used car for sale is considered "as is", and no warranty is provided or implied. Therefore, if the car breaks down after you have sold it, you are under no obligation to refund the buyer's money or pay to have it repaired. If you have sold a car to someone who took it for inspection at a garage and the mechanic found nothing wrong with it, you have done all you can to protect yourself and the buyer.

The best way to feel peace of mind after selling your used car is to make sure you did everything correctly. This means being open about the condition of the car before the sale and timely and complete in transferring DMV paperwork after the sale.

When done correctly, selling a used car can be a win-win situation. You have turned your used car into cash and provided reliable transportation for the next owner. Focus on the benefits to both parties and you are likely to have a smooth and profitable experience.

Questions

1. What are the ten steps of selling your car?

2. How should one do to negotiate the best price?

3. What should one do after the sale?

APPENDIX

I Vocabulary

A

accelerator [æk'seləreitə] *n.* 加速者，加速器

accelerometer [æk,selə'rɔmitə] *n.* 加速计

activate ['æktiveit] *v.* 使……活动，对……起作用；启动，开动

actual ['æktʃuəl] *adj.* 实际的，真实的；现行的，目前的

adhere to 黏附，黏着

advertising ['ædvətaiziŋ] *n.* 广告

air bag 气囊

air conditioner 空调

air filter 空气滤清器

air flow meter 空气流量计

air flow sensor 空气流量传感器

air injection 空气喷射，(特指废气净化系中的)二次空气喷射

air-fuel mixture 混合气

air-fuel ratio 空燃比

alignment [ə'lainmənt] *n.* 呈直线，准直

alternating [ɔːl'təːnitiŋ] *adj.* 交互的，交替的

alternating current 交流电

alternative [ɔːl'təːnətiv] *n.* 替换物；取舍 *adj.* 两者择一的；供选择的

alternator ['ɔːltə(ː)neitə] *n.* 交流发动机

alternator drive belt 发电机皮带

altitude ['æltitjuːd] *n.* 高度，海拔；高地

ammeter ['æmitə] *n.* 安培计，电流表

analog system 模拟系统

anchor ['æŋkə] *vt.* 使固定，锚定

angular ['æŋgjulə] *adj.* 有角的

antifreeze ['antifriːz] *n.* 防冻剂

antiknock [,ænti'nɔk] *n.* 抗爆剂，抗爆，抗爆震的

anti-lock ['ænti]　*n.* 防抱死

anti-skid ['æntiskid]　*n.* 防滑装置

apart from…　除……之外

approach [ə'prəutʃ]　*n.* 接近；途径；方法　*v.* 靠近，接近

armature ['a:mətʃə]　*n.* 盔甲，电枢(电机的部件)

as a result　结果，因此

as expect　如所期望的

assemble [ə'sembl]　*v.* 装配

at worst　在最坏的情况下

atmospheric [ˌætməs'ferik]　*adj.* 大气的，大气层的

attribute…to　把……归因于，把……归咎于

automatically [ˌɔ:tə'mætikəli]　*ad.* 自动地

automotive [ɔ:tə'məutiv]　*adj.* 汽车的，自动推进的

auxiliary [ɔ:g'ziljəri]　*n.* 帮助者；辅助物；助动词　*adj.* 附加的，辅助的

axle ['æksl]　*n.* 轮轴，车轴

B

back up　倒退

backbone ['bækbəun]　*n.* 脊骨，支柱；骨干

baffle ['bæfl]　*n.* 挡板；隔板；障碍

baffle plate　挡板，缓冲板，折流板

ball joint　球形接头

band [bænd]　*n.* [机]传送带，传动带

bare skin　裸露皮肤

basic advance angle　基础点火提前角

beam [bi:m]　*n.* 梁，横梁

bearing journal　支承轴颈

behavior [bi'heivjə]　*n.* 行为，举止

belt pulley　皮带轮带式运输机滚筒

boil [bɔil]　*n.* 沸点，沸腾；疖子　*v.* 煮沸；激动

bolt [bəult]　*n.* 门闩；螺钉；闪电；跑掉　*v.* 上门闩；囫囵吞下；逃跑

booster ['bu:stə]　*n.* 助力器，加力器；附加装置，辅助装置

bore [bɔ:]　*n.* 孔，口径；令人讨厌的人或事　*v.* 钻孔，凿孔

bottom dead center　下止点；下死点

brake band　制动带

brake booster　制动助力器

brake caliper　制动钳

brake fluid　制动液

budget ['bʌdʒit]　*n.* 预算

buffer ['bʌfə]　*n.* 缓冲器

built-in　内置

bumper ['bʌmpə]　*n.* 汽车保险杠；防撞器；缓冲器

bypass valve　旁通阀

byproduct ['bai,prɔdʌkt]　*n.* 副产品

C

cab [kæb]　*n.* (机车、卡车等的)驾驶室

cable ['keibl]　*n.* 电缆，海底电报，缆，索

caliper ['kæləpə]　*n.* 卡钳

cam lobe　凸轮的凸角

Cam Position Sensor　凸轮轴位置传感器

camshaft play　凸轮轴端隙

canister ['kænistə]　*n.* (放咖啡、茶叶、烟等的)小罐，筒；[军](防毒面具的)滤毒罐

carbon monoxide　(化)一氧化碳

carburetor [kə:bə'retə(r)]　*n.* 化油器

carrier ['kæriə]　*n.* (货运)运载工具[装置]；托[支，悬，车]架底盘；行车装置

cartridge ['kɑ:tridʒ]　*n.* 弹药筒

catalyst ['kætəlist]　*n.* 催化剂，触媒

catalytic [,kætə'litik]　*adj.* 催化的，接触反应的

catalytic converter　(汽车等的)催化式排气净化器

CD-ROM　*n.* 光盘驱动器

center electrode　中央电极

centrifugal [sen'trifjugəl]　*adj.* 离心的；利用离心力的

centrifugal fan　离心式鼓风机，离心式风扇

cerametallic　*adj.* 金属陶瓷的

cetane ['si:tein]　*n.* 十六烷

chamfer ['tʃæmfə]　*n.* 锥角；切角面；圆角

charging system　充电系统

chassis ['ʃæsi]　*n.* 底盘

chemical energy　化学能

circuit ['sə:kit]　*n.* 电路；一圈；周游，巡回

circumference [sə'kʌmfərəns] *n.* 圆周；胸围

clamp [klæmp] *n.* 夹子 *v.* 夹紧

clientele [ˌkliːɑːn'teil] *n.* 老主顾

clog [klɔg] *v.* 阻塞

close to the closing　临近尾声

clutch [klʌtʃ] *n.* 离合器；控制 *v.* 抓住；攫取

clutch fork　离合器分离叉

clutch housing　离合器壳

clutch linkage　离合器操纵杠杆机构

clutch pack　离合器压盘

clutch pedal　离合器踏板

coast [kəust] *vi.* 惯性滑行，滑[溜]下

coefficient [kəui'fiʃənt] *n.* 系数

coil [kɔil] *v.* 盘绕，卷

coil spring　螺旋弹簧，圈弹簧

collapse [kə'læps] *n.* 倒塌，崩溃，*vi.* 倒塌，崩溃，瓦解

combustible [kəm'bʌstəbl] *adj.* 易燃的，燃烧性的，*n.* 燃质物，可燃物

combustion [kəm'bʌstʃən] *n.* 燃烧，燃尽；发火；爆震燃烧

combustion chamber　燃烧室

comfort ['kʌmfət] *n.* 安慰，舒适，安慰者 *vt.* 安慰，使(痛苦等)缓和

communicate with　与……连通，和……互通

compact [kəm'pækt] *adj.* 紧凑的，紧密的

comparatively [kəm'pærətivli] *adv.* 比较地；　相对地

competitor [kəm'petitə] *n.* 竞争者

component [kəm'pəunənt] *n.* 元件，组件 *adj.* 组成的，构成的

compound ['kɔmpaund] *n.* 混合物 *adj.* 复(混)合的，合成的 *vt.* 混合；调合；妥协

compression ratio　压缩比

compression ring　压缩环，气环

compressor [kəm'presə] *n.* 压缩物，压缩机

computerization [kəmˌpjuːtəraiˈzeiʃən; -riˈz-] *n.* 计算机的使用，计算机化

concave ['kɔn'keiv] *adj.* 凹的，凹面的

concentric [kɔn'sentrik] *adj.* 同心的；同轴的

condenser [kən'densə] *n.* 冷凝器；电容器

condenser fins　冷凝器肋片

confirmation [ˌkɔnfəmeiʃən] *n.* 确认

conical ['kɔnikəl] *adj.* 圆锥形的，圆锥的

connecting rod 连杆；结合杆；活塞杆

considerable [kən'sidərəbl] *adj.* 相当地，可观地，重要地

consistent [kən'sistənt] *adj.* 一致的；调和的；坚固的[数、统]相容的

contact point 触点

contamination [kən,tæmi'neiʃən] *n.* 污染，污染物

continuously [kən'tinjuəsli] *adv.* 不断地，连续地

contra-rotating gears 反转齿轮

conventional [kən'venʃənl] *adj.* 惯例的，常规的

conversion [kən'və:ʃən] *n.* 变换，转化

convert [kən'və:t] *vt.* 使转变；转换，使……改变信仰

convert into 把……转变成

convex ['kɔn'veks] *n.* 凸状；凸透镜 *adj.* 凸面的

convolute ['kɔnvəlju:t] *v.* 回旋，卷绕，盘旋 *adj.* 旋绕的

cooling jacket 冷却水套

cork [kɔ:k] *n.* 软木塞，软木制品

counter-balanced weight 配重，平衡重

countershaft ['kauntəʃa:ft] *n.* 中间轴

crank arm 曲柄臂

crankcase ['kræŋkkeis] *n.* 曲柄箱，曲轴箱

crankshaft ['kræŋkʃa:ft] *n.* 曲轴

crash sensors 碰撞传感器

cruise [kru:z] *n.* 巡航，漫游 *v.* 巡航，巡航于，航游于，慢速行驶于

cushion ['kuʃən] *n.* 垫子，软垫，衬垫

customer satisfaction 客户满意

cylinder block 汽缸体

cylinder head 汽缸盖

cylindrical [si'lindrik(ə)l] *adj.* 圆柱的

D

dashboard ['dæʃ,bɔ:d] *n.* 仪表盘

database 数据库

database ['deitobeis] *n.* [计]数据库，资料库

deceleration [di:,selə'reiʃən] *n.* 减速

deform [di:'fɔ:m] *v.* 使……残缺，使……变形

dehumidify [ˌdiːhjuː'midifai] v. 除湿，使……干燥

demo ['deməu] n. 演示

deploy [dipləi] v. 展开，调度

deposit [di'pɔzit] vt. 存放，堆积；使沉淀 vi. 沉淀 n. 押金；存款；定金；堆积物

descriptive [dis'kriptiv] adj. 叙述的

destruction [di'strʌkʃən] n. 损坏，破坏

detonation [detəneiʃən] n. 爆震，爆燃

deviate ['diːvieit] vi. 脱离；越轨

diagnose ['daiəgnəuz] v. 诊断

diagnosis [daiəg'nəusis] n. 诊断

diagnostic [ˌdaiəg'nɔstik] adj. 诊断的，(有)特征的

diaphragm ['daiəfræm] n. 膜片；膜片泵；隔板；遮光板；薄膜

diesel ['diːzəl] n. 柴油机；内燃机

differential [ˌdifə'renʃəl] adj. 差动[速，示](的)，(有)差别[异]的 n. (传动系)差速器

differentiate [ˌdifə'renʃieit] v. 区分，分别；使变异

dilute [dai'ljuːt] adj. 冲淡的，稀释的；微弱的

diode ['daiəud] n. 二极管

dipstick ['dipstik] n. 油尺，水[油]位指示器

disc brake 盘式制动器

discharge [dis'tʃɑːdʒ] 放出，流出，排出

disposal [dis'pəuzəl] n. 处理；消除；销毁

dissipation [ˌdisi'peiʃən] n. 耗散，损耗，散逸；能量耗散；损耗

distortion [dis'tɔːʃən] n. 变形，扭曲；扭转

distribute [dis'tribju(ː)t] vt. 分发，分配；散布；分区 v. 分发

distribution [ˌdistri'bjuːʃən] n. 分配，分销

distributor cap 分电器盖

diverter valve 分流阀

dog clutch 牙嵌[爪式]离合器

dominant ['dɔminənt] adj. 占优势的；主导的；显性的 n. 主宰者

double helical 人字齿轮

doughnut ['dəunʌt] n. 油炸圈饼；圆环图

drag link 转向直拉杆

drainage ['dreinidʒ] v. 排水 n. 排水系统；污水

drive belt 传动皮带

drive shaft　传动轴

drive train　动力传动系统

drive wheel　驱动轮

dry clutch　干摩擦离合器

duralumin [djuə'ræljumin]　n. 硬铝，杜拉铝

dynamic [dai'næmik]　adj. 动态的，有活力的　n. 动力力学

E

eccentric [ik'sentrik]　n. 偏心轮　adj. 偏心的，偏心装置

efficient [i'fiʃənt]　adj. 效率高的；胜任的

EGR　废气再循环装置

elastic [i'læstik]　adj. 弹性的，有弹力的

electric arc　电弧

electrochemical [i'lektrəu'kemikəl]　adj. 电化学的，电化的

electrode [l'lektrəud]　n. 电极

electromagnet [i'lektrəu'mægnit]　n. 电磁铁，电磁

electromagnetic [i,lektrəumæg'netik]　adj. 电磁的

electromagnetic field　电磁场

eliminate [i'limineit]　vt. 消除

embarrassed [im'bærəs]　adj. 尴尬的，局促的

emergency [i'məːdʒnsi]　n. 紧急情况，突然事件，非常时刻，紧急事件

emission [i'miʃən]　n. 排放物

emit [i'mit]　vt. 发出，放射，吐露；散发；发表，发行

engage [in'geidʒ]　vt. 使忙碌；雇用；预定；使从事于，使参加　vi. 答应；从事；交战[机]接合，啮合

engine performance　发动机性能

engine speed and position sensor　发动机转速和位置传感器

entrepreneur [,ɔntrəprə'nəː]　n. 企业家

equivalence [i'kwivələns]　n. 等效(性)，等值(性)

equivalent [i'kwivələnt]　等价的

essential [i'senʃəl]　n. 要素，要点　adj. 必要的；重要的；本质的

essentially [i'senʃəli]　adv. 本质上；本来

evaluate [i'væljueit]　vt. 评价，估……的价

evaporation [i,væpə'reiʃən]　n. 蒸发；消失；脱水，干燥

evaporator [i,væpə'reiʃən]　n. 蒸发器，脱水器

evaporator core　蒸发器芯

evasive [i'veisiv]　*adj.* 逃避的

evolution [ˌi:və'lu:ʃən]　*n.* 进化；进展

evolve [i'vɔlv]　*v.* (使)发展，(使)一体化

excess air ratio　过量空气系数

exciter [ik'saitə]　*n.* 振荡器，激发器，励磁机

exhaust [ig'zɔ:st]　*vi.* 排气　*n.* 排气；排气装置

exhaust gas　排气，废气

exhaust manifold　排气歧管

exhaust valve　排气阀

expansion valve　膨胀阀

F

fabricate ['fæbrikeit]　*v.* 制造，组装；伪造，杜撰；装配

fail to do　不能做……

fail-safe mode　故障安全模式

fasten ['fæsn]　*vt.* 拴紧，使固定

feature [fi:tʃə]　*n.* 外貌、特征

feed [fi:d]　*v.* 供应

fender ['fendə]　*n.* 挡泥板

fiberglass ['faibəglɑ:s]　*n.* 玻璃纤维，玻璃丝

filler cap (汽油箱)加油口盖

fin [fin]　*n.* 鳍；鳍状物

final drive　主减速器，主传动

finger ['fiŋgə]　*n.* 手指；指状物；钩爪；机械手；指针；箭头；塞尺

flammability [ˌflæmə'biləti]　*n.* 易燃的，可燃性的

flange [flændʒ]　*n.* [机]凸缘，法兰

flat [flæt]　*adj.* 平坦的；单调的；扁平的　*adv.* 平直地；干脆地　*n.* [英]公寓

flow back　回流

fold [fəuld]　*v.* 折叠，笼罩；对折起来

fraction ['frækʃən]　*n.* 片断，片刻，小部分

frame [freim]　*n.* 车架；结构

fresh charge　吸入的新鲜混合气

friction ['frikʃən]　*n.* 摩擦，摩擦力

front suspension　*n.* 前悬架

frontal ['frʌntl]   n. 前沿

front-end collision   前端碰撞

frostbite ['frɔstbait]   n. 冻伤，冻疮   v. 使.冻伤

fuel filter   燃油滤清器

fuel injection   燃油喷射

fuel injection system   燃油喷射系统

fuel pump   燃油泵

fuel-metering system   燃油计量系统

fulcrum ['fʌlkrəm]   n. 支点，支轴，支柱

G

gap [gæp]   n. 缺口，间隙，缝隙；差距

gas tank   汽油箱

gasoline engine   汽油机

gear box   齿轮箱

gear combination   齿轮啮合

goal [gəul]   n. 目的，目标；守门员；球门，(球赛等的)得分

governor ['gʌvənə]   n. [机]调节器，调速器

GPS-based   基于 GPS 的

grill [gril]   n. 烤架，铁格子   vt. 烧，烤

groove [gru:v]   n. 槽，凹槽；切口，vt. 开槽   vi. 开槽；使……快活

grove [grəuv]   n. 树丛，小树林

gyroscope ['gaiərəskəup]   n. 陀螺仪

H

Halt [hɔ:lt]   n. 停止，暂停，中断   vt. 使停止，使立定   vi. 立定，停止，踌躇，有缺点

Hassle ['hæsl]   n. 激战

headlight ['hedlait]   n. 前大灯

heat dissipation   热消散，热散逸

heat transfer   热传导，传热

helical ['helikəl]   adj. 螺旋状的

high-pressure liquid refrigerant   高压液态制冷剂

hinge [hindʒ]   n. 铰链；折叶；关键   vt. 用铰链装

hood [hud]   n. 车篷，遮罩   vt. 覆盖

horsepower ['hɔ:s,pauə]   n. 马力

hub [hʌb] *n.* (轮)毂；(兴趣、活动的)中心

hump [hʌmp] *n.* 小圆丘，小丘 *vt.* (使)隆起，弓起

hydraulic [hai'drɔ:lik] *adj.* 水力的，水压的

hydrocarbon ['haidrəu'ka:bən] *n.* 碳氢化合物

hydrogen ['haidrəudʒən] *n.* 氢

hydroplaning 湿路打滑

I

ideal [ai'diəl] *adj.* 理想的；观念的

IGf signal 点火反馈确认信号

ignite [ig'nait] *vi.* 着火，发光 *vt.* 点燃，(使)燃烧，引发

ignition coil 点火线圈

ignition distributor 点火分电器

ignition key 点火开关

ignition system 点火系统

ignition timing 点火定时

IGt signal 点火信号

illuminate [i'lju:mineit] *v.* 照亮，发光

impeller [im'pelə] *n.* 叶[涡，工作，泵]轮，转子

implement ['implimənt] 实现，实施

import [im'pɔ:t] 调入

impurity [im'pjuərit] *n.* 杂质；夹杂物；不纯

in the event of 如果……发生

inadvertently ['inəd've:təntli] *adj.* 不经心的，疏忽的

inconvenient [,inkən'vi:njənt] *adj.* 不便的，有困难的

incorporate [in'kɔ:pəreit] 合并，并入

indicator lamp 指示灯

induce [in'dju:s] *vt.* 诱导，诱发，引起，导致

inertia [i'nə:ʃjə] *n.* 惯性，惯量

infinitely ['infinitli] *adv.* 无限地，无穷地

inflate [in'fleit] *vt.* 使膨胀；使得意；使(通货)膨胀；使充气 *vi.* 充气，膨胀

inlet(intake) valve 进气阀

install [in'stɔ:l] *vt.* 安装；安置；使就职

institute ['institju:t] 创立，开始；制定

instrument panel 仪表板

intake air temperature sensor　进气温度传感器

intake ducting　进气管

intake manifold　进气歧管

intensity [in'tensiti]　n. 激烈、强烈

interconnecting　互相连接

interior [in'tiəriə]　adj. 内部的，内地的，国内的　n. 内部，内在

intermeshing [ˌintə'meʃiŋ]　adj. 相互啮合的

intermittent [ˌintə'mitənt]　adj. 间歇的

internally [in'tənəli]　adv. 内部地，国内地，内在地

interrupt ['intə'rʌpt]　v. 中断，打断

intricate ['intrikit]　adj. 复杂的；难懂的

inventory ['invəntri]　n. 库存

K

kinetic [kai'netik]　adj. 运动的

kinetic energy　动能

king pin　主销

L

lag [læg]　vi. 走得慢　n. 落后

landmark ['lændma:k]　n. 重大事件；里程碑；地界标

lap [læp]　n. (坐时的)大腿前部，膝盖，下摆

lateral acceleration　横向加速度

layshaft t ['leiʃa:ft]　n. 中间轴

leaf spring　钢板弹簧

leakage ['li:kidʒ]　n. 泄漏，漏损物，漏损量

lean mixture　稀混合气

linkup ['liŋkʌp]　n. 连接，联系，会合

logic probe　逻辑探测仪

longitudinal ['lɔndʒi'tju:dinəl]　adj. 纵向的

lot [lɔt]　n. 车场，车店

lubricate ['lu:brikeit]　v. 使润滑，涂油，起润滑剂作用

lubrication [ˌlu:bri'keiʃən]　n. 润滑

lubrication oil　润滑油

lubrication system　润滑系

M

magnetic induction　磁感应

magnetic switch　磁力开关

main bearing cap　主轴承盖

maintenance　['meintinəns]　*n.* 维护，保养

manifold　['mænifəuld]　*n.* 歧管；总管；多种；复印本，*adj.* 多种的，多方面的

manifold pressure sensor　歧管压力传感器

manifold runner　歧管通道

market penetration　市场渗透

marketing　['ma:kitiN]　*n.* 市场营销

marketing mix　营销组合

market-skimming　撇脂定价

mass　[mæs]　*n.* 质量

mass marketing　完全市场覆盖

master cylinder　制动主缸

maze　[meiz]　*n.* 曲径；迷宫，迷津[C]

mechanism　['mekənizəm]　*n.* 机械机构

meet and greet　欢迎与问候

mesh　[meʃ]　*n.* 网孔，网丝，网眼；圈套，陷阱，[机]啮合　*vt.* 以网捕捉；啮合；编织 *vi.* 落网，相啮合

microprocessor　['maɪkrəu'prɑsesə]　*n.* 微信息处理机，微处理器

mileage　['mailidʒ]　*n.* 英里数，英里里程

moderate　['mɔdərit]　*n.* ；*v.* 缓和，缓冲；减轻，节制

modulator　['mɔdjuleitə]　*n.* 调节器

monitor　['mɔnitə]　*n.* 监督员，监控器；*v.* 监控

monoxide　[mə'nɔksaid]　*n.* 一氧化物

motor　['məutən]．　*n.* 发动机；电动机

mount　[maunt]　*vt.* 设置，安放，固定在……上

muffler　['mʌflə]　*n.* 消声器

multi-disk clutch　多片式离合器

multipoint fuel injection　多点喷射

N

navigation　[ˌnævi'geiʃən]　*n.* 航海，导航，航行

needle　['ni:dl]　*n.* 指针

neutral ['nju:trəl]　*n.* [机]空挡

nitrogen ['naitrədʒən]　*n.* [化]氮

noxious ['nɔkʃəs]　*adj.* 有害的

nozzle ['nɔzl]　*n.* 喷嘴

O

obsolete ['ɔbsəli:t]　*adj.* 过时的

obstacle ['ɔbstəkl]　*n.* 障碍(物)

occupant ['ɔkjupənt]　*n.* 占有人，占有者

octane ['ɔktein]　*n.* 辛烷

oil filter　机油滤清器

oil pump　油泵

oil-control ring　控油环，油环

one-way clutch　单向离合器

optimum ['ɔptiməm]　*n.* 最适条件，最适度

oscillate ['ɔsileit]　*v.* 摆动；振动；摇摆

oscillation [ˌɔsi'leiʃən]　*n.* 振动；动摇

oscilloscope [ɔ'siləskəup]　*n.* 示波器

outweigh [aut'wei]　*v.* 胜过，优于

over-charging　过充电

overdrive ['əuvə'draiv]　*vt.* 超速传动

overload [ˌəuvə'ləud]　*vt.* 使超载，超过负荷　*n.* 超载，负荷过多

override switch　超越控制开关

P

Pad [pæd]　*n.* 衬垫，垫块

parameter [pə'ræmitə]　*n.* 参数

parking brake　驻车制动

passenger compartment　驾驶室

pedestal ['pedistl]　*n.* 轴承座；轴架；支座

penetration [peni'treiʃən]　*n.* 渗透，穿透；侵入

periphery [pə'rifəri]　*n.* 周边，周线，外围

personal selling　人员推销

petroleum [pi'trəuliəm]　*n.* 石油

phosphorus ['fɔsfərəs]　*n.* 磷

pinion ['pinjən] *n.* 小齿轮

piston head 活塞顶部

piston land 活塞环槽岸

piston pin hole 活塞销孔

pitman arm 转向摇臂

pivot ['pivət] *n.* 枢；旋转 *vt.* 装枢轴于；以……为中心旋转

planet carrier 行星齿轮架

planetary gear set 行星齿轮系统

plate [pleit] *n.* 板材，电容器板，(蓄电池)极板

platinum ['plætinəm] *n.* 白金，铂

plunger ['plʌndʒə] *n.* 柱塞；冲杆；模冲；活塞

pollutant [pə'lu:tənt] *n.* 污染物

positive displacement type 主动容积式

potential [pə'tenʃ(ə)l] *adj.* 潜在的

potentiality [pə,tenʃi'æliti] *n.* 可能；(用复数)潜能，潜力，可能性

power stroke 做功行程

power train 动力传动系

preferential [,prefə'renʃəl] 优先的，特惠的

prematurely [,pri:mə'tjuəli] *adv.* 过早地；早熟地

primary ['praiməri] *adj.* 第一位的，主要的；初步的，原来的

primary winding 初级绕组

product-variety marketing 专门化市场

progressive [prə'gresiv] *adj.* 前进的；(税收)累进的，进步的

prominent ['prɔminənt] *adj.* 显著的，突出的，杰出的

promise the sun and moon 对天发誓

promotion [prə'məuʃən] *n.* 促销

propel [prə'pel] *v.* 推进；驱使

propeller shaft 传动轴

property ['prɔpəti] *n.* 属性，特性

pros and cons 正反两方面

prospective [prəs'pektiv] *adj.* 预期的

protrude [prə'tru:d] *vt.* 使伸出，突出

public relations 公共关系

puddle ['pʌdl] *vt.* 使泥泞；把……做成胶土；搅拌 *vi.* 搅泥浆 *n.* 水坑，胶土

pulse [pʌls] *n.* 脉搏，脉冲

purge valve　排气阀

PVC　曲轴箱正压通风装置

R

radially　['reidiəli]　*adv.* 径向地；放射状地

radiator　['reidieitə]　*n.* 散热器，暖气片；辐射体

radiator cap　散热器盖，水箱盖

rampant　['ræmpənt]　蔓生的；猖獗的

rear suspension　*vt.* 后悬架

rear wheel drive　后轮驱动

reasonably　['ri:zənəbll]　*adv.* 适度地，相当地

reburn　['ri:'bə:n]　*v.* 在燃烧

receiver　[ri'si:və]　*n.* 接收者，接收器，收信机

Recharging the AC system　空调重新加注制冷剂

reciprocate　[ri'siprəkeit]　*v.* 互给；酬答；互换；报答

reciprocating　[ri'siprəkeitiŋ]　*n.* 往复(摆动，往复式发动机)　*adj.* 摆动的

referral　[ri'fə:rəl]　*n.* 介绍，指引；推荐人

refrigerant　[ri'fridʒərənt]　*adj.* 制冷的　*n.* 制冷剂

refrigerator　[ri'fridʒəreitə]　*n.* 电冰箱，冷藏库

regulator　['regjəleɪtə]　*n.* 调节器

relay　['ri:lei]　*n.* 继电器　*vt.* (消息，货物等)分程传递；使接替；转播

release lever　分离杠杆

reliable　[ri'laiəbl]　*adj.* 可靠的，可信的

relief valve　安全阀，卸压阀，溢流阀

remanufacture　[ri:'mænju'fæktʃə]　*n.* 再制造、改制

remove…from…　从……中除(消)去

repeat the cycle　重复循环

resistance　[ri'zistəns]　*n.* 反抗，抵抗，抵抗力；阻力，电阻，阻抗

resistance to knock　抗爆震

resonance　['rezənəns]　*n.* 谐振，共振

restraint　[ris'treint]　*n.* 抑制，制止，克制

restriction　[ris'trikʃən]　*n.* 限制，约束

retainer　[ri'teinə]　*n.* 止推挡圈；定位器

retard　[ri'ta:d]　*n.* 减速；延迟；阻滞　*v.* 延迟，阻止，使减速；减慢

retardation　[,ri:ta:'deiʃən]　*n.* 延迟

retrieve [ri'tri:v] *v.* 更正，纠正，弥补

reverse [ri'və:s] *n.* 倒挡；倒退，倒转；反向

rich mixture 浓混合气

riding environment 驾乘环境

rigid ['ridʒid] *adj.* 刚性的；刚硬的，坚硬的；不易变形的

ring gear 齿圈

road wheel 车轮

rocker contact pad 摇臂接触部位

roller ['rəulə] *n.* 蜗轮

rotor ['rəutə] *n.* 转子；涡轮

rug [rʌg] *n.* 小地毯

run on 涉及

rust [rʌst] *n.* 锈 *v.* 生锈 *vt.* 生锈，使……生锈

S

safety sensors 安全传感器

sales promotion 促销

sales volume 销量

satellite ['sætəlait] *n.* 人造卫星

seep [si:p] *v.* (液体等)渗漏

segmentation [ˌsegmən'teiʃən] *n.* 市场细分

sensitive ['sensitiv] *adj.* 敏感的

sensor ['sensə] *n.* 传感器

serial ['siəriəl] *adj.* 连续的；一系列的

servo ['sə:vəu] *n.* 伺服，伺服系统

shift [ʃift] *vt.* 替换，转移，变速 *vi.* 转换；移动，转变；推托；变速

shock [ʃɔk] *n.* 振动

shock absorber 减震器

shoe [ʃu:] *n.* (汽车轮的)制动器

silicone ['silikəun] *n.* 聚硅氧；硅铜；硅树脂

simplex type 单缸式

single point fuel injection 单点喷射

single-piston floating caliper 单活塞，浮钳盘式制动器

slant [sla:nt] *n.* 倾斜，斜面；个人观点或见解；倾向性 *vt.* 使倾斜 *vi.* 倾斜

sleeve [sli:v] *n.* 衬[轴，护]套，套筒，空心轴；管接头，外[套]盒；(发动机)缸套

slide [slaid] *vi.* 滑动，滑落 *vt.* 使滑动，使滑行

slightly ['slightly] *adv.* 轻微地；微小地；稍微地；纤细地

slosh [slɔʃ] *n.* 晃动 *v.* 搅动；把……泼溅出

solenoid ['səulinɔid] *n.* [电]螺线管；电磁线圈

solenoid-actuated 电磁阀动作的

spark [spɑːk] *n.* 火花；瞬间放电

spark plug 火花塞

speed up 加速

spherical ['sferikəl] *adj.* 球的，球形的

spin [spin] *v.* 旋转；纺，纺纱 *n.* 旋转

spindle ['spindl] *n.* 轴，转轴

spiral cable 螺旋电缆

spline [splain] *vt.* 用花键连接 *n.* [机]花键，键槽，齿条

splined hub 花键毂

spoke [spəuk] *n.* 轮辐[C]

spray [sprei] *v.* 喷雾；扫射；喷射

sprocket ['sprɔkit] *n.* 链齿；带齿盘；星轮

squeeze [skwiːz] *v.* 压榨，挤，挤榨

stability [stə'biliti] *n.* 稳定性

stage [steidʒ] *n.* 阶段；舞台；驿站 *vt.* 上演；实行，进行

stall [stɔːl] *n.* 货摊；畜栏，厩；出售摊 *v.*(使)停转，(使)停止，迟延

starter ['stɑːtə] *n.* 起动器，起动钮

starter motor 起动机

starting a fire 着火

starting system 起动系统

stator ['steitə] *n.* 定子，固定子[片]；(点火系)定子，感应传感器；(变矩器)导轮

steering arm 转向节臂

steering column 转向管柱

steering gear 转向齿轮，转向器

steering knuckle arm 转向节臂

steering knuckle 转向节

steering shaft 转向轴

steering system 转向系

steering wheel 转向盘

stick shift 换挡杆换挡

storage ['stɔridʒ] *n.* 贮藏(量)，贮藏库，存储

straddle ['strædl]   v. 跨骑

strap [stræp]   n. 带子；皮带；布带；金属带   v. 用带捆扎；拼命工作

streamlined ['stri:mlaind]   adj. 流线型的   v. 使……流线化

strive [straiv]   vi. 努力，争取；斗争，奋斗

stud [stʌd]   n. 柱头螺栓，螺柱

supercharger ['sju:pətʃɑ:dʒə]   n. 增压器

supervision [ˌsju:pə'viʒən]   监督

supplement ['sʌpliment]   v. 增补，补充   n. 增补，补充；增刊，副刊

supplemental restraint system   辅助约束系统

surge [sə:dʒ]   n. 电涌；冲击波；浪涌   v. 汹涌；澎湃

suspension [səs'penʃən]   n. 悬架，悬挂装置

sport utility vehicle(SUV)   n. 运动多用途车

swept volume   有效容积

swirl [swə:l]   n. 漩涡，涡状形

synchronizer ['siŋkrənaizə]   n. 同步装置

T

tailpipe ['teilpaip]   n. 排气管

tailpipe [teilpaɪp]   n. 排气管

tappet ['tæpit]   n. (凸轮)挺杆；气门推杆

target marketing   密集单一市场

temperature sensor   温度传感器

terminal ['tə:minl]   n. 端子，终端，接线端

terminate ['tə:mineit]   v. 终止，结束，终结

theoretical [θiə'retikəl]   adj. 理论(上)的

thermal energy   热能

thermostat ['θə:məstæt]   n. 节温器；自动调温器；温度调节装置

thermo-time switch   热限时开关

throttle body   节气门体

throttle plate   节气门

throttle position sensor   节气门位置传感器

throttle valve   节气门

throwout bearing   分离轴承

tie-rod   转向横拉杆

tolerance ['tɔlərəns]   n. [机]公差，容限

top dead center 上止点，上死点

torque [tɔ:k] *n.* 转[扭]矩，扭转力矩

torque converter 液力变矩器

torsion bar 扭杆弹簧

transaxle [træns'æksl] *n.* 变速驱动桥

transmit [trænz'mit] *vt.* 传输，传送；代代相传；传达

transportation [ˌtrænspɔ:'teiʃən] *n.* 运输；交通业；输送

transverse [træns'və:s] *adj.* 横向的

trap [træp] *n.* 诱捕，捕捉

tremendous [tri'mendəs] *adj.* 巨大的；可怕的；非常的

tuck [tʌk] *n.* (衣服等的)褶裥；打褶

turbine ['tə:bin] *n.* 涡轮

turbocharger ['tə:bəu,tʃɑ:dʒə] *n.* 涡轮增压器

turbulence ['tərbjuləns] *n.* 紊流，涡流；喧嚣，骚乱，狂暴

typical ['tipikəl] *adj.* 典型的；象征性的

U

under normal driving conditions 正常行驶状态

understeer ['ʌndəstiə] *n.* 驾驶盘失灵

uniform ['ju:nifɔ:m] *adj.* 一致的，统一的 *n.* 制服 *vt.* 穿制服

unison ['ju:nizn] *n.* 和谐，一致

universal joint 万向节

V

vacuum ['vækjuəm] *n.* 真空；空间；真空吸尘器 *adj.* 真空的

vacuum-advance mechanisms 真空提前装置

valve body 阀体总成

valve clearance 气门间隙

valve gear 气门机构，配气机构

valve stem 气门杆，阀杆

van [væn] *n.* 货车

vapor lock 气阻

vaporization [ˌveipərai'zeiʃne] *n.* 汽化器，喷雾器，蒸馏器

vaporize ['veipəraiz] *v.* (使)蒸发

Variable Advance Spark Timing (VAST) 可变点火正时

variable coil pitch spring   变螺距弹簧

various   ['vɛəriəs]   *adj*. 各种各样的

varnish   ['vɑːniʃ]   *n*.   油漆；掩饰；清漆   *v*. 粉饰，装饰；涂油漆于

vehicle manufacturer's guidelines   车辆制造者指导规范

venturi   [ven'tuəri]   *n*. 文氏管，喉管

vibration   [vai'breiʃən]   *n*. 振动；颤动

vibration damper   振动阻尼器   减震器

viscosity   [vis'kɔsiti]   *n*. 黏度，黏性

vital   ['vaitəl]   *adj*. 重大的；生命的；生机的；至关重要的，所必需的

voice prompts   声音提示

volatility   [ˌvɔlə'tiliti]   *n*. 挥发性，挥发度

voltage gauge   电压表

voltmeter   ['vəult'miːtə]   *n*. 电压表，伏特计

W

warning light   警告灯

warrant   [wɔrənt]   *v*. ；*n*. 认为正当，担保；正当理由，根据

wash off   冲洗，洗去

water jacket   *n*. 水冷套，水套

water pump   水泵

wheel cylinder   制动轮缸

winding   ['waindiŋ]   *n*. 绕，缠；绕组，线圈

wire   ['waiə]   *n*. 金属丝，电线

worm   [wəːm]   *n*. 蜗杆

worm gear sector   扇形蜗轮

wrist   [rist]   *n*. 手腕，腕关节

Y

yaw   [jɔː]   *n*. 偏航；偏离角

II Abbreviation

缩　写	英　文　含　义	中　文　含　义
A/C	Air Conditioning	空调
AT	Automatic Transmission	自动变速器
ACC	Air Condition Clutch	空调离合器
ACT	Air Charge Temperature	进气温度
AFC	Air Flow Control	空气流量控制
AFS	Air Flow Sensor	空气流量传感器
AI	Air Injection	二次空气喷射
ACL	Air Cleaner	空气滤清器
AIV	Air Injection Valve	空气喷射阀
ALCL	Assembly Line Communication Link	总装线测试插座
ALDL	Assembly Line Diagnostic Link	总装线诊断插座
ALT	Alternator	交流发电机
APS	Absolute Pressure Sensor	绝对压力传感器
ATS	Air Temperature Sensor	空气温度传感器
AP	Accelerator Pedal	加速踏板
ABS	Anti-lock Brake System	防抱死刹车系统
ATF	Automatic Transmission Fluid	自动变速箱油液
A/F	Air Fuel Ratio	空燃比
ATDC	After Top Dead Center	上止点后
ANT	Antenna	天线
ASSY	Assembly	总成
B+	Battery Positive Voltage	蓄电池正极
BP	Barometric Pressure Sensor	大气压力传感器
BAT	Battery	电瓶
BTDC	Before Top Dead Center	上止点前
BDC	Bottom Dead Center	下止点
C3I	Computer Controlled Coil Ignition	计算机控制点火
CMFI	Central Multiport Fuel Injection	中央多点燃油喷射
CFI	Central Fuel Injection	中央燃油喷射
CID	Cylinder Identification Sensor	汽缸传感器
CL	Closed Loop	闭环
CPS	Crankshaft Position Sensor	曲轴位置传感器

续表

缩　写	英　文　含　义	中　文　含　义
CTS	Engine Coolant Temperature Sensor	发动机水温传感器
CAT	Catalytic Converter	触媒转换器
CO	Carbon Monoxide	一氧化碳
CYL	Cylinder	气缸
CPC	Clutch Pressure Control	离合器压力控制
CPU	Central Processing Unit	中央处理器
CHG	Charge	充电
DLC	Data Link Connector	数据传递插接器
DFI	Direct Fuel Injection	直接燃油喷射
DI	Distributor Ignition	分电器点火
DTM	Diagnostic Test Mode	诊断测试模式
DTC	Diagnostic Trouble Code	诊断故障码
DLI	Distributorless Ignition	无分电器点火
DS	Detonation Sensor	爆震传感器
DIFF	Differential	差速器
EATX	Electronic Automatic Transmission	电控自动变速器
EC	Engine Control	发动机控制
ECA	Electronic Control Assembly	电子控制总成
EFI	Electronic Fuel Injection	电控燃油喷射
EGOS	Exhaust Gas Oxygen Sensor	氧传感器
EGR	Exhaust Gas Recirculation	废气再循环
EGRV	Exhaust Gas Recirculation Valve	废气再循环阀
EX	Exhaust	排气
ELD	Electrical Load Detector	电子负载检测器
FC	Fan Control	风扇控制
FP	Fuel Pump	燃油泵
FIA	Fuel Injection Air	燃油喷射进气
IA	Intake Air	进气
IATS	Intake Air Temperature Sensor	进气温度传感器
IAC	Idle Air Control	怠速控制
IACV	Idle Air Control Valve	怠速空气控制阀
ICM	Ignition Control Module	点火控制模块
IMA	Idle Mixture Adjustment	怠速混合比调整
L/C	Lock-up Clutch	锁定离合器
LSD	Limited Slip Differential	防滑差速器
LED	Light Emitting Diode	发光二极管

缩　写	英　文　含　义	中　文　含　义
M/C	Mixture Control	混合气控制
MAP	Manifold Absolute Pressure	歧管绝对压力
MCU	Microprocessor Control Solenoid	微处理控制单元
MFI	Multipoint Fuel Injection	多点燃油喷射
MAF	Mass Air Flow Sensor	空气流量计
NPS	Neutral Position Switch	空挡开关
NO$_X$	Nitrogen Oxides	氮氧化合物
PCV	Positive Crankcase Ventilation	曲轴箱强制通风
PSP	Power Steering Pressure	动力转向压力
PROM	Programmable Read Only Memory	可编程只读存储器
PMR	Pump Motor Relay	油泵马达继电器
RAM	Random Access Memory	随机存储器
RM	Relay Module	继电器模块
RPM	Reliability Performance Messure	可靠性能测定
SBEC	Single Board Engine Control	单板发动机控制
SEFI	Sequential Electronic Fuel Injection	次序电控燃油喷射
SFI	Sequential Fuel Injection	次序燃油喷射
SPI	Single Point Injection	单点喷射
SOL	Solenoid	线圈
SRS	Supplemental Restraint System	安全气囊系统
SW	Switch	切换开关
TB	Throttle Body	节流阀体
TBI	Throttle Body Fuel Injection	节流阀体燃油喷射
TP	Throttle Position	节流阀位置
TPS	Throttle Position Sensor	节流阀位置传感器
TPS	Throttle Position Switch	节流阀位置开关
TWC	Three Way Catalytic Converter	三元催化反应器
TDC	Top Dead Center	上止点
VAT	Vane Air Temperature	进气温度
VSS	Vehicle Speed Sensor	车速传感器
VSV	Vacuum Solenoid Valve	真空电磁阀
VVIS	Variable Volume Intake System	可变进气系统

III Special Words

中 文	英 文	中 文	英 文
发动机	engine	前支柱	front pillar
曲柄连杆机构	crank connecting rod mechanism	门	door
配气机构	valve mechanism	门嵌板	door panel
供油系统	fuel system	挡风玻璃	windshield
排气系统	exhaust system	车身后部	body rear garter
冷却系统	cooling system	行李箱盖	luggage compartment lid
润滑系统	lubrication system	驾驶室	cab
点火系统	ignition system	座椅	seat
起动系统	starting system	安全带	safety belt
底盘	chassis	加速踏板	accelerator pedal
传动系统	drive line	制动踏板	brake pedal
离合器	clutch	离合器踏板	clutch pedal
液力偶合器	hydrodynamic coupling	变速杆	gearshift lever
变速器	gearbox	照明	lighting
自动变速器	automatic transaxle (transmission)	车头灯	headlamp
分动器	transfer case	车头灯控制开关	headlamp control
传动轴	propeller shaft	示宽灯	clearance lamp
万向节	universal joint	转向灯	turn-signal lamp
主减速器	final drive	转向灯开关	direction indicator switch
差速器	differential	反光灯(镜)	reflector
半轴	half-axle	倒车灯	reversing lamp
桥壳	axle housing	牌照灯	number plate lamp
行驶系统	running gear	雾灯	fog lamp
车架	frame	紧急信号灯开关	warning flasher switch
悬架	suspension	点火-起动开关	ignition-starter switch
钢板弹簧	leaf spring	雨刮器	windshield wiper
减震器	shock absorber	雨刮器及洗涤器开关	windshield wiper and washer control
驱动桥	drive axle	仪表	instrument
从动桥	driven axle	车速里程表	speedometer and odometer

续表

中　文	英　文	中　文	英　文
前桥	front axle	发动机转速表	engine tachometer
后桥	rear axle	冷却剂温度表	coolant temperature gauge
车轮	wheel	燃油表	fuel gauge
轮胎	tire	充电指示灯	charging control lamp
转向系统	steering system	机油压力报警灯	oil pressure warning light
转向盘	steering wheel	手制动报警灯	hand brake warning light
转向器	steering gear	喇叭	horn
转向油泵	steering oil pump	空调	air conditioning
转向油罐	steering oil tank	压缩机	compressor
制动系统	braking system	电磁离合器	electromagnetic clutch
制动踏板	service brake pedal	冷凝器	condenser
制动主缸	master brake cylinder	贮液罐	liquid tank
制动轮缸	wheel brake cylinder	膨胀阀	expansion valve
制动毂	brake drum	蒸发器	evaporator
制动盘	brake disc	鼓风机	blower
制动蹄	brake shoe	气囊	air bag
摩擦片	friction drum	碰撞传感器	impact(dash) sensor
车身	body	保护(碰撞)传感器	saving impact(dash) sensor
保险杠	bumper	转向盘螺旋弹簧(游丝)	steering wheel spiral spring
散热器护栅	radiator grille	控制单元	control unit
(发动机)盖	hood	工具	tools
前翼子板	front wing		

IV   Example of Engine Specifications

Engine Code	G9
Fuel - Petrol (Gasoline)	Octane - *95 RON
Firing order	1-3-4-2
Emission level	Stage III
Bore	78 mm
Stroke	83.6mm
Cubic capacity	1598 cm³
Power output	77 kW (105 HPs) at 6000 rpm
Maximum Torque	145 Nm at 4000 rpm
Max. engine speed (intermittent)	6850 rpm
Max. engine speed (continuous)	6500 rpm
Throttle Actuation	Accelerator cable
Idle speed – manual transaxle	700 ± 50 rpm
Idle speed – automatic transaxle	750 ± 50 rpm
Intake Manifold	Tuning IMTV & IMRC Valves
Ignition System	Coil on Plug (COP)
Fuel Injection	PFI - Sequential
Camshaft Drive	Chain
Variable Valve Timing	Yes – Intake camshaft only
Valve Actuation	Selective – Tappet thickness

V   2016 Volkswagen Passat Technical Data

SUMMARY	Body Style Sedan
	Vehicle Name: Volkswagen Passat
ENGINE	Displacement 2.0 L/120
	SAE Net Horsepower @ RPM150 @ 4000
	Fuel System: Direct Diesel Injection
	Engine Type: Intercooled Turbo Diesel I-4
	SAE Net Torque @ RPM236 @ 1750
STEERING	Steering Type: Rack-Pinion
	Turning Diameter - Curb To Curb (Ft): 36.4
INTERIOR DIMENSIONS	Front Leg Room (in): 42.4
	Front Shoulder Room (in): 56.9
	Passenger Volume (ft): 102
	Front Head Room (in): 38.3
	Second Shoulder Room (in): 57
	Passenger Capacity: 5
	Second Leg Room (in): 39.1
	Second Head Room (in): 37.8
EXTERIOR DIMENSIONS	Width, Max W/O Mirrors (in): 72.2
	Length, Overall (in): 191.9
	Height, Overall (in): 58.5
	Track Width, Rear (in): 61
	Wheelbase (in): 110.4
	Track Width, Front (in): 62.1
	Min Ground Clearance (in): 5.4
ELECTRICAL	Cold Cranking Amps @ 0 F (Primary): 380
	Maximum Alternator Capacity (Amps): 140
MILEAGE	EPA Fuel Economy Est - City (MPG): 30
	EPA Fuel Economy Est - Hwy (MPG): 44
	Fuel Economy Est-Combined (MPG): 35
CARGO AREA DIMENSIONS	Trunk Volume (ft): 15.9

WHEELS	Front Wheel Material: Aluminum
	Spare Wheel Size (In): Compact
	Spare Wheel Material: Steel
	Rear Wheel Material: Aluminum
	Front Wheel Size (in): 19 X 8
	Rear Wheel Size (in): 19 X 8
WEIGHT INFORMATION	Base Curb Weight (lbs) 3444
SUSPENSION	Suspension Type: Front (Cont.) Strut
	Suspension Type: Rear Multi-Link
	Suspension Type: Rear (Cont.) Multi-Link
	Suspension Type: Front Strut
TRANSMISSION	Fifth Gear Ratio (:1): 0.86
	Trans Description Cont.Manual: W/OD
	Final Drive Axle Ratio (:1): 3.68
	Third Gear Ratio (:1): 1.26
	Second Gear Ratio (:1): 1.96
	Trans Type: 6
	DrivetrainFront Wheel Drive
	Sixth Gear Ratio (:1): 0.72
	First Gear Ratio (:1): 3.77
	Reverse Ratio (:1): 4.56
	Fourth Gear Ratio (:1): 0.87
FUEL TANK	Fuel Tank Capacity, Approx (Gal) 18.5
TIRES	Rear Tire Size: P235/40HR19
	Front Tire Size: P235/40HR19
	Spare Tire Size: Compact
BRAKES	Rear Brake Rotor Diam X Thickness (in): 10.7
	Disc - Rear (Yes Or): Yes
	Brake ABS System: 4-Wheel
	Disc - Front (Yes Or): Yes
	Front Brake Rotor Diam X Thickness (in): 12.3
TRAILERING	Dead Weight Hitch - Max Tongue Wt. (lbs): 100
	Dead Weight Hitch - Max Trailer Wt. (lbs): 1000
	Wt Distributing Hitch - Max Trailer Wt. (lbs): 1000
	Wt Distributing Hitch - Max Tongue Wt. (lbs): 150

参 考 文 献

[1] 宋红英. 汽车实用英语[M]. 北京：高等教育出版社，2010.

[2] 黄少炯. 汽车专业英语[M]. 北京：人民交通出版社，2013.

[3] 陈淑芬. 汽车专业英语[M]. 北京：人民交通出版社，2013.

[4] 姚嘉. 汽车专业英语[M]. 北京：北京大学出版社，2013.

[5] 廖忠诚. 汽车专业英语[M]. 北京：化学工业出版社，2015.

[6] 王风丽. 汽车专业英语[M]. 北京：人民邮电出版社，2015.

[7] 杨玲，柏杨. 汽车专业英语[M]. 重庆：重庆大学出版社，2015.

[8] 刘涛，王顺利. 汽车专业英语[M]. 南京：东南大学出版社，2015.

[9] 侯锁军，王旭东. 汽车专业英语图解教程[M]. 2版. 北京：北京大学出版社，2016.

[10] 宋进桂. 汽车专业英语读译教程[M]. 2版. 北京：机械工业出版社，2016.

[11] John B. Heywood. *Internal Combustion Engine Fundamentals*[M]. Massachusetts Institute of Technology，McGraw-Hill, Inc., 2000.